Modern Economic Analysis 2

Modern Economic Analysis 2

Edited by

D. H. Gowland

Lecturer in Economics at the University of York

BUTTERWORTHS
LONDON BOSTON
Durban Singapore Sydney Toronto Wellington

First published 1983

British Library Cataloguing in Publication Data

Modern economic analysis. 2
1. Economics
I. Gowland, D. H.
330 HB171

ISBN 0-408-10771-5
ISBN 0-408-10772-3 Pbk

Typeset by Photoset by Butterworths Litho Preparation Department
Printed and Bound in Great Britain by Redwood Burn Ltd.,
Trowbridge, Wilts.

Preface

It is both reassuring and flattering to be asked to write a sequel to a book, in that it reveals that the first work has proved useful. We hope that those who have found *Modern Economic Analysis* useful will also find this volume to be of value. Both volumes seek to provide short, non-technical summaries of important areas of economics, especially those areas where the alternative literature is either not easily accessible or highly specialized.

An additional objective of this book is to provide an economic analysis of the present Conservative Government's economic policy. Whether Mrs Thatcher is Prime Minister for another 20 years or whether she has resigned before this book is published, it is clear that her policy is and will remain the most controversial of the last half of the twentieth century. Her Government's policy represents a far more fundamental break with the orthodoxy of economic policy and political practice than anything seen since 1945 or even proposed by either Mr Benn or the SDP.

The Government is avowedly monetarist. It is not clear precisely what this term means, or rather it is clear to everyone but the answer differs from one person to the next. Nevertheless, monetarism must involve the control of the money supply. In fact, the Government has failed signally to control the quantity of money. There has been a major debate about how to control it. The failure and the debate are discussed in Chapter 1. Moreover, both experience and debate since 1979 have emphasized the importance of interest rates and in consequence the theory of the determination of interest rates which is discussed in Chapter 2.

This Government has argued that it is necessary to control the quantity of money because this is both essential and sufficient for the control of inflation. Their argument is that no alternative policy, such as an incomes policy, could work, an issue considered in Chapter 4. Traditionally, economists have argued that there is a trade-off between unemployment and inflation. Sir Geoffrey Howe denies this, and argues instead that inflation causes unemployment:

> 'The pay rises of recent years have caused a lot of today's unemployment and our problems have been getting worse for a long time under governments of both parties. The figures show that very clearly: take inflation; under each new government – Labour or Conservative – prices have gone up faster than under the one before. Less than 3% a year at the end of the first Conservative Government after the war, 4½% under Sir Harold Wilson's first Labour Government of the 1960s, 9% under the last Conservative Government and 15% under Mr Callaghan. *Some people think we can choose between inflation and unemployment*. Let inflation rise a bit they say to get unemployment down. *But it doesn't work like that*. The two go together. Higher inflation means higher unemployment. *It's like an addictive drug, the more you need and the more damage it does to you*. The figures show that. They show that the average level of unemployment under each of those Governments has been climbing steadily as well; 400 000 up to 1964, half a million by 1970, three-quarters of a million by 1974, and one and a quarter million under the last Labour Government. So the problem goes back 20 years. All this time we've avoided reality at the cost of rising prices and rising unemployment.'
>
> (Budget broadcast, 10 March 1981, emphasis in official transcript of broadcast.)

Sir Geoffrey Howe's views are analysed in Chapters 4 and 5.

Paradoxically, both its critics and its defenders are united in rejecting orthodox economics in favour of new theories of macroeconomics which challenge monetarist and Keynesian orthodoxy alike. For example, the Labour 'Alternative Economic Strategy' is based in part on 'New Cambridge' arguments; Mrs Thatcher's Chief Economic Adviser is an international monetarist. All these theories are analysed in Chapter 3, together with the American New Right, so crucial to an understanding of economic policy under President Reagan.

Mrs Thatcher was originally elected in large part because of an anti-union sentiment and trade unions are regarded by many as primarily responsible for the UK's economic ills. Chapter 6 is devoted to an analysis of the economics of industrial relations and strikes. The present government is also avowedly devoted to the free market. Many argue that this reflects ignorance of the modern evolution of the company, an issue discussed in Chapter 7. The whole case for and against state intervention is discussed in Chapter 8. The most controversial areas disputed between the state and the market are health, housing and education, discussed in Chapters 9, 10 and 11 respectively.

Hence we believe that this book provides the background essential to an understanding of the debate which surrounds economic policy in the UK in the 1980s. To quote the preface of the earlier volume, 'we hope that teachers and students alike will find this book useful as a demonstration of the power and scope of economic analysis'.

Contributors

David Gowland is a lecturer in economics at the University of York and is also Director of In-Service Training. He was the editor of *Modern Economic Analysis* and contributed six chapters to it. He worked in the economic section of the Bank of England from 1971 to 1973. He was founder co-author of the Rothschild Intercontinental Bank *Monthly Review* in 1974. Between 1975 and 1979 he worked as a consultant on domestic and international monetary and financial policy to the 10 Downing Street Policy Unit. He has written various articles on aspects of monetary economics and securities markets and is the author of several books including *Controlling the Money Supply*.

Mark Austin is a lecturer in economics at the University of Leeds. He was a contributor to *Modern Economic Analysis*. He was formerly a lecturer at the University of York and is currently engaged in research into the influence of company financial behaviour on investment.

Nick Jennett is a lecturer at Wolverhampton Polytechnic and was formerly a lecturer in industrial relations at Paisley College of Technology. His research interests include strike patterns and international comparisons of strike behaviour.

Alan Maynard is a reader in economics at the University of York. He was a contributor to *Modern Economic Analysis*. He has worked for the EEC Commission, the Organization for Economic Cooperation and Development (OECD), the Royal Commission on the Distribution of Income and Wealth, and the Royal Commission on the National Health Service. He is the author of numerous articles on economic aspects of social policy and of the book *Health Care in the European Community*.

Alan Williams is a professor in the Department of Economics at the University of York. He was a contributor to *Modern Economic Analysis*. He is currently a member of the National Water Council. He is the author of several books and numerous articles on public expenditure appraisal, including a recent book *The Principles of Practical Cost-Benefit Analysis*. Between 1966 and 1968 he was seconded to HM Treasury as a consultant on programme budgeting and cost-benefit analysis, and also served on various working parties concerned with the application of these techniques in local government. He has been a member of the Yorkshire Water Authority and of the Royal Commission on the National Health Service and is currently directing further empirical research on the economics of health and welfare services.

Contents

1
Techniques of Monetary Control

D. H. Gowland

1.1 INTRODUCTION

This chapter has two principal objectives. The first is to analyse the methods of monetary control used by the Conservative Government from 1979 to 1981. The other is to analyse the debate about the desirability of money base control that took place in the UK in 1979–1981 and the resulting changes in the techniques of monetary policy foreshadowed in a statement by Sir Geoffrey Howe on 24 November 1980, announced in the Budget on 10 March 1981 and introduced between then and 20 August 1981 when the new scheme was officially inaugurated.

The *modus operandi* of UK monetary control have had about the same degree of permanence as Italian premiers (see p.14ff). Accordingly, it is all the more necessary to emphasize the basic theory of monetary control (section 1.2) including the case for and against price and quantity controls which is presented in section 1.3. Within this context the kaleidoscopic pattern of UK monetary control can be analysed (1.4). Given these problems and the apparent failures of monetary policy in the UK, the argument for an alternative is obvious. The only alternative which *might* be politically feasible is some form of reserve base control, so this system is analysed (1.5). The Bank of England has argued forcefully that any system of reserve base control is both undesirable and unnecessary so this argument is considered (1.6). Finally the latest changes are examined (1.7 and 1.8).

1.2 THE ANALYTICAL FRAMEWORK

There are various ways of presenting the alternative menu of techniques of monetary control, but the most useful is the flow-of-funds approach: it is both the simplest framework and the one used by the UK authorities. This analysis starts with a definition of the money stock:

Money ≡ (Non-bank private sector holdings of) Currency + Residents' (bank) Deposits*. (1.1)

This is the open economy flow-of-funds model; the simple closed economy model is in Gowland (1979)[1].

The definition of money is a broad one such as the UK M_3 or sterling M_3 (or with an appropriate definition of bank PSL_2).

Bank deposits are held either by residents or by foreigners so:

Bank Deposits ≡ Residents' Deposits + Foreign-owned Deposits. (1.2)

Bank deposits are bank liabilities, and for simplicity the other liabilities are ignored[2], so:

Bank Deposits ≡ Bank Liabilities. (1.3)

The familiar balance sheet identity is

Bank Assets = Bank Liabilities. (1.4)

So, from (1.3) and (1.4):

Bank Deposits = Bank Assets. (1.5)

Bank assets include bank loans, premises, computers and so on but all assets other than loans are ignored. The consequences of relaxing this assumption are discussed in note 2. Therefore,

Bank Assets = Bank Loans (1.6)

and

Bank Deposits = Bank Loans. (1.7)

* Words in brackets are omitted on subsequent lines.

Bank loans can be made to foreigners, the public sector, or the non-bank private sector, so

Bank Loans = Bank Loans to Foreigners + Bank Loans to the Public Sector + Bank Loans to the (non-bank) Private Sector. (1.8)

Equations (1.2) and (1.8) can be combined to form (1.9):

Residents' Deposits + Foreign Deposits = Bank Loans to Foreigners + Bank Loans to the Public Sector + Bank Loans to the Private Sector. (1.9)

Bank loans to foreigners less foreign deposits can be presented as a net item, Bank Claims on Foreigners, so

Residents' Deposits = Bank Claims on Foreigers + Bank Loans to the Public Sector + Bank Loans to the Private Sector (1.10)

So, substitution (1.10) into (1.1):

Money = Currency + Bank Claims on Foreigners + Bank Loans to the Public Sector + Bank Loans to the Private Sector (1.11)

It is convenient to rewrite this equation as a flow, i.e. in changes, using the symbol Δ to indicate 'change in'.

Δ Money = Δ Currency + Δ Bank Claims on Foreigners + Δ Bank Loans to the Public Sector + Δ Bank Loans to the Private Sector. (1.12)

By definition,

Δ Bank Loans to the Public Sector ≡ Δ Total Loans to the Public Sector − Δ Non-bank Loans to the Public Sector. (1.13)

Δ Total Loans to the Public Sector is equal to the public sector borrowing requirement (PSBR) since lending to anyone must equal their borrowing, so

$$\Delta \text{ Bank Loans to the Public Sector} = \text{PSBR} - \Delta \text{ Non-bank Private Sector Loans to the Public Sector,} \quad (1.14)$$

or

$$\Delta \text{ Bank Loans to the Public Sector} = \text{PSBR} - (\Delta \text{ Currency} + \Delta \text{ Overseas Loans to the Public Sector} + \Delta \text{ Non-bank Private Sector Loans to the Public Sector).} \quad (1.15)$$

Equation (1.15) can be substituted into equation (1.12) in which case Δ Currency appears once as a positive and once as a negative term and thus cancels out, giving

$$\Delta \text{ Money} = \text{PSBR} + \Delta \text{ Bank Loans to the Private Sector} - \Delta \text{ Non-bank Private Sector Loans to the Public Sector} + (\Delta \text{ Bank Claims on Foreigners} - \Delta \text{ Overseas Loans to the Public Sector).} \quad (1.16)$$

This is the basic flow-of-funds equation. It must be emphasized that 'overseas loans to the public sector' means transactions with the overseas sector whereby the government acquires *sterling*, so it does not include government borrowing in foreign currency[3]. The bracketed items are usually called the overseas impact on the money supply, so (1.16) can be written in more familiar form[4]:

$$\Delta \text{ Money} = \text{PSBR} + \Delta \text{ Bank Loans to Private Sector} + \Delta \text{ Non-bank Private Sector Loans to the Public Sector} \pm \text{Overseas Impact.} \quad (1.17)$$

This equation is invaluable in many ways; it is necessary to emphasize that it is the money creation equation[5]. Money will be created if and only if one of the items on the right-hand side changes. A change in the PSBR will, *ceteris paribus*, have the effect of changing the money supply by precisely the amount of the increase in spending or reduction in taxation. To illustrate this, the example of a £100 wage payment to a teacher will be taken. She could receive this in currency, in which case there is obviously an increase in the money supply. It is more likely that she will receive a cheque for £100. This will be paid into her bank account in which case the bank's assets and liabilities will rise simultaneously by £100, and hence so will the money supply. The increase in bank assets is its claim on the government (the cheque), and the increase in bank liabilities is her deposit of £100, i.e. the increase in the money supply. This is the primary, or direct impact of government spending and must be distinguished from any subsequent transactions. The bank may convert the cheque into some other asset; it may increase or reduce its lending to other borrowers because of the increase in its assets. If it does, some of these subsequent transactions could affect the money supply so there might be a secondary, or induced effect on the money supply; in a reserve base system there will be. However, it is crucial to distinguish direct effects from secondary ones. Moreover, it is vital to emphasize that the impact of the PSBR on the money supply is independent of any induced or secondary effects.

Changes in bank loans create money because 'every loan creates a deposit'; every creation of a bank asset involves the simultaneous creation of a bank asset and liability, i.e. money. Changes in non-bank loans to the public sector are identical in their effects to the PSBR. If I write a cheque to the government, the money supply will fall, whether it is to pay my taxes or to buy savings certificates (or to buy BP shares). Changes in the overseas impact work similarly to changes in the other three items[6].

1.2.1 The techniques of control

In principle, it is possible to restrict the output or consumption of a good by three methods:

(1) *by price*, e.g. a higher price to reduce consumption;
(2) *by quantity control*, usually some form of rationing;
(3) *by interference with methods of production*, usually by a device designed to make the industry less efficient, e.g. restricting the number of vines per acre to reduce (French) wine output.

In the case of money (3) is the reserve base system, which is designed to reduce the output of either bank deposits or loans below the industry's unconstrained equilibrium level. Such a system is used in the US, the Federal Republic of Germany, Australia, New Zealand, South Africa, Venezuela and Mexico, but not in the UK. Recently, it has been argued that it should be. Both the system and the arguments against its use are considered below (see section 1.5).

In the case of monetary control, either price or quantity controls can be used[7]. Moreover, both can be used on either the 'asset' or the 'liability' side of the balance sheet of the banking sector. The two flow-of-funds equations illustrate this:

$$\Delta \text{ Money} = \Delta \text{ Residents' Deposits} + \Delta \text{ Currency} \quad (1.18)$$

$$= \text{PSBR} + \Delta \text{ Bank Loans to the Private Sector} - \Delta \text{ Non-bank Private Sector Loans to the Public Sector} \pm \text{Overseas Impact} \quad (1.19)$$

The first equation represents the liabilities (or demand) approach, the second the assets approach. Before examining the techniques in detail, two points must be made. The first is that, because assets equal liabilities, to alter one necessarily involves changing the other. The distinction is between seeking direct manipulation of bank liabilities (i.e. deposits) and accepting, as a consequence, a change in bank assets and, on the other hand, causing a change in bank assets so as to effect the desired change in bank liabilities, i.e. the money supply. The second preliminary remark is that the right-hand side variables in both (1.18) and (1.19) are not necessarily independent of each other. For example, a bond-financed increase in public spending has no effect on the money supply because the increase in the PSBR is offset by the larger (negative) impact of the private loans item. Similarly there is no point in direct manipulation of currency because deposits are likely to respond in order to offset the initial effect. Omitting direct manipulation of currency there are still nine major ways of controlling the money supply[8].

1.2.1.1 Price effects on bank deposits

The rationale for this method is to raise the rate of return on alternative assets relative to that on bank deposits in order to induce a shift out of bank deposits. In practice this method cannot be used because bank interest rates are far less sticky than those on some of the alternatives, especially, in the UK, building society deposits. Thus the authorities could raise the rate of return on some of the alternatives to bank deposits, e.g. savings certificates. The banks would follow suit but building society deposit rates would remain unchanged. Hence, bank deposits would attract money from building societies and the effect on the money supply would be perverse.

1.2.1.2 Quantity controls on bank deposits

The rationing of bank deposits is one obvious – if crude – method of controlling the money supply. The main example occurred in the UK where the authorities imposed ceilings on IBELs (interest-bearing eligible liabilities, i.e. deposits) from 1974 to 1980[9]. The general arguments for quantity controls are discussed below, in section 1.4. A major problem is evasion, which arose originally through the 'bill leak'[10]. A bank can perform the normal banking function by introducing a borrower to a lender and guaranteeing the loan. In this case, the transaction does not appear in the bank's balance sheet even though the investor holds a bank-guaranteed claim and the borrower has obtained funds through the banking system. If a bank lends by discounting and accepting a bill of exchange, and sells this to a potential depositor, this is what has happened. Thus, the form of the control is satisfied but the authorities' intention is evaded. This was sometimes also called the 'letter of acceptance' leak, from the name of a particular type of bill.

1.2.1.3 Price effects on bank lending

The *modus operandi* of this device is to reduce the level of the demand for bank credit below that at which it would otherwise have been by forcing up the rate of interest on borrowing from banks. This reduction in bank assets necessarily means that their liabilities are lower[11]. This policy was, or was intended to be, the centrepiece of the 'new approach' to *Competition and Credit Control* in the UK in 1971–1973. It was also a key element of the Conservative Government's policy from 1979.

In addition to the general problems with the use of price effects (see p.11ff below), there are a number of problems which apply peculiarly to using interest rates to control bank lending. The first is that there is no clear evidence that bank borrowing is interest sensitive. A Bank of England research study suggested that it was not[12]. The next is that even if it is, the authorities have to react quickly to changing circumstances. Otherwise inflationary expectations can accelerate, thus lowering the real rate of interest and increasing the demand for credit. If the authorities then raise (nominal) rates, the increase is too late to do more than partially offset the fall in real rates. A vicious cycle can develop in which rising nominal rates fail to catch up with accelerating inflationary expectations. This problem occurred in 1973 and 1979–1980.

Finally, the authorities' attempts to move along a demand curve may be offset by shifts of the curve. For example, in 1979–1980 the authorities found that the demand for credit accelerated because the depression shifted the demand for credit function by more than enough to offset any interest rate effect.

1.2.1.4 Quantity controls on bank lending

Credit ceilings in various forms work in the same way as interest rates; it does not matter why bank lending changes, the monetary consequences are identical. They were widely used in the UK from 1952 to 1971 and have been endemic in France[13]. They are subject to all the problems of direct controls discussed below – evasion, inefficiency, ineffectiveness, distortion of statistics, etc.

1.2.1.5 Price effects on non-bank private sector lending to the public sector

This device seeks to make public sector debt more attractive. This induces greater purchases by the non-bank private sector. They pay for the securities by writing cheques, or using currency, and so both bank deposits and bank assets (loans to the public sector) fall[14]. Usually, a higher interest rate is used to make government securities more attractive. However, this technique must not be confused with others – such as (1) and (3) above – that also involve higher interest rates because different interest rates are involved. In fact, increasing an interest rate for one purpose can make another technique work less well. For example, if bank loan rates go up, so do bank deposit rates and so the attractiveness of government debt falls relative to that of bank deposits. Hence, it has been argued that relative interest rates are more important for monetary policy than absolute levels. Since 1974, the UK government has manipulated interest rates so as to sell public sector debt – 'the Duke of York strategy'[15].

1.2.1.6 Quantity controls on non-bank purchases of public sector debt

If the authorities compel individual companies or institutions to purchase public sector debt, the money supply will be reduced in exactly the same way as if they had purchased it voluntarily. This *monetary* effect of a forced loan seems to have been the main reason why Keynes invented 'post-war credits'[16]. Otherwise, forced loans have had a bad press in the Anglo-Saxon world, being one of the ultimate 'bad things' in the words of *1066 and all that*. Richard II, Richard III, and Charles I all lost their thrones (and lives) partly because of imposing them. They are unconstitutional in the US. Nevertheless, the Jenkins squeeze in 1968–1969 seems to have been in large part effective because of the forced loan effect of import deposits. Moreover, the technique is used by the German and Belgian authorities, so perhaps the Anglo-Saxon prejudice is unjustified, although the author does not think so. In any case, all the problems of direct controls apply (see section 1.3).

1.2.1.7 PSBR

Any act of government spending and taxation, or any purchase or sale of an asset, will necessarily affect the money supply, although two transactions may cancel each other out as in the case of bond-financed expenditure. Thus, it is not surprising that, in recent years, the authorities in the UK have regarded the monetary effects of public sector actions as the major factor in determining the appropriate level of the PSBR and thus, of spending and taxation. This revolution in official attitudes has been as significant as the famous Kingsley Wood budget of 1941, which inaugurated Keynesian 'demand management'.

The PSBR can be influenced in many ways. Expenditure and tax policy can be altered: thus, for example, the *increase* in petrol tax in the 1981 budget 'to *reduce* inflation'. Nationalized industries can be made more profitable or their losses can be cut: hence, the increase in gas prices 'as an essential part of our anti-inflation strategy', to quote a Cabinet Minister in 1980. A Keynesian could offer an alternative explanation of why these policies could reduce inflation, but he could not explain why the sale of BP shares or the Gleneagles Hotel are thought by the Government to reduce inflation. However, in the flow-of-funds framework the explanation is obvious; asset sales reduce the PSBR as much as tax increases and have identical monetary effects. In fact, one of the major merits of flow-of-funds analysis is that it is the only way in which it is possible to explain or understand the rationale of the policy of the Conservative Government elected in 1979 and so to criticize (or defend) it.

Asset sales, however, are not a particularly good method of

trying to control the money supply. One of the problems with any technique is that it may be offset by a change in another financial aggregate. However, this is probably most serious with asset sales. For example, if the government sells BP shares in order to reduce the money supply, any of the following may occur.

(1) They may be bought by foreigners in which case there is a counterbalancing change in the overseas impact (i.e. the domestic borrowing requirement is unchanged)[17].
(2) They may be bought with a loan from the public sector – as with many sales of council houses.
(3) They may be bought instead of public sector debt, e.g. gilt-edged or national savings.
(4) They may be bought by a bank.
(5) They may be bought with finance provided by a bank.

In all these cases, there is no effect on the money supply.

1.2.1.8 Price effects on the overseas impact

This device seeks to induce a deterioration of the balance of payments (appropriately defined) in order to reduce the money supply. The mechanism is somewhat complex[18] but the intuitive idea is clear as in the analogous gold standard mechanism. Normally this technique means varying the exchange rate. Hence, Mr Healey let the exchange rate rise in November 1977 and his successor welcomed the rise in the exchange rate in 1979–1980 as it would help control the money supply.

1.2.1.9 Quantity effects on the overseas impact

This technique uses exchange control or other quantity methods in order to improve the balance of payments and cause monetary expansion or to worsen it and facilitate contraction. Hence, the German and Swiss authorities have imposed inward exchange control to prevent capital flows that would lead to monetary expansion, e.g. the Bardepot[19]. The House of Commons Treasury Committee recommended a similar scheme in the UK. The UK government adopted the variant of removing outward exchange control in November 1979 to encourage capital outflows so as to influence money and, hence, inflation.

1.3 THE CHOICE OF TECHNIQUE

There are three major categories of techniques of monetary control; price effects, quantity or direct controls, and the reserve base system. The first two have been used in the UK but, it has been argued, their inadequacies are such that base control should be introduced. This argument is explored later (section 1.5), but in this section the advantages and disadvantages of direct and price controls are set out. This is especially relevant, both to the reserve base debate as this system has some features of both of the others, and to the conduct of monetary policy in the UK where both types of control have been used so often and with such bewildering variations. Most of the arguments are based on elementary microeconomic theory, and, in particular, the elementary analysis of rationing and the consequent black market.

Direct controls are ineffective

This argument follows directly from the standard proposition that rationing creates an incentive to evade the control (profitably!), i.e. that a black market may emerge. Such evasion will frustrate the authorities' objectives. The most obvious relevant examples are the evasion of the ceilings on bank lending which led to the 'new approach' in 1971, and the erosion of the IBELs ceiling in 1978–1980 prior to its abandonment.

Direct controls are inefficient

By definition, direct controls override allocation by the price mechanism. Any system of allocation other than by price leads to a (Pareto) inefficient allocation of resources, at least on certain assumptions. This resource allocation argument for the price mechanism is discussed in Chapter 8.

Direct controls are inequitable

Since direct controls impede different groups in different ways, they are likely to be unfair. For example, in the UK in the 1960s established banks lost out to new institutions because the controls gave an unfair advantage to them. At the least, those who observe the regulations lose business to those who evade its spirit.

Direct controls distort statistics

This is probably the strongest argument against direct controls. No one will make a point of informing the authorities of a successful method of evading controls. Hence, the authorities will be unaware of the volume of black market transactions. Thus, they lack the information necessary for policy-making. If the distorted money supply statistics show a level of £60 000 m and the optimal level is £65 000 m, it is not clear whether policy is too slack or too tight because one does not know if the volume of black market transactions is more or less than £5 000 m. Moreover, direct controls in themselves cause structural changes which distort statistics. The last days of the IBELs ceiling in the UK in 1980 illustrate the problem vividly. The money supply grew 5% in one month after the ceiling was removed. How much was genuine and how much cosmetic, the result of black market transactions merely re-entering official statistics[20]? No one knows, yet the answer is vital to any assessment of monetary policy in 1979–1980. Even with hindsight, no one knows precisely what was happening. Distorted statistics make policy-making much more difficult.

Direct controls enable the money supply to be controlled with lower interest rates

If direct controls work, this is self-evident. The objective may be sought for political or distributional reasons but there is an economic case for it.

Direct controls permit more stable interest rates

This is also self-evident. The motive may be political but it can be justified on economic grounds. Stability is normally desirable in itself to facilitate better private sector decision-making. However, greater certainty about the rate of interest may be offset, or more than offset, by less certainty about the availability of credit.

Direct controls facilitate planning

This argument is based largely on French experience; the authorities have used credit controls as a major weapon in inducing industry to conform to the targets set by indicative plans.

Direct controls are biased towards investment

If the debatable proposition that more investment is desirable is accepted, this is an argument for direct controls. The argument is often based on casual empiricism; consumer loan demand is less interest sensitive than industrial demand. However, there is a sound theoretical case as well. The effect of higher interest rates on investment is clearly negative; the effect on consumption is ambiguous (see p.131 below)[21]. It is, however, worth pointing out that it may be stock investment rather than fixed investment which is favoured.

Interest rate changes are unfair to the building industry

Most buildings are erected by builders who depend upon bank credit to finance their operations. Most buildings are purchased with the aid of loans (lovers of atrocious puns may note that a building provides concrete security). The nature of net present value calculations is that the longer-lived an asset the more its desirability is affected by interest rate changes[22]. Buildings have the longest lives of all assets.

This completes the catalogue of arguments for and against direct controls. I should like to conclude by offering a series of general conclusions, or a list of personal prejudices.

(1) To be effective monetary policy must hurt sometimes and no technique can avoid this. Political will, even ruthlessness, is necessary to make any system work. With this, any system can work – at a price.

(2) Given existing political constraints, and the highly laudable Anglo-Saxon commitment to liberalism, direct controls cannot work in the UK for very long. Evasion is too easy, as is exemplified and argued below. In addition, no direct control can be effective without exchange control. Nevertheless,

(3) Direct controls have a role whenever the authorities make mistakes. A direct control seems to play a significant short-term role while it takes time for the effects of interest rates to work through. For example, the IBELs ceiling made it much easier to restrain monetary growth in May 1978 than in autumn 1979 when no effective direct control was available. So long as direct controls are used infrequently and for short periods, they will be effective because it is not worthwhile evading them; evasion is not costless.

An optimist would say that the above argument is invalid because it rests on an assumption of official fallibility. A cynic would argue that it is invalid because it ignores official fallibility, no politician will accept an infrequent short-term weapon. He will make it a frequently used, permanent weapon – and render it useless. Whether a fallible but prudent official decision-taker can exist, or has existed, is, perhaps, a moot point but the author is optimistic.

1.4 MONETARY CONTROL IN THE UK

It is useful to start this review of monetary control in the UK by emphasizing that one mechanism has not been used: the reserve base/minimum reserve ratio system, *pace* many elementary textbook statements. There have been a variety of ratios in the UK – including the 11% cash ratio in the 1920s, 8% cash ratio, 28 and 30% liquidity ratios, a 12½% reserve assets ratio after 1971 and (for the clearing banks) 1½% of liabilities held as balances with the Bank of England. However, none have been designed, or could hvae worked, as a textook reserve base system/minimum reserve ratio system in which, for example, the authorities have imposed a ratio of 20% and changed the base by 1 so as to change the money supply by 5. The evidence for this proposition is legion[23]. Bagehot emphasized it in his classic *Lombard Street* (1873). Both the evidence to and the report of the Macmillan Committee stressed the point in the 1930s – with Keynes, Lord Norman, Mckenna, Bradbury and Ernest Bevin in unique agreement. Radcliffe confirmed the irrelevance of the textbook model. More recently the authorities have stressed the point. The Governor's keynote speech introducing *Competition and Credit Control* could scarcely have been more explicit:

> 'It is not to be expected that the mechanism of minimum reserve ratio and special deposits can be used to achieve some precise multiple contraction or expansion of bank assets. Rather the intention is to use our control over liquidity, which these instruments will reinforce, to influence the structure of interest rates. The resulting change in relative rates of return will then induce shifts in the current portfolios of both the public and the banks'[24].

The Consultative Document produced by the Bank and the Treasury in 1980 stressed the same point once more[25]. Indeed, there would have been no point in the acrimonious debate about monetary control in 1980 if there had been a reserve base system. There would be no point in passionate advocacy of the introduction of a reserve base system or vehement opposition to it if such a system had already been in force. It was a comment both on the debate and on the increasing importance of monetary control that BBC's Radios 1 and 2 made a visit by the monetarist Karl Brunner to Mrs Thatcher to argue for base control their lead news item in September 1980. Friedman was quoted in the press as describing the opposition of Bank and Treasury officials to base control as sabotage. This heated and prolonged debate would have been meaningless if reserve base control were or had been in force.

The UK authorities have not used reserve base control. Instead they have used virtually every other control known to economic analysis. In the 1950s, the 'old approach' was inaugurated. From 1952 to 1971 this involved control of monetary aggregates by means of quantity controls on bank lending to the (non-bank) private sector[26]. In 1971 these were abandoned, and the 'new approach' was introduced. The reason was that evasion had, or at least so the authorities believed, both rendered the controls ineffective and so distorted the statistics that it was impossible to determine the appropriate monetary policy: the analysis is presented in 1.3 above. The evasion had taken various forms, usually called 'disintermediation' and 'parallel markets'[27].

The authorities responded in classic elementary microeconomic fashion: if rationing does not work, rely on the price mechanism. This was called the new approach to *Competition and Credit Control*. The authorities resolved to control all relevant financial aggregates by means of the effect of interest rates on bank lending to the private sector[28]. In 27 months, M_3, the target variable of this regime, rose by 60% and the scheme was abandoned in December 1973. There were a number of reasons why the *Competition and Credit Control* era was such a fiasco, but the major problem was the unwillingness of the authorities to accept the implications of the scheme in terms of either high or variable (nominal) interest rates.

The authorities introduced yet another regime of monetary control at the end of 1973, often called the 'new "new approach"'. This was introduced without the fanfare which marked similar changes in 1971 and 1979–1980 but was equally fundamental. There were three prongs to the new 'new approach'[29]. The first was the reintroduction of ceilings, so the authorities had to eat their brave words about the desirability of allocation by the price mechanism and the inevitable failure of ceilings. The ceiling was now on bank liabilities, the IBELs ceiling on bank deposits (not bank assets), so the authorities could preserve a fig-leaf of consistency. Moreover, there was a penalty if the ceiling was broken: supplementary special deposits. These had to be lodged on an interest-free basis with the Bank of England and were calculated as a percentage of the excess above the ceiling, the percentage rising with the amount of the excess. This, together with the effect of the depression and of the secondary banking crash, appeared to enable the new ceiling to be effective. The other weapons of the new 'new approach' were the use of the PSBR as a monetary weapon, see pp.9–10 above, and an aggressive gilt-edged marketing strategy called the Duke of York policy[30].

The new 'new approach' worked successfully until about the end of 1978. There were faults in the execution of monetary policy, notably a period of excessive optimism and complacency in late 1977–early 1978 which was abetted by poor statistics. The resultant explosion in monetary growth – to 16.2% in 1977–1978 – led to a property price boom and to problems for incomes policy[31]. In brief, the events of 1971–1973 were replayed in a minor key but vigorous action in May 1978 enabled the authorities to regain control of the situation and monetary growth was on target in 1978/79 at 13%.

Towards the end of this period, however, there were growing signs that the IBELs ceiling was starting to be evaded by the 'bill leak' described above. The Bank of England *Quarterly Bulletin* provided estimates of the 'bill leak' which suggest, as argued above, that the control was evaded because it was used for too long. Earlier evasion was on a small scale so the IBELs ceiling was still usable in September 1978 but by June 1979 it was being evaded on a substantial scale.

Hence it is possible to consider the weapons for monetary control which were available to the incoming Conservative Government. The Labour Government had pioneered variation of the PSBR for monetary control purposes, using both expenditure cuts and assets sales (especially of BP shares) for this purpose. The 'Duke of York' strategy had just worked again and was to be used three times in the first 15 months of the new government's life. Moreover, the authorities were experimenting with public sector debt policy. The use of 'part paid' issues made it possible to divorce the time of sale of gilts from the receipt of the funds and so reduce the variability in monetary growth. Limited experiments with 'tender' gilts, which gave the authorities more control over the quantity sold, had also been tried[32]. Mr Healey had also made national savings a weapon of monetary control, reversing the conventional wisdom of the 'new approach' embodied in the Page report[33]. This had involved both vigorous marketing of existing securities at more competitive rates (e.g. NSB accounts) and new types of security, e.g. the index-linked SAYE and 'Granny bonds'. The author has always been a passionate advocate of indexation on grounds of equity, efficiency and improved monetary control, but even less enthusiastic supporters welcomed both the flexibility and the success of the new departure[34]. Mr Healey had also broken another taboo in October 1977 by letting the exchange rate rise in order to curb monetary growth. To summarize, the major weapon of the new 'new approach' was in danger of becoming useless because of excessive and prolonged application, but many supplementary weapons were available and in good order.

This is not the place to analyse monetary policy from 1979 to 1981 in detail[35], but the salient feature of the period is that monetary growth accelerated to over 20% per annum despite a plethora of new techniques of control. At times the review of techniques conveyed the appearance of panic. Here, the techniques and their defects will be examined. The authorities put considerable and understandable emphasis on controlling overseas flows, both by means of price effects – allowing and on occasions forcing the exchange rate to rise – and by means of quantity controls. This involved the abolition of exchange control in November 1979, which in turn meant that the IBELs ceiling became totally ineffective, as argued above. The overseas tactics worked in that, in 1979–1980, the overseas influence was negative by over £2 bn despite a current account surplus, but the cost of this was that no quantity or direct control could any longer be used. The government placed considerable reliance on adjustment of the PSBR, especially by means of asset sales which, as argued above,is not a foolproof device. the Duke of York strategy continued to work; at the end of 1979, spring 1980, and July–August 1980. Further experiments with tender gilts followed and so did expansion of indexation, in December 1979 and November 1980. Of considerable technical significance, 'sale and repurchase agreements' were introduced with the banks on a regular basis whereby the banks sold gilts to the authorities but arranged to buy them back at a specified price on a given date. Of symbolic importance, the Bank 'spat on the flag' by reducing the tap price of gilt-edged securities in advance of a market fall, previously regarded as impossible.

Despite this plethora of new and well-established devices, the authorities put most reliance on the effect of interest rates on bank lending, a return to the spirit if not the practice of the 'new approach'. The *Quarterly Bulletin* of the Bank of England expressed its scepticism in surprisingly blunt terms: 'even sharp increases in interest rates may have little impact on the money supply'[36]. It is necessary to examine the problems associated with this technique and why it failed to curb bank borrowing, which accelerated sharply in the period after a very sharp increase in MLR to 17% on 16 November 1979. One problem, discussed above, is that the increase was too late by several months to avoid setting off a vicious cycle in which rising nominal rates failed to keep up with rising inflationary expectations, fuelled by the VAT increase in the June 1979 budget. Another problem stemmed from the government's own transmission mechanism. This was

(1) To curb monetary growth in order to
(2) Squeeze corporate liquidity so as to
(3) Reduce corporate spending (below the level at which it would otherwise have been) and, in particular, to
(4) Reduce spending on wages by containing wage settlements.

In addition, (1) would also tend to push up the exchange rate and so reinforce (3). Moreover, the pressure of demand would be such that price increases would not be a practicable means of maintaining liquidity.

Unfortunately for the Government, firms could also reduce their wage bill by reducing employment and cut their spending by reducing stocks or investment. In these cases the impact of monetary policy would be on output and not on inflation; in fact all four reactions took place, except the fall in investment, which held up surprisingly well. However, another reaction was to borrow more from banks so the policy was counter-productive. In other words, the squeeze shifted the demand for credit by more than the higher interest rate moved it along the demand curve. To be logical, the authorities should have raised interest rates still more but there were both economic and political reasons for hesitation[37].

To summarize, the authorities had a plethora of techniques available but most of them had problems which impaired their use. Moreover, they lacked an effective direct control. Thus the failure of monetary policy was not surprising. Hence, the authorities' attention was focused on possible alternatives. There was really only one: a reserve base system[38]. This issue was canvassed by the authorities[39] but the Bank remained resolutely opposed to it. The outcome of a prolonged debate was a series of changes in monetary control. The system, its merits and demerits and the results are discussed in the next three sections.

1.5 THE RESERVE BASE SYSTEM

The normal presentation of the reserve base system starts by defining money:

$$\text{Money} \equiv \text{Deposits} + \text{Non-bank Private Sector Holdings of Currency.} \tag{1.20}$$

(If not all Deposits are defined as part of the money supply, this equation can be amended without any consequences for the formal structure of the system.)

Next, it is *assumed* that the private sector holds a fixed percentage of its money holdings as currency (and a fixed percentage as deposits). If this fixed proportion is written as e,

$$\text{Currency} = \text{eMoney.} \tag{1.21}$$

The crux of the system is that the authorities impose a minimum reserve ratio on the banks such that their holdings of certain specified assets, the reserve base, is always at least equal to some specified proportion of their deposits. This proportion will be written as Z. (If the reserve ratio were 20%, Z would be ⅕.) Thus

$$\frac{\text{Reserves}}{\text{Deposits}} \geqslant Z. \tag{1.22}$$

The next step is to assume that banks are *short-run* profit maximizers and so never hold excess reserves. (Long-run profit-maximizing banks hold excess reserves so as to be able to facilitate increased lending if demand rises.) In this case

$$\frac{\text{Reserves}}{\text{Deposits}} = Z \tag{1.23}$$

or

$$\text{Deposits} = \frac{\text{Reserves}}{Z}. \tag{1.24}$$

Equations (1.24) and (1.21) can be substituted into equation (1.20):

$$\text{Money} = \frac{\text{Reserves}}{Z} + \text{eMoney} \tag{1.25}$$

which can be rearranged to form the basic equation, usually called the ratios equation:

$$\text{Money} = \frac{\text{Reserves}}{Z(1 - e)} . \tag{1.26}$$

The authorities can then, in principle, alter the money supply by changing Z (the reserve ratio) or the quantity of reserve assets in existence.

1.5.1 The behavioural underpinnings

Equation (1.26) implies nothing about behaviour nor does it offer any explanation of how the system might work. These questions are normally answered by reinterpreting the equation as a supply of credit equation[40]. The banks' balance sheet can be presented as

$$\text{Liabilities} \equiv \text{Assets}, \tag{1.27}$$

i.e.

$$\text{Deposits} = \text{Reserve Assets} + \text{Non Reserve Assets}. \tag{1.28}$$

Non Reserve Assets are defined as Credit so

$$\text{Deposits} = \text{Reserve Assets} + \text{Credit} \tag{1.29}$$

or

$$\text{Credit} = \text{Deposits} - \text{Reserves}, \tag{1.30}$$

i.e. using equation (1.24)

$$\text{Credit} = \frac{\text{Reserves}}{Z} - \text{Reserves} \tag{1.31}$$

$$= \frac{\text{Reserves } (Z - 1)}{Z} . \tag{1.32}$$

A story is told to justify this. Reserve assets are increased by the authorities by 10, in a system with a 20% reserve ratio. A bank receives these as a deposit of 10. It then retains 2, as reserves against its deposits, and loans 8. This 8 is paid as a deposit into another bank which loans 6.4 (80% of 8) and so on *ad infinitum*. The increase of 10 in reserve assets leads to loans of 40 (the supply of credit) which together provides the counterpart of the increased deposits of 50. This familiar credit mulitiplier story has many defects of which one is that it ignores the fact that some of the loans may be held as currency. In this case, the story might go as follows:

Round 1: Reserve assets increase by 10, received as a bank deposit;
Round 2: Bank loans out 8;
Round 3: Private sector retains half the 8 as currency and re-deposits 4;
Round 4: Bank receives 4 and loans 3.2, etc.

In this example, the crucial nature of the assumption about a fixed currency : deposit ratio becomes apparent (equation 1.21 above). If the general values e and Z are inserted in the story, the first round is Change in Reserves, the second (1 − Z)·Change in Reserves, the next round of loans is (1 − Z)·(1 − e)·Change in Reserves, etc. This is a geometric series whose sum to infinity is equation (1.26). In other words, there is a behavioural justification for (1.26). This model is normally presented as shown in *Figure 1.1a*. The supply of credit is drawn as an inelastic supply curve, dependent on Z and the quantity of reserves. This intersects with a demand curve to give an equilibrium rate of interest (r_1) and quantity of credit (Q_1).

The inelastic supply of credit seems unrealistic so the next change in the model is to assume that banks hold excess reserves but that the quantity falls as interest rates rise. In this case, Z and the quantity of reserve assets determine a maximum value of credit, shown as S_{max} in *Figure 1.1b*. The actual supply curve (S) is upward sloping and is asymptotic to S_{max}. The 'new view of money' of Tobin draws an upward supply curve on a priori grounds and ignores all the preliminaries. The author is an advocate of the 'new view' but for a defence of the 'multiplier approach' see Coghlan (1980).

In the reserve base system, the authorities seek to shift the supply curve for credit, as shown in *Figures 1.1c* and *1.1d*, so as to change the quantity of credit in order to change the money supply.

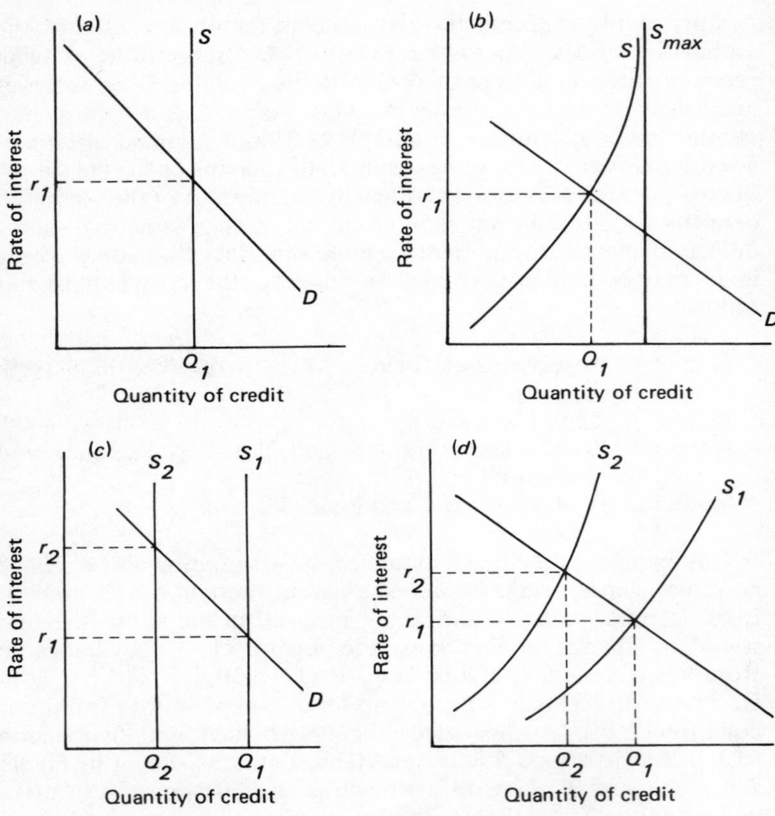

Figure 1.1 Money base control

An element of the case against reserve base control is that when S_{max} is changed there is no reason why the shift in the actual supply of credit should be even predictable, let alone parallel or of equivalent size.

1.6 THE RESERVE BASE SYSTEM: FOR AND AGAINST

The extent of the divergence of opinion about the reserve base system can be seen in the following quotes:

> 'A determined control of the monetary base, technically achievable by any central bank, is sufficient (and necessary) to ensure that no monetary aggregates can run away.' (Brunner, 1981)

> 'This approach [monetary base control] therefore is intended to provide a means for the markets to generate the interest rates necessary [to control the money supply].' (Bank, 1980)

The Bank views the reserve base system merely as a means of adjusting interest rates, 'as interest rate control in disguise' as Lewis put it (1980), in contrast to Brunner (and Friedman) who regard it as a genuine alternative.

The Bank's argument against reserve base control can be divided into two propositions (see Bank, 1980 and Foot *et al.*, 1979):

(1) At best reserve base control is the same as interest rate control.
(2) In fact it is likely to be ineffective and may suffer all the problems of direct controls.

However, they concede

(3) That movements in bank portfolios may act as a signal which conveys information on the basis of which the authorities may act.

Base control is, at best, the same as interest rate control

This argument can be examined best in the context of *Figures 1.1c* and *1.1d*. The effect on the money supply obtained by shifting the supply curve from S_1 to S_2 is exactly the same as, and could have been achieved by, increasing interest rates from r_1 to r_2. In the Bank's view, reserve base control is merely a means of changing interest rates. Friedman, on the other hand, accepts that reserve base control involves a change in rates but denies both that this causes the change in money and that there is a definite relationship between the change in money and that in interest rates.

Moreover, the Bank stresses the unpredictability of the shift in the supply curve in response to changes in the quantity of base assets. However, as argued in Gowland (1982), if there is not perfect knowledge of the demand curve for credit, base control may lead to more certain control of money at the cost of greater variability in interest rates. It is, however, *possible* that a reserve base system could be manipulated so as to produce less variability in rates by avoiding a variant of 'overshooting'[41].

To summarize, the Bank argues that the authorities can move along a demand curve (for credit) more easily by changing prices than by shifting the supply curve. Brunner and Friedman argue the opposite.

Base control will be ineffective

The Bank's basic proposition is that base control is another direct control and so it is subject to evasion, inefficiency and inequity, and likely to distort statistics and so on. Basically, this is true but one crucial distinction must be noted. Direct controls, like ceilings, put a limit on each bank. The reserve base system places the limit on the banking system as a whole so banks can compete with each other for base assets. This means that in some respects the system is a half-way house between price and quantity controls. The Bank would no doubt argue, with much justice, that it combines the worst of both worlds.

There are many ways in which a reserve base system can be evaded. One obvious method, also used to evade the IBELs ceiling, that some banks appear to have implemented, is to book banking transactions overseas. A bank can make a loan in any currency and in any centre of its choice and, so long as spot and forward exchange markets are available, the customer is indifferent to the currency and the place. A loan in, say, Hong Kong dollars in Dubai is the same as a loan in sterling in London so long as the transaction can be covered by a (forward) purchase of Hong Kong dollars. However, the bank has moved its assets outside the purview of UK monetary control. The bank can also transfer its deposits to a foreign branch. All negotiations could take place in London but the transactions would appear in the bank's books in, say, Paris. Thus reserve base requirements would be evaded. This happened on a large scale in the 1960s to evade US reserve requirements[42]. It is clear that such transactions would lead to both evasion and distortion of statistics. Without exchange control, base control could not operate in the UK.

This danger of evasion is the major argument, to me at least, in the case against reserve base control but there are other problems. These can be summed up in three questions.

(1) WHAT IS A BANK?

It is not clear to which organization reserve base requirements should apply, in other words 'what is a bank?' The notorious problem of non-member banks which are exempt from Federal Reserve requirements exemplifies this in the US[43]. There is no clear-cut distinction between banks and non-banks. Any boundary will be arbitrary and unfair. Moreover, those lucky enough to be on the non-bank side will be given a competitive advantage and will expand so as to produce evasion.

(2) WHAT IS MONEY?

The problem is to define those liabilities against which reserves should be held, i.e. what is money. There is no clear-cut answer and again any definition would produce evasion since the assets excluded would grow disproportionately fast because of the obvious incentive to increase supply. 'Goodhart's law' would apply with full force; to control (a definition of money) is to distort (its significance).

(3) WHAT SHOULD THE BASE BE?

The authorities need to be able to control the quantity of base assets, police the total and (at least at the margin) be the sole source of issue. The Bank has argued that no definition of the base would give this degree of control in the UK[46]. The authorities can fix a price at which reserve assets are available but this, in the Bank's view, makes base control equivalent to the effects generated by alteration of interest rates.

There are a number of possible solutions to these problems. The main effect is that the distinction between base control and interest rate control is blurred, or at least that is the conclusion reached by Lewis (1980) and Gowland (1982). However, one alternative has been mooted and widely debated. This is 'non-mandatory' base control analysed by the Banks as 'the Swiss system'[44]. If there is an asset which banks believe they must hold in a fixed proportion to their deposits and for which there is no substitute, then a (non-mandatory) base system can be operated by official manipulation of this aggregate. Unfortunately, there is no evidence that such an asset exists. Banks must hold *some* cash but the minimum may be as low as ¼ or ⅓% of their deposits. A credit multiplier of 300 or 400 is daunting enough but the value would be unstable; any squeeze on cash would drive the banks' minimum down. Non-mandatory base control seems impracticable in the light of present knowledge and evermore sophisticated banking techniques.

1.6.1 The debate: some conclusions

The Bank has reaffirmed the position it took at the time of the *new approach*: money can be controlled only by interest rates. Any other method of control, whether by means of a ceiling or a reserve base system, can only operate if, and inasmuch as, it influences interest rates. These other methods of control are likely to produce distortion of official statistics and so render an effective monetary policy impossible. Moreover, it is probable that they will be evaded and they are likely to be inequitable and inefficient both because of misallocation of resources and the wasteful expenditure that takes place on evasion. Finally, the Bank stresses that there is a choice between interest rate stability and stability in monetary growth. The new elements are that the Bank is now less wedded to interest rate stability and would accept that observation of the composition of bank assets might be a good way of judging when to raise or lower rates, even going so far as to suggest a quasi-automatic system (Bank, 1980, pp.12–15) which has found few other supporters.

This position is intellectually impeccable but depends upon

(1) There being a stable, interest elastic demand for credit, for which the authorities possess knowledge of the parameters. Moore and Threadgold (1980) have re-emphasized the doubt about this.
(2) The authorities having the political will to raise interest rates to the required level when necessary.
(3) The authorities having the knowledge and the will to adjust interest rates quickly enough. Delay may be disastrous for the reasons discussed above.

Doubt may be expressed on all three points. The implications are that a satisfactory method of monetary control does not, and perhaps cannot, exist in the UK. The new package introduced in 1980–1981 has done nothing to diminish this worry.

1.7 THE NEW MEASURES

On 24 November 1980, Sir Geoffrey Howe produced the monetary policy equivalent of a Budget, e.g. reducing MLR and announcing a new money supply target. He also introduced some longer-term, more tentative measures[45]. More measures, many of which confirmed the November package, followed in his Budget on 10 March 1981. Further changes followed culminating in the abolition of MLR on 20 August 1981. These measures will be examined and analysed in this section. They are described in Bank (1981) and Treasury (1981.)

First of all, the Chancellor announced that monetary base control would not be introduced. However, steps would be taken to investigate whether there was a meaningful monetary base and to collect statistics on this aggregate and to monitor it. It was hinted that the authorities would experiment to see if they could control the aggregate and that in the long run this might be equivalent to a non-mandatory base system. The Bank produced several alternative definitions of base[46]. The Chancellor announced the phasing out of the 12½% reserve assets ratio. The ratio would be reduced to 10% from 7 February 1981. It was further reduced to 8% in the Budget and then abolished in August. As the ratio had not been very effective in its objective as a device to influence short-term rates, this was logical[47]. The authorities also abolished the clearing banks' obligation to hold an amount equal to 1½% of their eligible liabilities interest-free with the Bank of England. Instead, all banks were required to lodge ½%. This was associated with a prolonged discussion of prudential ratios.

In addition to the new base statistics the authorities started to collect data for an American-definition M_2 series, i.e. currency, demand deposits and retail (less than £100 000) time deposits. This is Friedman's preferred definition of money. The authorities have also added two very broad definitions of money, called PSL_1 and PSL_2 (private sector liquidity). As 'credit proxy' data are also available in addition to two EEC-defined money series (L_1 and L_2) there are now official statistics for eight definitions of money (M_1, M_2, £M_3, M_3, L_1, L_2, PSL_1, PSL_2), not to mention DCE and credit proxy data. This is still modest compared with the New York Fed's output of about 40 series[48]. The additional information should prove valuable and emphasizes the advantages of setting multiple targets rather than a single aggregate. In similar vein, the authorities committed themselves to continued experiments with weekly monetary data.

The authorities continued to introduce new methods for debt management policy. They extended indexation to some new gilt-edged stock but restricted its purchase to pension funds. Two issues followed, £1 bn in March 1981 and £750 m in July 1981, both of which offered a real rate of return of over 2%; they were sold by tender. As a further measure, the age restriction on 'Granny bonds' (index-linked national savings) has been removed and an issue of oil bonds announced.

It would be difficult to criticize any of the above policies. Flexibility and a desire for knowledge are welcome in policy-makers. Both were exemplified in the new measures. Moreover, the experiments with gilts were a preparation for the eventual breakdown of the Duke of York strategy, should that manoeuvre ever cease to work. Nevertheless, all of these policy changes were tentative and on a small scale. The other changes, which involved dealing policy and intervention rates, were more controversial.

In a brilliant sally, Griffiths had accused the Bank of being a lender of first rather than last resort[49]. The substance of the charge involved the optimal choice between variability of interest rates and money. The Bank agreed that it had put too much emphasis on price and not enough on quantity so it changed its dealing strategy in the money markets in an American direction. The authorities would no longer deal at predetermined prices in securities with more than seven days to mature. Instead they would respond to offers of the Treasury bills concerned at a price (i.e. interest rate) within a narrow band which would be unpublished and would vary according to market conditions. The new policy was first seen in action in early July. Whilst 'new' this change fitted in with the Bank's traditional desire to maximize its freedom of action. It also inspired the most publicized change, the abolition of MLR on 20 August. Once the new dealing strategy was introduced MLR had little remaining practical significance. The Bank had already changed its official interest rate twice each time both in order to depoliticize it and to avoid being constrained by it. Bank Rate was abolished in 1972 and replaced by MLR so that rates could be raised covertly, and to make the rate less political. The formula by which it was normally fixed was abolished in May 1978 to increase official freedom of action (the authorities had always retained effective control of the rate but often the cost of adjustment was too high). The move from a published and publicized MLR fixed with pomp and ceremony to an intervention rate varied up to twice a day at the authorities' discretion was the logical culmination of the process. In summary, the authorities

(1) Showed flexibility in debt management, especially by accepting creeping indexation.
(2) Did not entirely close the door on radical changes, e.g. a non-mandatory base system, but for the time being ruled them out.
(3) Accepted more variability in rates in order to achieve greater control of money.
(4) Collected more data.
(5) Obtained more freedom of action in day-to-day operations.

1.8 THE IMPLEMENTATION

After 15 controversial years and prolonged debate the authorities had restated the Bank's traditional position; that monetary control could be achieved only by manipulation of the level and, especially, the structure of interest rates. This manipulation would be facilitated considerably by more discretion in fixing day-to-day interest rates. In fact there was only one substantial difference compared to views expressed in the new approach of 1971 and the abolition of Bank Rate in 1972. This was that far greater, and ever increasing, emphasis was placed on sales of public sector debt to the non-bank private sector and far less on the control of bank lending. This emphasis was encouraged in 1981–82 by the ease with which public sector debt was marketed and the problems in predicting let alone influencing bank lending.

Public sector debt policy in 1981–82 continued to show both imagination and flexibility. In the 1982 Budget, index linked gilts were made available to all purchasers. This – and the real interest rate of 3 per cent – meant that private investors, like their Victorian predecessors, could plan expenditure and saving without the uncertainty engendered by inflation. In the 1982 Budget the revolution in National Savings policy since 1973 was completed. In 1973 (Page, 1973), national savings had been a 'social service' not 'an instrument of economic policy'. From 1978, the authorities had used national savings as an instrument of economic policy but with the restricted objective of maximizing sales. From 1981–82 onwards there were to be precise targets as a major element of monetary management. When in July 1982 it seemed that sales were less than the target the authorities raised the holding limit on index-linked national savings certificates and, crucially, introduced a new security, designed to compete with many market funds, called the Income Bond. These imaginative innovations in debt policy were matched by a vigorous policy of asset sales e.g. Amersham, Cable and Wireless and the Wych farm fields. These, however, were far less adeptly handled.

On the other hand whilst debt management revealed a new level of flexibility and skill at hitting targets, bank lending appeared almost totally out of control. The impact of the revision may have been to shift massively the corporate demand for liquidity (and so precautionary borrowing to build up liquid balances). In any case corporate borrowing rocketed, e.g. sterling lending by banks to the UK private sector rose by over £9 billion in the first half of 1982. In consequence the authorities sold ever more debt to offset this avalanche of bank lending. The result was from August 1981 onwards, sales of public sector debt nearly always exceeded the PSBR. Thus the authorities were in a position to reduce their indebtedness to the banking system. However, this would have had certain undesirable effects, such as the disappearance of Treasury bills, which would have made short-term control of interest rates much harder. Therefore instead of reducing bank loans to the public sector the authorities purchased large quantities of assets from the banks in the form of commercial bills, some £8 billion in 1981–82. Additionally, by increasing the banks' secondary liquidity, the change fitted in with the abolition of the 'lender of first resort' and the consequent reduction in primary liquidity. This was one of the two major changes in monetary policy in 1981–82, the other being the concession to academic and city opinion made in the 1982 Budget by the introduction of targets for M_1 and PSL_2 as well as £M_3.

Notes

1 This sub-section is an extension of the closed economy model in Gowland (1979), pp.2–5. The earlier text is much simpler and should preferably be consulted first. Gowland (1982) presents the model in more depth in Chapter 2, sections 2.3 and 2.5.
2 The other liabilities are owners' capital (including reserves) and debentures etc. If the other liabilities and assets are included, an extra term, 'net non deposit liabilities', appears. See Gowland (1982), Chapter 2, Appendix A.
3 See Gowland (1979), pp.28–31 and the fuller explanation in Gowland (1982), Chapter 2, section 2.5.
4 This is also known as the DCE equation, see Gowland (1979), p. 4.
5 See Gowland (1979), pp. 26–27 and Gowland (1982), Chapter 2, section 2.2.
6 See Gowland (1979), p. 28 and Gowland (1982), Chapter 2, section 2.5.
7 See Gowland (1979), pp. 5–7 for a condensed treatment of this material.
8 See Gowland (1982), Chapter 2.
9 For the IBELs scheme see Gowland (1982), Chapter 8.
10 Detailed references are in Gowland (1978).
11 The technique is discussed at more length in Gowland (1982).
12 Moore and Threadgold (1980).
13 See Gowland (1982), pp. 34–37 and references cited there.
14 This is explained in more detail in Gowland (1982).

15 See Gowland (1982), Chapter 8, section 8.2. The name is because rates are 'marched to the top of the hill and down again'.
16 See Keynes's papers, reprinted in Keynes (1971).
17 For the DBR see Gowland (1979) and, for an extended version of the present argument, Gowland (1982), Chapter 10.
18 See Gowland (1982), Chapter 2, section 2.5.
19 See Gowland (1979), Chapter 4.
20 The issue is discussed in Gowland (1982), Chapters 9 and 10.
21 For the effect on investment see Austin's chapter in Gowland (1979).
22 See the fuller version of this argument in Gowland (1982), p. 33.
23 For a more extended version of this argument see Gowland (1982), pp. 11–12 (where full references are provided) and also Gowland (1979), pp. 13–14 and Gowland (1978), p. 30ff.
24 Reproduced in Bank (1971).
25 Bank (1980): see also Foot *et al.* (1979) for an analysis by Bank economists.
26 See Gowland (1979), pp. 7–10 and Gowland (1982), Chapter 5, sections 5.1 and 5.2.
27 See references cited in note 26.
28 Gowland (1978), Chapter 2; Gowland (1979), pp. 10–18; and Gowland (1982), Chapter 5. See also Zawadzki (1981).
29 Gowland (1979), pp. 18–26; Gowland (1978), Chapter 8; and Gowland (1982), Chapters 8 and 9.
30 See references cited in note 29 and the additional references cited therein.
31 See Gowland (1982), Chapter 9, sections 9.5 and 9.6.
32 See Gowland (1982), pp. 93 and 175 and Bank (1979).
33 Page (1973).
34 See e.g. Gowland (1978), Chapter 9 and Bank (1979).
35 See Gowland (1982), Chapter 10.
36 Vol. 20, no. 2 (June 1980), p. 173.
37 See Gowland (1982), Chapter 10, esr p. 185.
38 See Gowland (1982), Chapter 3.
39 SeeFoot *et al.* (1979) and Bank (1980).
40 See e.g. Culbertson (1972).
41 See the discussion in Gowland (1982) and the references cited therein.
42 See Gowland (1979), Chapter 3.
43 See Gowland (1978), Chapter 7 and Gowland (1982), Chapter 3.
44 See Bank (1980), p.9.

45 See *Bulletin*, Vol, 20, no. 4 (December 1980), pp. 390 and 428.
46 See *Bulletin*, Vol. 21, no. 1 (March 1981), p. 59.
47 'it presented particular short-term difficulties' (Bank, 1980, p. 18); on the RAR see Bank (1980), pp. 16–20, Gowland (1978), pp. 30–35, and Gowland (1979).
48 See Gowland (1978), Chapter 9; Gowland (1982), Chapter 8; Foot (1981); and Buiter (1980).
49 For example in IEA (1980).

Guide to further reading

This chapter is intended to be a complement to the first chapter of Gowland (1979). The analysis presented here can also be found in an extended and more rigorous form in Gowland (1982). In both cases, I have provided extensive cross references. Foot *et al.* (1979), Bank (1980), and Lewis (1980) are the most useful analyses of the reserve base system. Bank (1981) is invaluable. Valuable, more general studies of monetary policy include Artis (1978), Tew (1978), Dennis (1980), Goodhart (1973 and 1981), Pepper and Wood (1976), Smethurst (1979), and Artis and Lewis (1981).

Bibliography

ARTIS, M. J. (1978), 'Monetary Policy, Part II', in BLACKABY, F. T. (ed.), *British Economic Policy 1960–74*, Cambridge University Press; Cambridge

ARTIS, M. J. and LEWIS, M. K. (1981), *Monetary Control in the UK*, Philip Allan, Oxford

BAGEHOT, W. (1873), Lombard Street, John Murray; London (reprinted by *The Economist*, in his collected works, ed. by N. St. John-Stevas, 1965)

BANK (1971), *Competition and Credit Control*, Bank of England

BANK (1979), 'The Gilt Edged Market', *Bank of England Quarterly Bulletin,* Vol. 19, No. 2 (June), p. 137

BANK (1980), *Monetary Control*: A Consultation Paper by HM Treasury and the Bank of England, Cmnd 7858, HMSO; London

BANK (1981), 'Monetary Control Provisions', *Bank of England Quarterly Bulletin*, Vol. 21, No. 3 (September), p. 323

BRUNNER, K. (1981), 'Monetary Policy', *Lloyds Bank Review*, No. 139 (February), p. 1

BUITER, W. (1980), *The Superiority of Contingent Rules over Fixed Rules in Models with Rational Expectations*, Bristol Discussion Paper 80/80, University of Bristol

COGHLAN, R. T. (1980), *Theory of Money and Finance*, Macmillan; London

CULBERTSON, J. M. (1972), *Money and Banking*, McGraw-Hill; New York

DENNIS, G. E. J. (1980), 'Money Supply and its Control', in MAUNDER, W. P. J. (ed.), *The British Economy in the 1970s*, Heinemann Educational Books; London

FOOT, M. D. K. W. *et al.* (1979), 'Monetary Base Control', *Bank of England Quarterly Bulletin*, Vol. 19, No. 2 (June), p. 149

FOOT, M. D. K. W. (1981), 'Monetary Targets: Their Nature and Record in the Major Economies', in GRIFFITHS, B. and WOOD, G. E. (eds.), *Monetary Targets*, Macmillan; London

GOODHART, C. A. E. (1973), 'Monetary Policy in the UK', in HOLBIK, K. (ed.) *Monetary Policy in Twelve Industrial Countries*, Federal Reserve Bank of Boston; Boston

GOODHART, C. A. E. (1981), 'Problems of Monetary Management', in COURAKIS, A. S. (ed.), *Inflation, Depression and Economic Policy in the West*, Mansell and Alexandrine Press; London

GOWLAND, D. H. (1978), *Monetary Policy and Credit Control: The UK Experience*, Croom Helm; London

GOWLAND, D. H. (ed.) (1979), *Modern Economic Analysis*, Butterworths; London

GOWLAND, D. H. (1982), *Controlling the Money Supply*, Croom Helm; London

IEA (1980), *Is Monetarism Enough*, IEA Readings No. 24, IEA; London

KEYNES, J. M. (1971), *Collected Writings*, Macmillan; London, for the Royal Economic Society, Vol. XVI

LEWIS, M. (1980), 'Is Monetary Base Control Just Interest Rate *Control* in Disguise', *Banker* (September), p. 35

MOORE, B. J. and THREADGOLD, A. R. (1980), 'Bank Lending and the Money Supply', *Bank of England Discussion Paper No. 10* (July)

PAGE, H. (1973), *Report of the Official Committee on National Savings*, Cmnd 5273, HMSO; London

PEPPER, G. T. and WOOD, G. E. (1976), 'Too Much Money . . .?', *Hobart Paper 68*, Institute of Economic Affairs

SMETHURST, R. G. (1979), 'Monetary Policy', in MORRIS, D. (ed.) *The Economic System in the UK* (2nd edn.), Oxford University Press, Oxford

TEW, B. (1978), 'Monetary Policy, part I', in BLACKABY, F. T. (ed.), *British Economic Policy 1960–74*, Cambridge University Press; Cambridge

TREASURY (1981), 'New Monetary Control Arrangements', *Economic Progress Report*, No. 137 (September)

ZAWADZKI, K. K. F. (1981), *Competition and Credit Control*, Basil Blackwell; Oxford

2
Interest Rates

D. H. Gowland

2.1 INTRODUCTION

Interest rates have always fascinated economists because they provide the most convenient tool with which to analyse two of the most fundamental and intractable problems in economics. Interest rates provide a link between the real and financial sectors of the economy. Such links are crucial to any analysis of monetary policy. Interest rates also provide the simplest and most realistic means of analysing decisions across time. There are alternatives, of which the best known is that suggested by Arrow and Debreu, namely to label goods according to their date and use conventional microeconomic tools to analyse production and consumption decisions. The normal apparatus of indifference curves, isoquants, etc. can be applied for baked beans for delivery in 1981 and to those for delivery in 1982 just as easily as to baked beans and tomatoes. However, there are a number of limitations to this analysis so it is preferable to recognize that decisions involving the future normally involve interest rates and the financial system.

It is one of the main institutional features of a modern economy that the monetary system is used in nearly all transactions in some form or other, including cash, cheques, credit cards and other means of deferred payment. Goods are purchased with money and labour is sold for money by most private individuals. They do not trade goods for goods or labour for goods; barter in any form is unusual. However, both conventional microeconomic theory and the elementary Keynesian model implicitly assume a barter economy, or rather that the existence of money and a financial system does not affect any results derived for a barter economy. This assumption is relaxed in monetary economics and it is the role of the monetary theorist to construct a model of the financial sector to interact with these models of the real sector. Monetary theory usually gives pride of place to interest rates which are the inverse of the price of financial assets (see below). Moreover, if the barter assumption, usually called the classical veil or classical dichotomy, is to be relaxed, some mechanism is required whereby developments in the financial sector and the real sector interact. As the rate of interest has an important role in real sector decision-making (section 2.3), it provides a highly flexible link. Any development in the financial sector affects the equilibrium rate of interest and so the optimal decisions in the real sector. This disturbance in the real sector will feed back into the rate of interest and so disturb equilibrium in the financial sector. This iterative process continues until a new equilibrium is reached. The most frequently analysed of such processes is the transmission mechanism of monetary policy whereby the authorities deliberately seek to influence the financial sector so as to produce a different real sector equilibrium.

Similarly, any disturbance to the real sector must affect the equilibrium rate of interest and so throw the financial sector into disequilibrium and set off a chain of financial–real interactions until a new equilibrium is reached. In this way it is possible to analyse such questions as whether the impact of a 'real shock', for example a change in government spending, is dependent on its method of finance.

In this chapter interest rates are considered, first in financial markets (section 2.2), then in real markets (section 2.3). In section 2.4 a model for the determination of interest rates is developed. However, there is not just one interest rate: there are many, dependent on who borrows, with what security and for how long. The multi-dimensional nature of interest rates is examined in section 2.5. Finally, the most important distinction, time, is examined in section 2.6 which is devoted to an analysis of the term structure of interest rates, the relationship between long and short-term interest rates.

2.2 INTEREST RATES AND FINANCIAL MARKETS

Individuals, companies and governments can borrow in many ways. The simplest is a loan, e.g. a bank loan, that is due to be repaid on a specified date. In this case it is simple to calculate the rate of interest, although there are problems – should simple or compound rates be used, for example? Moreover, 10% per annum paid four times a year in equal instalments is a higher rate of interest than 10% per annum paid on 31 December, as the recipient can earn interest on the earlier instalments until 31 December in the first case. These problems led the government to introduce an official measure of the cost of credit, called the annualized percentage rate (APR). This was a recommendation of the Crowther Committee (1971) and was enacted under the provisions of the Consumer Credit Act 1973.

Most government and a large proportion of corporate borrowing is in the form of bonds and bills. The distinction is legal but usually bills are for a much shorter period than bonds. In both cases, the debt is marketable and the security, whether a bond or a bill, is £*x* per year interest plus (usually) a capital repayment of £*y* at some future specified date. The borrower sells this to the lender at an agreed price and the initial lender can resell the asset if he wishes. There is a nominal value of the loan, normally the amount to be repaid. There is a coupon rate, the payment per year as a percentage of the nominal value. These two amounts are fixed at the start of the loan and never vary. However, the market value need not be equal to the nominal value, nor need the effective interest rate be equal to the coupon rate. For example, the market value of a bond with a 5% coupon and a nominal value of £100 is currently about £50. This bond is really a claim to a payment of £5 per annum for a number of years and to a payment of £100 at a (specified) future date. The value of this stream of payments can be calculated using the discounting procedure outlined by Williams (in Gowland 1979). The net present value of the stream, at the prevailing rate of interest, will equal the market price of the bond. If interest rates rise, the NPV and so the bond's price will fall and vice versa for a fall in interest rates. This creates an inverse relationship between bond prices and interest rates. This fundamental relationship is seen most clearly in the case of an irredeemable security such as Consols and War Loan issued by the UK government. In this case, the bond is an entitlement to a constant (money) income for ever with no repayment, e.g. £100 nominal of 3½% War Loan entitles the holder to £3.50 per annum for ever (technically an annuity of £3.50). The change in value of this bond is exactly the inverse of the alteration in the rate of interest. It is easy to see that if interest rates were 7%, an annuity of £3.50 per annum would be worth £50, and if rates rose to 14%, the bond would be worth £25. Hence, if interest rates double, the value of the bond is halved. If a bond entitled the holder to £100 in one year's time, and no other payments, the rise in interest rates would reduce its value from £93 to £86. The relationship is still an inverse one, but in general the longer dated a bond is the greater its variation in price when interest rates change.

There are some other technical points concerning interest rates on securities. It is sometimes useful to distinguish between redemption rates or yields (the two terms are identical) and flat or running ones. The redemption yield is the interest rate used to discount the security in order to determine its price (or the interest rate which would make the NPV equal the price). The running or flat yield is the annual payment divided by the market price. If the price of a bond was £50, its coupon 5% and it was due for repayment in five years at £100, the flat yield would be 10% (5 ÷ 50). The redemption yield would include an allowance for the profit made in buying the bond at £50 and receiving £100 in five years; it is about 17%. Another point is that when securities are purchased by banks, they are sometimes said to be 'discounted'. Many central banks quote a discount rate, or rediscount rate as the Bank of England did until 1971 with Bank Rate. This is not the same sense of discount rate as used by economists such as Williams (Gowland, 1979) nor is it equal to an interest rate. If I sell a one year bill with a nominal value of £100 to a bank for £90, then the interest rate is 11.1% (10 ÷ 90). The discount rate is calculated as a percentage of the amount to be repaid and is 10% (10 ÷ 100).

As the fundamental relationship is between interest rates and bond prices, attempts have been made to extend the concept to include an inverse relationship between other asset prices and an implicit rate of return. Hence, it has been argued that a rise in house prices involves a reduction in the rate of return on houses, the flow of services divided by the price. This generalization of the notion of an interest rate was analysed extensively by Keynes (see Turvey 1965). Frequently, in modern monetary theory 'a rise in interest rates' means 'a reduction in a composite index of all asset prices'. The composition of this index has been a subject of controversy between monetarists and Keynesians. Leijonhufvud (1968) argued that this was one of the essential differences between the models used by Keynes and Keynesian models.

2.3 INTEREST RATES IN REAL MARKETS

In equilibrium, interest rates should be equal to the real rate of return on capital, the rate of time preference and the rate of transformation of current to future consumption. (All three will be discussed below.) If the interest rate, appropriately measured, is not equal to each of these, there is an incentive for agents to change their behaviour to increase their welfare and scope for Pareto improvements in social welfare.

It is easy to demonstrate that if companies maximize profits, the real rate of return on capital, Keynes's marginal efficiency of capital, will equal the rate of interest, see Austin (in Gowland, 1979). Analysis of consumer behaviour when facing problems of inter-temporal choice is more complex but equally necessary to enable the demand side to be added to the supply decisions implied by investment plans.

Inter-temporal consumer choice is usually analysed by using the normal tools of microeconomic theory. Here, a very simple example will be taken. (More complex studies can be found in Deaton and Muellbauer, 1980 and Hey, 1979.) This example is also central to the macroeconomic analysis of consumers' expenditure and saving (see p. 133 below). A consumer receives income in one period and spends it over two, the first period his working life, the second retirement. He must choose how much income to spend in period 1 and how much in period 2. To do this he needs to know the rate at which he can exchange (transform) present to future consumption, i.e. the inter-temporal budget line, and his preferences between consumption now and in the the future, the rate of time preference, i.e. his inter-temporal indifference curve (for the rate of time preference see Sugden and Williams, 1978 and Henderson, 1968).

The inter-temporal budget line can be constructed by taking his maximum consumption in each period and joining the two points; since the individual cannot influence prices, the budget line is a straight line. His maximum consumption in period 1 is his total income, (Y_1) shown as *OA* in *Figure 2.1*. His maximum consumption in the second period is that purchased by his income plus the interest he receives from investing it between receipt and consumption. Hence, if the interest rate is i, this is equal to $Y_1(1 + i)$. The purchasing power of $Y_1(1 + i)$ in period 2 will depend upon whether prices have changed between the two periods. If they have increased, this purchasing power will be reduced compared with that of an equivalent amount in period 1, so, if the rise in prices is p, it is necessary to divide $Y_1(1 + i)$ by $(1 + p)$ so that the quantity of goods can be compared with that shown on the vertical axis. This maximum consumption in period 2 is shown as *OB* in *Figure 2.1*. The budget line is accordingly shown as *AB*; $(1 + i)/(1 + p)$ is also the real rate of interest (r) and *OB* is also equal to $Y_1(1 + r)$. Alternatively, one could calculate the slope of the budget line by calculating the relative price of consumption between periods 1 and 2; this is obviously $(1 + i)/(1 + p)$ for the

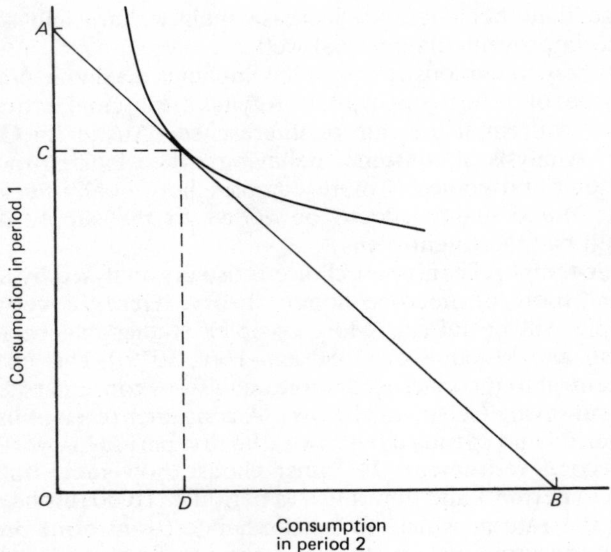

Figure 2.1 Consumption and saving

reason argued above, on each pound of forgone consumption one receives interest but its purchasing power can be affected by price changes. The consumer's inter-temporal preferences are shown by his indifference curves whose slope is determined by the (marginal) rate of time preference. In equilibrium, the indifference curve will be tangential to the budget line, so their slopes will be equal. So, the consumer's equilibrium consumption choice (*OC* in period 1 and *OD* in period 2) will be where his marginal rate of time preference is equal to the rate of transformation, determined by the real interest rate. Moreover, as *OA* is equal to income and *OC* to consumption, *AC* is equal to saving. The level of interest rates is, therefore, a determinant of the optimal level of saving as well as investment, of when to spend as well as when to produce.

2.4 THE DETERMINATION OF INTEREST RATES

Any model that seeks to analyse the determination of interest rates must explain the interaction between the real and financial factors that produce the equilibrium level of interest rates. Moreover, the model must be capable of illustrating official intervention in the determination of interest rates. In the last resort, the authorities can fix the level of interest rates by fiat, but in this case the operation is not costless and the role of the model is to elucidate the costs and benefits of such intervention. The IS–LM model is usually the context for the economic analysis of interest rates.

In summary, the IS–LM system consists of separate models of the real system, the goods market, the financial system and the money market. The rate of interest acts as the link between the two sectors so a shock to either system affects the other through its impact on the interest rate.

In more detail, two variables are determined within the system, the level of nominal income and the rate of interest. A diagram can be drawn (*Figure 2.2*) with the rate of interest (r) on the vertical axis and the level of nominal income (Y) on the horizontal axis. It is necessary to find all the combinations of Y and r that produce equilibrium in the goods market. The equilibrium condition is that desired expenditure should be equivalent to planned output or, more conveniently, that planned withdrawals (S, M and T) should equal planned injections (X, G and I). This relationship can be derived in three ways, algebraic, graphical and intuitive (see Laidler, 1974 and Gowland, 1979). The intuitive method will be presented here because it is both the simplest and the least well-known. It is assumed that one equilibrium combination is known: this is plotted as (Y_1 r_1). Next, another level of income (Y_2) is taken and it is necessary to deduce what the rate of interest would have to be if Y_2 were the equilibrium level of income. Y_2 exceeds Y_1 and so a higher (planned) level of withdrawals would be generated than at Y_1 (more saving and imports and higher tax yields). Therefore, if the goods market equilibrium is to be satisfied, a higher level of injections would have to be induced. Within the model, a higher level of injections could only have been induced by a lower rate of interest (more investment). Similarly, a higher rate of interest (r_3) would reduce planned injections. Hence, the equilibrium level of withdrawals would have to be lower and this in turn implies a lower level of income (Y_3). By taking all possible levels of income, considering what level of planned withdrawals each generates and the rate of interest necessary to induce this level of injections, all possible values of Y and r that satisfy the goods market equilibrium condition can be derived. Alternatively, one can take each rate of interest, consider the desired injections it would induce and the consequent level of income necessary to produce an equivalent level of planned withdrawals. The resulting points can be joined together to give the IS curve (investment and saving being representative injections and withdrawals). It is downward sloping as in *Figure 2.2a*.

Then it is necessary to derive a similar relationship between income and interest rates in order to show all the combinations of values that would produce equilibrium in the money market. The equilibrium condition in the money market is that the demand for money should equal the supply of money. The supply of money is assumed to be determined by official action, an illustration of the role of official action in the determination of interest rates. Accordingly, the supply of money is taken as fixed when determining the equilibrium level of interest rates. The demand for money is positively related to the level of income and negatively related to the rate of interest. This result can be derived in various ways. The most rigorous of these is also the simplest. This is the neoclassical theory which argues that money is an asset like any other and that its demand can be treated like the demand for other (durable) goods and assets such as cars and televisions. For all 'normal' goods, the income elasticity is positive (indeed, this is the definition of normal) and the price elasticity is negative. The price of holding money is the cost of not holding other assets. This is the rate of interest which could have been earned on these assets. The price of holding money is, therefore, the interest rate. The (negative) interest rate and (positive) income determinants of the demand for money follow from conventional price theory.

It is now possible to derive all possible equilibria in the money market in the same way as for the goods market, *Figure 2.2b*. (Y_1, r_1) is one equilibrium. If Y_2 were to be an equilibrium level of income what would the rate of interest have to be? Y_2 is greater than Y_1 so the demand for money would be greater than at (Y_1, r_1) if the interest rate were r_1. Instead, the rate of interest must be sufficiently high (higher than r_1) to offset the effect on the demand for money of the higher level of income because the demand for money must equal the fixed supply in equilibrium. This level is shown as r_2. Similarly, a lower rate of interest (r_3) would generate a higher demand for money so income would have to be lower (Y_3) to offset this. In this way all possible equilibria can be derived. For each variation in income, the necessary alteration in interest rates (or vice versa) can be calculated which would produce the original demand for money; this is necessary so that the demand for money will equal the fixed supply. If all these points are joined up, the result is the LM (liquidity money) curve, the locus of equilibria for the money market.

At all points on the LM curve, the financial system, the money market, is in equilibrium. At all points on the IS curve, the real system, the goods market, is in equilibrium. Where the two curves intersect, both markets are in equilibrium so the entire system is in

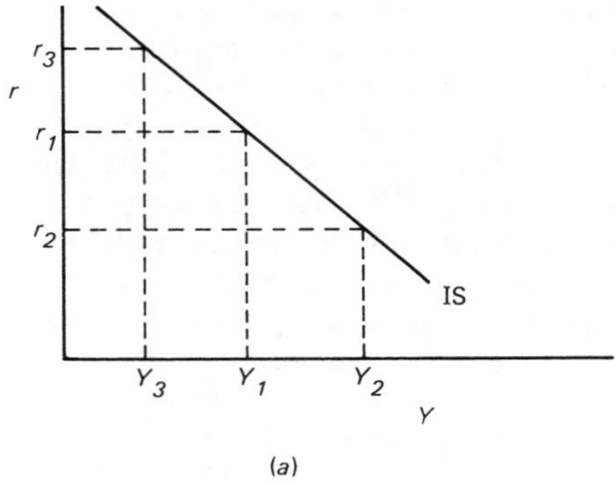

(a)

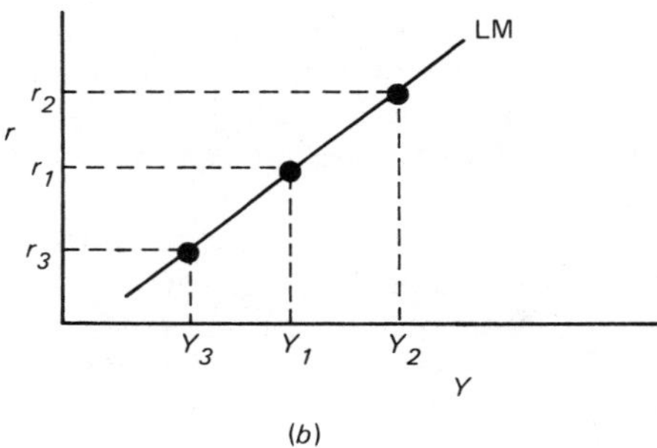

(b)

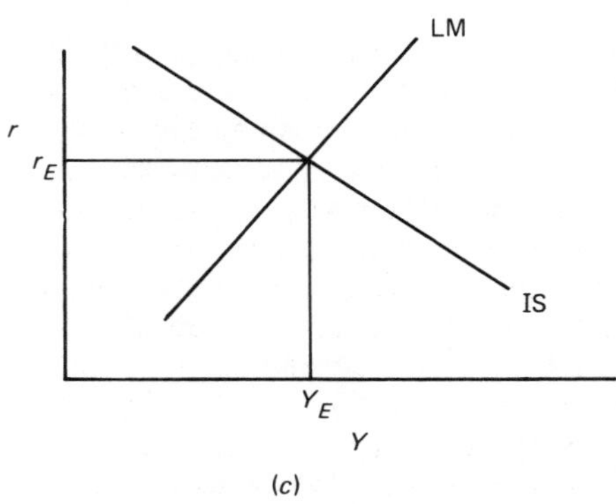

(c)

Figure 2.2 IS and LM curves

equilibrium. Hence, as shown in *Figure 2.2.c*, the equilibrium level of income and interest rates has been determined.

If the money supply is increased, at each *r* a higher income is required to generate a demand for money equal to the new higher money supply (and at each *Y* a lower *r*). Hence the increase in the supply of money shifts the LM curve to the right and the equilibrium rate of interest falls (and level of income rises). An increase in government spending means that the planned level of injections is higher at each rate of interest so a higher level of income would be necessary to generate it, i.e. the IS curve shifts to the right. (The shift is by the amount predicted by the elementary Keynesian multiplier because this shows the effect of government spending on income if financial factors are unimportant, in this model equivalent to holding the rate of interest constant.) In this case, the equilibrium rate of interest rises, and so does the equilibrium level of income. Other shocks to the goods market can be analysed in a similar manner – a rise in export earnings or the discovery of oil would also raise the equilibrium rate of interest, unless the money supply were increased. Finally, there are special cases – the monetarist and Keynesian extreme cases, see Gowland (1979), Chapter 5.

The IS–LM model has thus illustrated the interaction of monetary and real factors in determining interest rates and the pervasive role of government intervention, and the cost of this intervention in terms of income and money supply variations which may or may not be intended or desired.

2.5 'A MANY-SPLENDOURED THING'

It is conventional and convenient in monetary theory to refer to the rate of interest but in fact there are many different rates of interest and it is useful to distinguish among them. One important distinction is between nominal and real rates of interest. The nominal rate is the amount actually paid or received. The real rate is the borrower's income in the Hicks sense: 'the maximum value which he can consume and still expect to be as well off as he was at the beginning' (Hicks, 1946). If inflation affects the purchasing power of the lender's future stream of receipts (of interest and repayment of capital), he cannot spend all he receives and still be as well off as he was. Accordingly, it is usual to define the real rate of interest as the nominal rate of interest less the amount by which changes in the price level are *expected* to reduce the lender's capital asset (the NPV of future interest and repayment of principal). Hence, the real rate would be measured as the nominal rate adjusted for *expected* inflation over the period of the loan. If inflation were expected to be constant, it would simply be subtracted from the nominal rate. Unfortunately, inflationary expectations cannot be measured (see p. 103 below). Therefore, real rates cannot be measured, except on indexed securities but these have only recently become available in the UK. It is conventional to use past inflation as a proxy for expected inflation when measuring real rates or, with hindsight, to use the actual rate of inflation over the relevant period. Both methods are unsatisfactory for obvious reasons. Economists have tried to detect the relationship between inflation and interest rates, but with little success, ever since Fisher first pointed it out. Indeed, since Keynes they have been puzzled by the 'Gibson paradox', an apparently perverse relationship. Borrowers may not have to compensate lenders fully for anticiapted inflation; certainly, in the 1970s, real rates were negative by the usual measures and this suggests either that most inflation was unanticipated or that lenders were unable to obtain compensation for expected inflation.

Even if one is concerned only with nominal rates, it is not easy to measure them either in theory or in practice. First of all, it is necessary to specify the currency in which the interest rate should be measured. In some sense, 8% per annum interest on a lire loan and 3% per annum on a D-Mark loan are identical rates if the mark is expected to appreciate 5% per annum over the period of the loan, but the exact adjustment is as difficult to calculate as measuring real rates. If these problems are ignored, there are a number of practical problems. For example, many loans involve service charges, commissions, bonuses and other contractual arrangements which affect the effective rate of interest. The common practice of banks in many countries, including the US, of demanding a compensating balance affects the measurement of the rate of interest. An interest rate of 15% and an obligation to deposit 20% of the loan as an interest free (compensating) balance with the lending bank are equivalent to a rate of 18% without this condition. Loans may also involve additional terms which blur the distinction with equity capital; for example, bonds may be convertible into equity or the lender may receive some equity as a bonus.

Even when the rate of interest is clearly defined, there are a number of dimensions to a loan that cannot be compressed into one dimension. The most important are risk, which depends on who borrows and on what security, and the length of time for which the loan is made. The analysis of how interest rates vary according to the date of maturity (repayment) is given in section 2.6 below, but it is not even clear how this should be measured. In the case of a loan repayable instantly on demand or a five-year bond it is clear and, with difficulty, it is possible to measure the maturity of a loan due for repayment in stages (even if repayment is by drawing lots, as with Victory bonds when $x\%$ were repaid per annum, the lucky beneficiaries being determined by the luck of the draw). However, when there is a cost to repayment it is not. For example, if a loan is for five years but the lender can demand repayment by giving three months' notice and forfeiting a certain amount of interest, is it a three-month loan or a five-year loan? If a diagram is drawn with maturity on the horizontal axis and the rate of interest on the vertical one, then the yields on securities with different maturities, but otherwise identical, can be plotted. These can be joined and the result is called a yield curve. Yield curves are usually drawn for government securities. Alternatively, since this produces an unsmooth line which is hard to interpret, it is possible either to estimate the curve which best fits the data or to use theoretical methods which produce a hypothetical yield curve, e.g. the rate which would have to be offered on a new bond if it were to be issued with the market price equal to the issue price (Goodhart, 1976).

Risk is difficult to analyse in theory but in practice two simple methods have been used. One of these is the risk premium. It argued that there is a pure riskless rate for each maturity and that a risk premium would be paid in addition. If there is a 1 in 100 chance that the borrower will default, he would pay the pure rate of interest plus an amount sufficient to compensate the lender for accepting the risk (1% on a one-year loan in a risk neutral world, more if investors are risk averse). This method, used by many banks, implies that it is possible to argue that any interest rate can be converted into a 'certainty equivalent' and compared with any other. The certainty equivalent is the amount which a lender would regard as being of equal value, if it were to be paid with certainty, to the prospect he faces. For example, a rate of 5% on a one-year loan with certainty might be equivalent to 7% with the risk described above. Other economists have argued that return and risk cannot be conflated into a single measure. They treat them as separate goods (or rather one good and one bad) and use normal microeconomic choice theory to analyse individuals' behaviour towards more and less risky securities. Conventionally, risk is measured by some statistic (usually variance) which measures the dispersion of expected outcomes.

2.6 THE TERM STRUCTURE

Of all the distinctions between different interest rates discussed above the most important is the time to maturity. The relationship between interest rates of different maturities is called the term structure of interest rates. It is vital in the analysis of monetary policy because it provides both a probable transmission mechanism for monetary policy and a device to help control the money supply. Normally the authorities directly control only very short-term interest rates although they often intervene in a wider spectrum of markets. However, behaviour in real markets is commonly thought to be influenced by longer-term rates so the authorities need to understand the term structure of rates if they are to be able indirectly to manipulate longer-term rates by their activities in the short-term markets. This analysis is particularly relevant to the Tobin model (Gowland, 1979, Chapter 5; Chick, 1973). Even if the money supply is the be all and end all of monetary policy, then the structure of rates is probably as important as their level (p. 29 above). In order to manipulate the structure of rates and thus control the money supply it is necessary to understand what determines it. The authorities may also wish to manipulate the structure for other reasons, e.g. Keynesians have argued for high short-term rates to maintain a high exchange rate and low long-term ones to encourage investment ('operation twist' in the US is the best known example although it was carried out 20 years ago). Under Mr Healey's Chancellorship in 1977, the reverse twist was attempted in order to hold the exchange rate down and curb bank borrowing but with little success.

There are three theories of the term structure of interest rates which seek to explain the relationship between longer and shorter-dated securities, which are identical in all other respects. The oldest theory is the *expectations theory*, largely developed by Hicks. For simplicity, the exposition in this section will examine the relationship between a one and a two-year bond but the model can be generalized very simply. Hicks pointed out that, in a world of perfect certainty, the rate of return on a two-year bond held from 1982 to 1984 must equal that on two one-year bonds held from 1982 to 1983 and from 1983 to 1984 respectively, because they are perfect substitutes for each other and so must have identical prices. A two-year bond can be sold after one year at a known price, dependent on the known (one-year) interest rate then prevailing – a two-year bond in 1982, due to mature in 1984, is, of course, a one-year bond in 1983. This purchase and sale yields a return which can be compared with that on a one-year bond. No one will hold a one-year bond unless the return is as great as the (certain) return from holding a two-year bond for one year and then selling it. Two one-year bonds held from 1982 to 1983 and from 1983 to 1984 would be a perfect substitute for a two-year bond so no one would hold a two-year bond unless the rate of return was at least as great as that of two one-year bonds. Hence, arbitrage between two and one-year bonds will take place unless the returns from the investment policies outlined are identical, i.e.

$$\frac{R_1(1982) + R_1(1983)}{2} = R_2(1982), \tag{2.1}$$

where $R_1(1982)$ is the one-year rate in 1982 etc. (Strictly it should be a geometric average not an arithmetic one because of the possibility of reinvesting interest; for example, a 12% bond 1982–1983 and an 8% bond 1983–1984 offer a fractionally higher return (by 0.16%) – than a 10% two-year bond 1982–1984 because the extra 2% received in 1983 can be invested at 8% from 1983 to 1984 and is, therefore, worth more than the extra 2% due to be received in 1984 on the two-year bond.)

This type of relationship is central to Hicks's theory. The one and two-year interest rates are interdependent because one type of bond will be substituted for the other according to the level of *future* short-term interest rates. Moreover, if the future short rate exceeds the present short rate, the long rate must exceed the present short rate; this follows from (2.1), since the long rate is the average of the present and future short rates. Conversely, if the present short rate is greater than the future short rate, it will also exceed the present long rate. By reversing these relationships, forecasts of interest rates can be derived. If the long rate exceeds the present short rate, future short rates must exceed present short rates, i.e. (short) interest rates will rise. Similarly, if the short rate exceeds the long rate, interest rates must fall. To take two examples, if the one-year rate is 8% and the two-year rate is 10%, the one-year rate in one year's time must be 12% if (2.1) is to be satisfied. Similarly, if one-year rates are 10% and two-year rates 9%, the one-year rate will have fallen to 8% in a year's time. The yield curve necessarily incorporates a prediction of future movements in interest rates. This idea is crucial to the expectations model when it is amended to allow for uncertainty; it is, of course, rather empty to derive predictions in a world of certainty.

The expectations theory has two key elements even in a world of uncertainty.

(1) The relationship between one and two-year rates depends on future one-year rates which determine substitution between the two bonds.
(2) It is possible to derive forecasts of interest rate changes from observation of one and two-year rates or from the yield curve generally.

Hicks generalized the model for a world of uncertainty by substituting *expected* future short rates for their known equivalent in (2.1) and by adding a risk premium so that

$$\frac{R_1(1982)}{2} + \frac{E(R_1(1983))}{2} \pm l = R_2(1982), \qquad (2.2)$$

where $E(R)$ is the expected rate and l the risk premium (or liquidity premium). l can be either negative or positive because there are two types of risk involved in holding bonds. One is capital risk often called liquidity preference. If one holds a series of one-year bonds, their capital value will fluctuate less than longer term bonds (see p. 38 above) and is known with certainty for each date of maturity. If interest rates are higher than expected in one year's time, in 1983, the value of the two-year bond will be less than the £100 received by the holder of the one-year bond due to mature then. Thus, if the investor holding a two-year bond has to sell it after a year because of some unforeseen contingency, he will be worse off than if he had invested in a one-year bond (with the intention of reinvesting if no contingency arose). This risk more than offsets the chance of gain if rates are lower than expected in one year's time when the contingency occurs. A capital risk-averse investor will accordingly prefer to hold short-term bonds. If all investors are capital risk averse, l will be positive and there will be a liquidity premium because long rates will exceed short ones when no change is expected in (short-term) interest rates. Hicks expected that capital risk aversion would be the norm.

However, there is another sort of risk aversion – income risk aversion. The holder of a two-year bond knows what his income will be in both years of the life of the bond. The holder of two successive one-year bonds does not. His income in the second year will depend upon the level of (one-year) interest rates in a year's time. Therefore, if one wishes to guarantee (money) income, a long-term bond is preferable to a succession of short-term ones. An institution with known liabilities for a long period – such as a pension fund – should be in this position and has every reason to be income risk averse. The income risk averter will thus prefer longer dated bonds. If all investors were income risk averse l would be negative and short rates would exceed long ones when no change in interest rates was expected[1].

The relationship that would prevail between long and short-term rates if no change were expected is called the normal one. The yield curve corresponding to this pattern is called the normal slope. To generalize the argument above, this will slope upwards if capital risk averters dominate and downwards if income risk averters dominate, *Figures 2.3a* and *2.3b* respectively. Normal

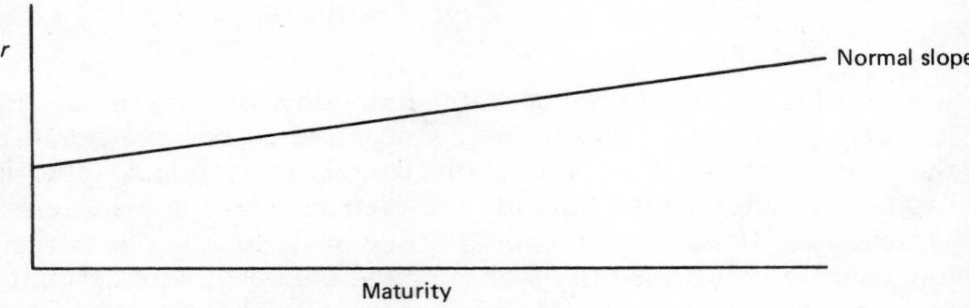

Figure 2.3a Yield curve: capital risk-averse investors dominate

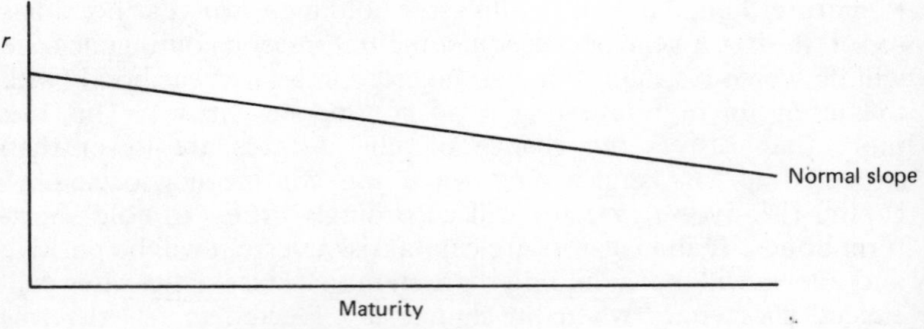

Figure 2.3b Yield curve: income risk-averse investors dominate

slopes can be derived from more complex assumptions. For example, Bank of England researchers (Goodhart, 1976) have on occasion hypothesized that income risk averters dominate in long-dated bonds and capital risk averters in short-term ones in such a way that the yield curve initially slopes upwards and then turns down, with the two halves joined between 4 and 8 years to maturity (sometimes called the 'walking stick' hypothesis from the consequent shape of the normal yield curve.

It is possible to derive forecasts of interest rate changes from any pair of (present) interest rates of different maturity, but the procedure is slightly more complex than when rates are known with certainty. It is not the case that rates are expected to rise if long rates exceed short rates (as in the certainty case) but they are expected to rise if long rates exceed short ones by more than the normal amount. This is most clearly seen using the yield curve. If the slope of the actual yield curve exceeds the normal slope, interest rates are expected to rise, as shown in *Figure 2.3c*. This can also occur if the yield curve is downward sloping but by less than the normal amount, as in *Figure 2.3d*. Similarly, if the yield

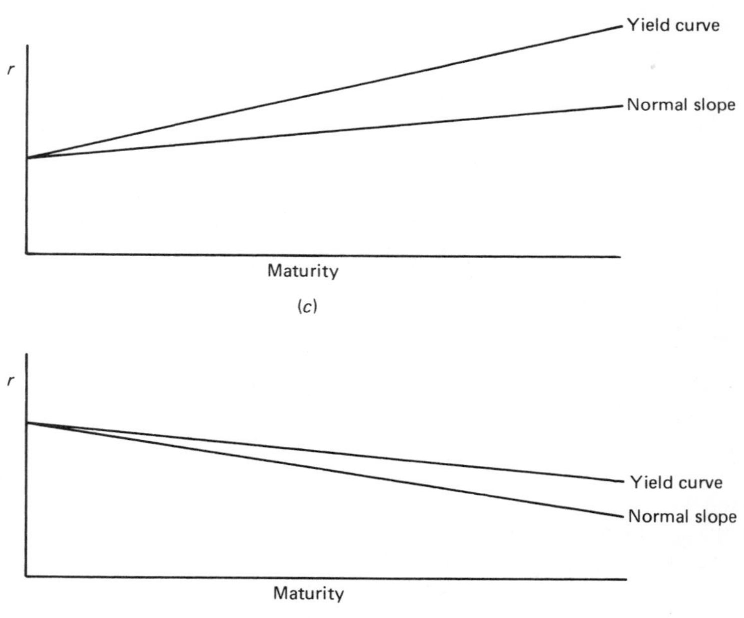

Figure 2.3c and d Yield curves: interest rates expected to rise

curve slopes downwards by more than the normal slope or, by extension, upwards by less than the normal slope, interest rates are expected to fall, as shown in *Figures 2.3e* and *2.3f* respectively.

The extreme rival theory to the expectations theory is the *market segmentation* theory associated with Culbertson and Ben Friedman (see Goodhart, 1976). Whereas the expectations theory is based on substitution between bonds of different maturities, the

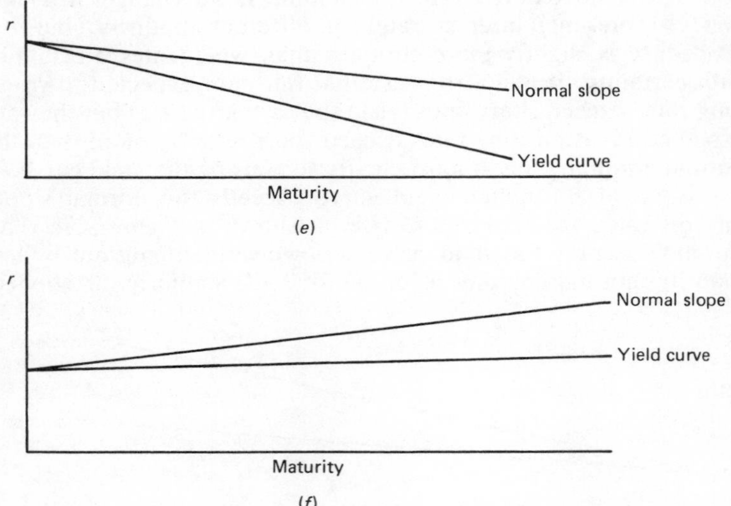

Figure 2.3e and f Yield curves: interest rates expected to fall

market segmentation theory denies the possibility of this ever occurring. Some investors, e.g. banks, prefer short-term assets for institutional and structural reasons. Others prefer longer-dated ones – insurance companies and pension funds are the classic examples. There is no relationship between the markets in long and short-term assets; the two are segmented, hence the name. Supply and demand factors will determine the equilibrium rate in each market independently and the yield curve can no more be 'explained' than any other sequence of unrelated events, such as a particular pattern of numbers which emerges at the roulette table.

The expectations and market segmentation theories were incorporated as polar extremes into the *preferred habitat* theory developed by Modigliani (Modigliani and Sutch, 1966). The market segmentation theory assumes no substitution between long and short-term bonds. Expectations theory assumes perfect substitution even in a world of uncertainty because arbitrage will occur to maintain the fixed differential between the actual and the 'pure expectations' long and short rates. Modigliani argued that substitution would occur but that the elasticity need not be infinite nor in consequence need the risk premium be constant. His theory incorporated the institutional and structural factors rightly stressed by the market segmentation theory but denied that these meant that no substitution would take place. Both those who issued bonds and those who held them had strong preferences for assets or liabilities of a specific date. However, they could be tempted away from this maturity, their 'preferred habitat', by an interest rate incentive. A bank might wish to hold a one-year bond but could be persuaded to hold a two-year one instead if the margin offered by the two-year bond were substantial enough. The bank would compare the two-year rate with that implied by the one-year rate and its expectation of the one-year rate in a year's time. According to the expectations theory, it would buy the bond if the margin exceeded a critical level (l); according to the market segmentation theory, it would never buy it. Modigliani argued that it would purchase it or not depending on the margin, the degree of certainty about its expectations, and other relevant considerations. Moreover, the decision need not be an 'all or nothing' one; the bank might shift part of its portfolio if the margin were ¼%, more if it were ½% and so on but never be prepared to move completely into longer bonds. Preferred habitat models are very similar in spirit to the neo-Keynesian version of Tobin's model (Gowland, 1979, Chapter 5) and the imperfect substitutability of preferred habitat would justify the neo-Keynesian transmission mechanism postulated by Tobin (so long as either long-dated financial assets are substitutes for real ones or spending on real goods is interest sensitive). As preferred habitat incorporates arbitrage, even though on a limited scale, the forecasting procedure developed from the expectations theory still holds. If the yield curve slopes upwards more steeply than the normal slope, rates are expected to rise and so on. However, the implicit increase is less than if the pure expectations theory were valid.

It is this feature of the 'preferred habitat' theory, its incorporation of implicit forecasts of movements in interest rates, which has cast doubt upon the theory. When tested as a theory, the model performed very well (see Goodhart, 1976 for a comprehensive survey of the literature). However, the implicit predictors of future interest rates could be tested and performed uniformly badly. (Hamburger and Platt were the first of a number of economists to do this; this literature is summarized by Goodhart, 1976). Moreover, the theory had to be reconciled with the rational and efficient markets hypothesis and with its empirical counterpart, the random walk (Goodhart and Gowland, 1977 and 1978), which were also upheld by the data. Most of the evidence seems to sustain the rational critique of the preferred habitat (Pippenger and Phillips, 1977); Carleton and Cooper, 1976), so it is necessary to examine this critique.

A rational market is a market in which all agents take any profits open to them[2]. An efficient market is one in which all agents process information optimally. There are three variants of the efficient market hypothesis according to the information involved: strong (all information), semi-strong or semi-weak (all information to which no one has privileged access), weak (past data on the price of the security concerned)[3]. These two theories can be treated as special cases of each other. Because knowledge of an opportunity to make a profit is a piece of information and to take the profit is a special case of optimization, the rational market hypothesis is a special case of the efficient one. On the other hand, processing information in any way which will yield a profit is a special method of 'operating rationally'.

The relevance of rational and efficient markets is that both of the hypotheses imply that the best predictor of the price of a security at any future date is its present price, whereas the preferred habitat theory denies this. In the rational world, if there is a better method of predicting the future price of a security, agents would use this information. For example, if the preferred habitat model implied a rise in bond prices, agents would buy bonds. However, if they bought bonds, the price would rise instantly and destroy the relationship. In equilibrium, demand must equal supply, i.e. desired holdings must equal the stock in existence. Thus equilibrium is inconsistent with a reliable forecast that prices will rise, because in this case the desire to purchase would mean that desired holdings would exceed actual ones. The bond market should always be in equilibrium because it has low transaction costs, a large number of buyers and sellers, no storage costs and so on. Hence there cannot be a method of predicting bond prices. The irresistible force of the preferred habitat model has met the immovable object of the rational–efficient hypothesis. So far this conflict has not been resolved.

Notes

1 If investors were capital risk loving l would also be negative (i.e. if they were gamblers) and l would be positive if they were income risk lovers.

2 For rational markets, see Muth (1961).

3 For efficient markets, see Fama (1970); for more readable versions of both rational and efficient markets, see Malkiel (1978) and Smith (1968).

Guide to further reading

On the early sections of the chapter, Turvey (1960) and Van Horne (1970) provide excellent introductions. On the term structure, Crockett (1977) is an excellent introduction and Goodhart (1976) a comprehensive guide, which includes an exhaustive bibliography.

Bibliobraphy

CARLETON, J. F. and COOPER, T. J. (1976), 'The Term Structure and Rationality', *Journal of Finance*, Vol. 63 (January), p. 837

CHICK, V. (1973), *The Theory of Monetary Policy*, Gray Mills; London

CROCKETT, A. (1977), *International Money*, Nelson; London

CROWTHER COMMITTEE (1971), *Report of the Crowther Committee on Consumer Credit*, Cmnd 4596, HMSO; London

DEATON, A. and MUELLBAUER, J. (1980), *Economics and Consumer Behaviour*, Cambridge University Press; Cambridge

FAMA, E. F. (1970), 'Efficient Capital Markets', *Journal of Finance*, (September)

GOODHART, C. A. E. (1976), *Money, Information and Uncertainty* (2nd edn.), Macmillan; London

GOODHART, C. A. E. and GOWLAND, D. H. (1977), 'The Relationship between Yields on Short and Long-Dated Gilt-Edged', *Bulletin of Economic Research*, Vol. 29 (November)

GOODHART, C. A. E. and GOWLAND, D. H. (1978), 'The Relationship between Long-Dated Gilt Yields and Other Variables', *Bulletin of Economic Research*, Vol. 30 (November)

GOWLAND, D. H. (ed.) (1979), *Modern Economic Analysis*, Butterworths; London

HENDERSON, P. D. (1968), 'Investment Criteria for Public Enterprises', in TURVEY, R. (ed.), *Public Enterprise*, Penguin; Harmondsworth

HEY, J. D. (1979), *Uncertainty in Microeconomics*, Martin Robertson; London

HICKS, SIR J. R. (1946), *Value and Capital* (2nd edn.), Oxford University Press; Oxford

LAIDLER, D. E. W. (1974), *The Demand-for-Money: Theories and Evidence* (2nd edn.), International Textbook Company; Scranton, Pa.

LEIJONHUFVUD, A. (1968). *On Keynesian Economics and the Economics of Keynes*, Oxford University Press; New York

MALKIEL, B. M. (1978), *A Random Walk Down Wall Street,* Macmillan; New York

MODIGLIANI, F. and SUTCH, R. C. (1966), 'Innovations in Interest Rate Policy', *American Economic Review*, Vol. 56, No. 2 (May)

MUTH, J. F. (1961), 'Rational Expectations and the Theory of Price Movements', *Econometrica*, Vol. 29 (July)

PIPPENGER, J. E. and PHILLIPS, D. (1977), *Rationality and the Term Structure of Interest Rates*, (unpublished mimeo), University of Wisconsin

SMITH, ADAM (1968), *The Money Game*, (UK edition), Michael Joseph and Pan; London ('Adam Smith' is a pseudonum, generally believed to be that of Professor Goodman)

SUGDEN, R. and WILLIAMS, A. (1978), *The Principles of Practical Cost-Benefit Analysis*, Oxford University Press; Oxford
TURVEY, R. (1960), *Interest Rates and Asset Prices*, Allen & Unwin; London
TURVEY, R. (1965), 'Does the Rate of Interest Rule the Roost?', in HAHN, F. H. and BRECHLING, F., *The Theory of Interest Rates*, Macmillan; London
VAN HORNE, J. C. (1970), *Function and Analysis of Capital Markets*, Prentice Hall, Englewood, N.J.

3

Issues in Macroeconomics

D. H. Gowland

3.1 INTRODUCTION

In this chapter I analyse a number of controversies in macroeconomics. The purpose is twofold. On the one hand, it is necessary to emphasize the relevance to economic policy of many theoretical developments. On the other hand, many of the arguments need to be put into perspective so that their relationship to the main body of economic thought is clear. It is worth stressing that most of these controversies lie outside the main monetarist–Keynesian debate[1]. Often the newer developments treat monetarists and Keynesians as partners in crime, united by more than they differ, rather as the free marketeer views Stalinists and Trotskyites.

3.2 MONEY, PRICES AND UNEMPLOYMENT: THE MAINSTREAM DEBATE

The major theoretical debate of the 1950s and 1960s concerned the effectiveness of reductions in prices and wages as a cure for unemployment. In particular, the argument was about the consequence of a balanced deflation, i.e. one involving an equal reduction in both wages and prices and so leaving real wages unchanged. This has always struck students as a rather sterile, pointless debate. In fact, it is crucial to macroeconomic policy in the 1980s because it involves, implicitly, the analysis of two more relevant questions:

(1) Would a sufficiently large increase in the money supply necessarily ensure full employment?
(2) Can inflation cause unemployment?

If a balanced deflation could cure unemployment, the answer to both these questions would be 'Yes'.

The debate was conducted initially within the ubiquitous IS–LM model developed by Hicks (1937) and popularized by Hansen (1953). This model determines simultaneously the equilibrium levels of interest rates and (usually) nominal income. This is achieved by analysing the interaction between the goods market and the money market. In particular, on a diagram with interest rates on one axis and income on the other, one curve represents all possible equilibria in the goods market (IS curve) and the other all possible equilibria in the money market (LM curve). Where the two intersect both markets, i.e. the whole system, are in equilibrium; hence the equilibrium level of interest rates and income has been determined. The IS curve is normally downward-sloping because a higher level of income would generate a higher level of withdrawals. To satisfy the equilibrium condition, that planned injections equal planned withdrawals, there would have to be more injections which would have to have been induced by a lower rate of interest. The LM curve is normally upward-sloping because, at all points along it, the demand for money must equal the (exogenous) officially-fixed money supply in order to satisfy the equilibrium condition, namely, that the supply of money equal the demand for money. Hence, the LM curve shows the combinations of interest rates and income which lead to demand for the same quantity of money. The demand for money is positively related to income and negatively related to interest rates so the effect of a higher level of income would have to be offset by that of a higher rate of interest to leave the market in equilibrium, i.e. the LM curve is upward-sloping[2].

This IS–LM model represented the macroeconomic consensus of the early 1950s. Within this model a balanced deflation led to a rise in output and so to a fall in unemployment. This can be seen by using either the nominal or the real income version of the model. With the nominal income model (*Figure 3.1a*), the IS curve shifts to the right by the exact amount of the price reduction since all real magnitudes in the goods market are unchanged and the LM curve is unchanged. In this case, the fall in nominal income is less than the fall in prices so real income has risen. Alternatively, if, as in *Figure 3.1b*, real income is on the horizontal axis, the IS curve is unchanged but the LM curve shifts to the right, because the same nominal income is needed to generate the equilibrium demand for money at each interest rate. If prices are lower, output must be higher to produce the same nominal income. (Alternatively, it can be argued that the same services are provided with a lower nominal quantity of money, because prices are lower, and hence, income must rise or interest rates fall otherwise the demand for money would not equal the supply.)

Hence, in the orthodox IS–LM model the answer was that a sufficiently large balanced deflation would eliminate unemployment. However, in the Keynesian special case of a horizontal LM curve (infinite interest elasticity or liquidity trap), this was not so. In *Figure 3.1a*, if the LM curve were horizontal at r_1 the fall in nominal income would be exactly equal to the fall in prices (i.e. to

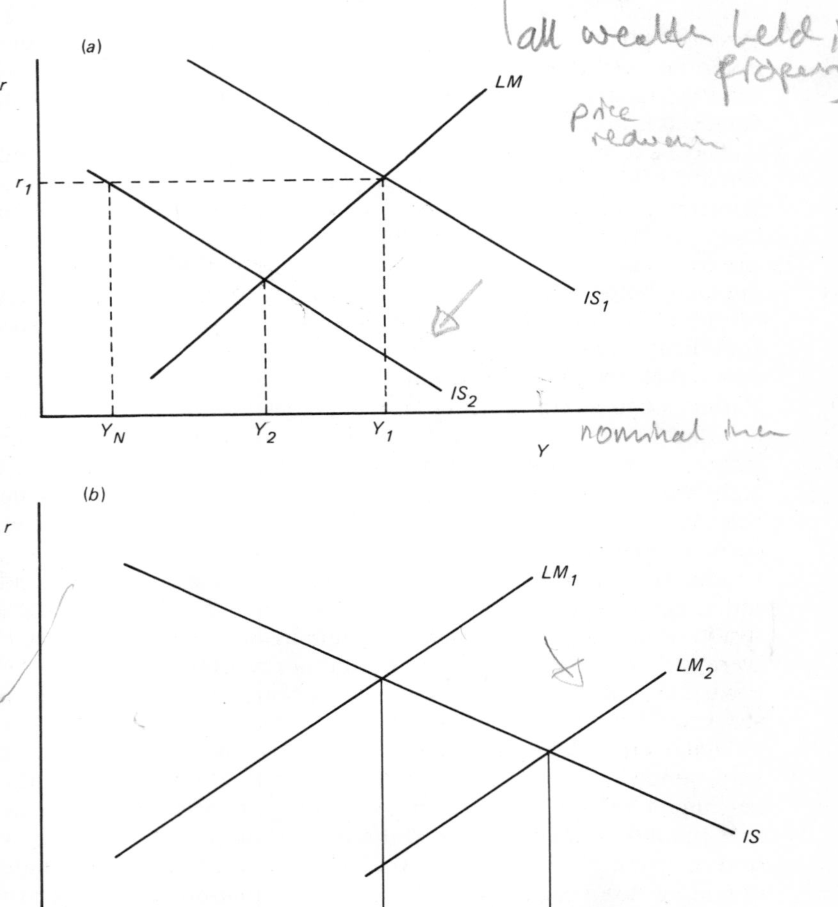

Figure 3.1 Balanced deflation

Y_N) so real income is unchanged. The LM curve no longer shifts in the real income diagram (*Figure 3.1b*), so real income is unchanged.

This latter result was challenged by Patinkin (1956, 1959) who introduced wealth effects. In particular, he drew attention to the real balance or Pigou effect. The argument was that the fall in prices increased the real value of money and, accordingly, made holders of money more wealthy. This extra wealth should induce more spending and so shift the IS curve in *Figure 3.1b* (or ensure that it falls by less than the fall in prices in *Figure 3.1g*). Accordingly, real income would rise. In principle, this argument could be extended to any asset denominated in money terms and by 1968, Leijonhufvud could count 14 different variants of real financial effects each involving different assets.

The next stage in the argument was the work of Gurley and Shaw (1960). Gurley and Shaw pointed out that Patinkin's analysis had ignored negative wealth effects on debtors. Many financial assets were another person's financial liability and a change in prices would make the debtor poorer just as it would make the creditor better off. There was no reason to assume that either wealth effect was bigger. Gurley and Shaw divided financial assets into inside assets, those matched by liabilities, and outside assets, those not matched by liabilities. The wealth effect used by Patinkin could only work on an outside asset.

The work of Gurley and Shaw, therefore, put the focus of the debate onto the existence of outside financial assets. In a gold standard world, gold was an outside asset but this was clearly of no relevance to modern economies. All financial institutions' assets were matched by liabilities and so were the assets of those who lent to the institutions, for example building society deposits and mortgages. Similarly, bank deposits matched by overdrafts were inside assets. In fact the only possible outside assets, it appeared, were government debt both in the form of currency and of securities, either national savings or bonds such as gilt-edged stocks etc.

However, it had already been denied by some economists that government obligations could be a form of net wealth, the so-called Chicago doctrine, later revived as the Ricardian doctrine (see below). If there were a counterbalancing liability to currency and government bonds, these would also be inside assets and there would be no outside assets at all. The foundation of the Chicago doctrine was that individuals take note of future tax liabilities in determining their consumption plans. Government bonds and currency, indeed all forms of government debt, will have to be serviced and ultimately repaid. Hence their existence implies that taxation will have to be levied in the future. Accordingly, rational individuals will plan their consumption on the basis of their contingent tax liability to redeem the national debt. Thus, if the real value of the national debt changes, so too does the contingent tax liability and hence, any real balance effect will be offset exactly by reductions in spending to finance the extra real burden of future taxation.

There are two distinct objections to this Chicago doctrine that individuals discount their future tax liabilities and that, therefore, changes in the real value of government debt are not perceived by the personal sector as changes in its wealth. One objection is that the Chicago argument is sheer fantasy as nearly all consumers are unaware of changes in the national debt and do not take its size into account when deciding whether to make purchases. This could obviously be tested but the Chicago proposition seems highly implausible. The counter argument is that, even if they did consider it, the change in the value of the national debt, represents an extremely illiquid liability to the taxpayer whereas the change in the value of currency and bonds represents an increase in liquid assets. Hence, even if real net wealth is unchanged, liquidity is higher and so spending will rise, i.e. the IS curve will shift as postulated by Patinkin. To deny this liquidity effect it is necessary to assume that no individual's borrowing is ever constrained. Tobin (1980) adds further to the list of implausible assumptions necessary for the Ricardian or Chicago doctrine.

Moreover, Pesek and Saving (1967) had shown the existence of another outside asset and so concluded this era of the debate in favour of the proposition that balanced deflation could cure unemployment. This 'new' outside asset consisted of the shares in banks and other financial intermediaries. These represented a claim on the assets and profits of the institutions. A part of their profits consisted of the difference between the interest rate at which they lent and that at which they borrowed. On existing contracts, at least, this was fixed and was fixed in money terms. If a bank had a £1 m deposit for five years at 5% and a £1 m loan for five years at 6%, then it had an asset equal to the the net present value of £10 000 per annum for five years. This asset was not matched by any liability and was an outside asset. *Reductio ad absurdum*, a balanced deflation would make bank shareholders sufficiently wealthy to ensure full employment. More practically, the area of portfolio analysis had been extended and the effect of monetary growth and inflation on bank profits emphasized. None of this was without relevance to the 1970s and 1980s.

Just as Pesek and Saving were finally winning the argument for the neoclassical viewpoint, it was challenged from another angle by Clower (1969) and Leijonhufvud (1968).

Clower and Leijonhufvud both argued that they were restating what Keynes had really meant but their exegesis is less important than the ideas. They claimed that various institutional arrangements inevitable in a modern economy might prevent a balanced deflation or monetary expansion from achieving full employment, and so by implication, that inflation could cause unemployment. The crucial factor is that modern economies are monetary rather than barter economies. Goods are exchanged for money and labour for (money) wages. Goods are rarely exchanged for other goods or for labour. Both the elementary Keynesian model and traditional microeconomic theory implicitly assume a barter economy in that they assume that this fact about a monetary economy could be ignored. Patinkin had claimed to integrate monetary and value theory but had not incorporated many of the basic elements, or so Clower and Leijonhufvud claimed.

Clower's proposition is usually called the 'dual decision' or 'sequential markets' hypothesis. Workers must sell their labour before they can buy goods; the two transactions do not take place simultaneously as is implicitly assumed in Walrasian general equilibrium. As a consequence, the (full employment) equilibrium may be unattainable. If the unemployed workers were to be employed by firms, they would buy the goods which would make it profitable for the firms to employ them. However, no firm can or will employ more workers because it would make a loss from doing so (unless all other firms were to expand employment simultaneously) since the firm's workers would spend only a small fraction of their income on the firm's products. If the firm could pay its workers in its own product, the problem would disappear, i.e. it would not exist in a barter economy. In this all firms would increase employment, paying wages with their output of steel, bread, etc. and the workers would exchange these among themselves. Thus the economy will remain at an underemployed level. In terms of notional demand, there is a full employment equilibrium, but this cannot be made effective in any way.

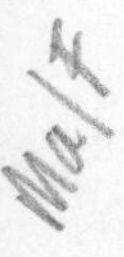

Clower used the idea of realized income constraints. The economists' optimization procedure only determined what an individual would like to do, Clower's notional demand. His actual spending, effective demand, might be very different. Institutional arrangements and limits to borrowing might make actual or realized income a binding constraint on spending. Clower made realized income constraints the centrepiece of his neo-Keynesian models. Leijonhufvud went further. He argued that 'the multiplier was an illiquidity phenomenon', that the downward spiral of contraction in income caused by an initial shock was caused by the forced reduction in consumption by the initially unemployed. If they had been able to borrow in unlimited amounts against future income, or sell labour forward, then there would be no slumps (see Appendix 3A). A market in human capital is illegal and anyway virtually every form of market failure would exist if it were not. Leijonhufvud argued that the absence of a 'futures market' in labour was the reason why unemployment could exist in an otherwise frictionless, perfectly competitive economy. This was related to the work of Arrow and Debreu who had shown that the existence of competitive general equilibrium depended on the presence of a complete set of futures markets and contingent markets, i.e. not merely could one sell or buy any product in a future market, but the transaction could be conditional. For example, one could sell 50 bushels of wheat for delivery in 2010, conditional on rainfall in the UK of at least 20 inches. In this way, Leijonhufvud started the process whereby macro and microeconomic theory became more closely related. The application of microeconomic theory by Leijonhufvud was simple. If the unemployed could sell their future labour, they would buy goods which would create a demand for their labour. Hence there was an excess supply of labour and an excess demand for goods but no way in which the two could be removed.

Leijonhufvud's most interesting proposition was to explain that the fundamental Keynesian proposition that planned savings and investment might diverge arose from the existence of monetary economy. In a barter economy an individual could only save by purchasing a claim to specific goods at a specific time. So, to trace an example, an individual increases his saving. He reduces his purchases of currently (1981) produced baked beans and buys a certificate entitling him to a washing machine in 1983. There is a reduced demand for baked beans for immediate delivery and an increased demand for future washing machines. This changes relative prices so there is an incentive for GEC to hire redundant baked bean production workers to build a factory to produce the washing machine for delivery in 1983. The price mechanism can ensure that a decision to save automatically produces a decision to invest. The decision to save involves a decision to purchase a specific good at a known future date. Relative price changes signal that it is profitable to supply this good, i.e. to invest so as to be able to do so. Hence, in a barter economy what is usually called Say's law would apply, and there would automatically be full employment. In a monetary economy, saving takes a monetary form and is, therefore, not specific so no signal is transmitted. The generality of money is one of its principal attractions because savers do not want to commit themselves to a specific good or a specific date of future purchase. Indeed, in many cases the saver has no idea when he will wish to spend his saving or what he will purchase. The existence of money allows savers to save in a non-specific form, and, in consequence, no signal is transmitted. Hence, there is no incentive to invest. Clower and Leijonhufvud and shown conclusively that balanced deflation would not ensure full employment. This has implications for economic policy, discussed at the start of this section.

At the risk of being either superficial or arrogant, it is necessary to appraise the effects of this debate which dominated macroeconomics for a quarter of a century. First of all, it emphasized the crucial role of wealth effects. All future macroeconomic models would incorporate wealth effects as a basic feature. Moreover, it was equally clear that it was necessary to look at liabilities as well as assets. The importance of these features for economic policy is discussed in Chapter 5 where they are seen to be crucial to the UK economy in the late 1970s. Clower and Leijonhufvud had shown that market failure might be crucial to macroeconomics. The microfoundations of macroeconomics were critical to the workings of a model. In particular, it was important how markets cleared, how transactions took place and in general what adjustment process occurred. In the 1970s many models were constructed to investigate this area. Barro and Grossman's (1976) model is the best known of these and is presented in a non-technical form by Davies (in Gowland, 1979). Malinvaud (1977) surveys and interprets this area in order to categorize unemployment according to the market conditions which cause it – 'classical', 'Keynesian', etc.

3.3 INTERNATIONAL MONETARISM

International monetarism, sometimes known as the monetary theory of the balance of payments, was developed in the late 1960s and the early 1970s largely by Johnson (Frenkel and Johnson, 1976) and Dornbusch (1980), although neither of these pioneers was ever an extreme adherent of the school. Its best-known UK supporters have been the London Business School forecasting team, one of whose leading lights, Terry Burns, became Chief Economic Adviser to the Treasury in 1979. It must be emphasized that international monetarism denies all the fundamental results of monetarism, notably the link between money and nominal income or prices. Nevertheless, the newer view is often presented as a natural open economy extension of monetarism, e.g. by Crystal (1979). Accordingly it is interesting to compare international and orthodox monetarism in order to understand how international monetarism differs from, and evolved from, the parent creed. Moreover, the resulting analysis throws considerable light on how international monetarists see the world and on the merits and limitations of their model.

A simple monetarist model can be constructed by assuming that each person wishes to maintain a constant ratio between his expenditure, his holdings of money, and his holdings of all other assets (both real and financial). The latter can be aggregated into one composite asset, hereafter just called assets. This assumption will produce all the results of the quantity theory and is an extension of what is sometimes called the Cambridge equation. If the economy is initially in equilibrium, and the government increases the supply of money, the following process occurs. Individuals have excess holdings of money and dispose of the surplus by buying either goods or assets. The resultant increase in the demand for goods and assets will lead to an increase in either their price or their quantity, depending on the elasticity of supply of goods and assets (some assets, e.g. Rembrandts, should be in perfectly inelastic supply!). In consequence, there is an increase both in the level of nominal income (price times output) and in the value of assets. Moreover, according to the theory, nominal income and the value of assets will both have increased by an amount exactly equal to the initial increase in the money supply. Similarly, if the money supply is reduced, individuals will sell assets and reduce expenditure, so creating an excess supply of both goods and assets and a consequent effect on income and asset values. In brief, the transmission mechanism is from money to either excess supply or excess demand in both the goods and the asset markets. As a result, there is a change in nominal income and in the total value of assets (as either their price or their quantity has changed).

The international monetarist accepts the behavioural assumption about the constancy of the desired ratio of money : expenditure : assets. When the authorities change the supply of money in the monetarist parable, he amends it to a change in the domestic supply of money or domestic credit expansion. However, he still accepts the initial excess (or deficient) supply of money and the consequent excess demand for (or supply of) goods and assets. At this point, the international monetarist parts company with his orthodox colleague. The whole of any excess supply of both goods and assets is bought by foreigners at the previously prevailing price. Similarly, the whole of any excess demand for goods and assets is satisfied by overseas suppliers without any change in price. Consequently, there is no change either in domestic output or in the quantity of assets in existence. Hence, all the basic monetarist propositions are denied. Neither domestic prices nor output have changed so an official action, such as an open market operation or an act of expenditure, has not led to any change in nominal income. Asset prices (and the value of assets) are also unchanged. However, there has been an impact on the balance of payments, as the overseas sector has either bought large quantities of goods and assets from the domestic residents or sold to them. Either way, both capital and current account have been affected. Moreover, by selling to (buying from) foreigners the domestic sector obtains (disposes of) money to re-attain equilibrium. Because the final level of income and the value of assets is unchanged, the equilibrium money stock must also remain unchanged. Domestic monetary policy creates a disequilibrium in the money market which is removed by transactions with the overseas sector so that equilibrium is re-attained with the original levels of income, money and the value of assets. An increase in DCE leads to a temporary balance of payments deficit and a contraction in DCE produces a temporary surplus. The resulting change in the money supply exactly counterbalances the initial change in DCE so as to return the money supply to its original value.

The international monetarist position can also be examined in the context of the flow-of-funds equation, and the equilibrium condition for the money market:

$$\text{Money Supply (M)} = \text{DCE} + \text{Overseas Impact on the Money Supply } (O) \quad (3.1)$$

$$\text{Demand for Money} = \text{Supply of Money} \quad (3.2)$$

The orthodox interpretation is that DCE and *O* interact to determine the change in the money supply. Keynes and Friedman both argued for sterilization operations so that DCE was automatically adjusted to offset *O* and maintain stability in monetary growth or interest rates. In practice, orthodox analysts argue that *O* and DCE both influence the money supply. The change in the money supply induces a change in either interest rates or income which will ensure that (3.2) is satisfied.

The extreme international monetarist interpretation is that the demand for money is exogenous, because its determinants, income and interest rates, are. This demand for money accordingly determines the change in the money supply. In equation (3.1) O adjusts to the difference between the domestic supply of money (DCE) and the predetermined level of money. The rationale for this is that the private sector buys or sells goods and assets in order to dispose of excess monetary holdings or to increase monetary holdings, as discussed above. In schematic form:

Orthodox School

$$\left.\begin{matrix}\text{DCE}\\ O\end{matrix}\right\}\ \text{determine } M$$

International Monetarism

$$\left.\begin{matrix}M\\ \text{DCE}\end{matrix}\right\}\ \text{determine } O$$

Orthodox School

Y and r adjust so that the money market is in equilibrium.

International Montetarism

O adjusts to ensure money market equilibrium.

There is a further feature to international monetarism. The foreign demand for sterling may depend on the exchange rate so the exchange rate may be determined simultaneously with O. Thus, one may compare the interpretations of the two schools, as follows:

Orthodox School

Change in DCE ⇒ Change in M ⇒ Change in Y
(with probable effects on the balance of payments and exchange rate)

International Monetarism

Change in DCE ⇒ Change in O and exchange rate

International monetarism is necessarily true for a small economy, i.e. one that has a perfectly elastic supply and demand curve for its goods and assets and for foreign goods and assets. It this is not the case, then orthodoxy is valid. Hence, the question is which economies, if any, are 'small' in this sense. Luxembourg, since the formation of its monetary union with Belgium, and the Republic of Ireland, at least until 1979 when the punt–pound link was broken, are almost certainly small. The USA is large. There is disagreement about the status of the Federal Republic of Germany, the UK and France. Almost certainly they are not small, as for example Dornbusch (1980) admits. Thus, the role of international monetarism is as a polar case in analysing medium-sized economies. Moreover, its development has

(1) introduced 'stock models' and the consequent analysis of the balance of payments as a temporary disequilibrium. Flows, such as income, rather than stock adjustment were the centrepiece of traditional models, even in Friedman's or Tobin's portfolio balance models.
(2) emphasized the link between monetary policy and the exchange rate.
(3) shown that economists should build explicitly open economy models rather than tack an overseas sector onto a closed economy model.

The international monetarist doctrine was not necessary for any of these propositions but their incorporation into conventional wisdom is a consequence of its development.

3.4 THE GOVERNMENT BUDGET CONSTRAINT

This area of economics originated with Blinder and Solow (1973) and has been investigated since then by numerous economists, e.g. Hillier (1977) and Turnovsky (1977). Its most dramatic result has been to question a proposition about which both monetarists and Keynesians agreed, that money-financed expenditure is more expansionary than bond-financed. The model is an application of flow-of-funds analysis and starts with one of the flow-of-funds equations for a closed economy (equation 1.6 above):

$$\text{PSBR} = \Delta \text{ Currency} + \Delta \text{ Bank Lending to the Public Sector} + \Delta \text{ Non-bank Private Sector Lending to the Public Sector} \quad (3.3)$$

Bank lending to the private sector is assumed to be zero, for simplicity, so (from equation 1.5):

$$\text{PSBR} = \Delta \text{ Money} + \Delta \text{ Non-bank Private Sector Lending to the Public Sector} \quad (3.4)$$

The PSBR is then divided into interest payments on the national debt (*IP*) and the remaining components (Other PSBR – *OPSBR*).

$$OPSBR + IP = \Delta \text{ Money} + \Delta \text{ Non-bank Private Sector Lending to the Public Sector} \quad (3.5)$$

This is the basic budget constraint model and all the results depend upon the impact of past levels of the PSBR upon the size of the national debt, and, hence, on the size of interest payments.

The orthodox comparison of money and bond-financed government deficit (spending) is shown in *Figure 3.2* (i.e. of an increase in the PSBR financed by an increase in currency or bank lending to the public sector compared with non-bank private sector lending).

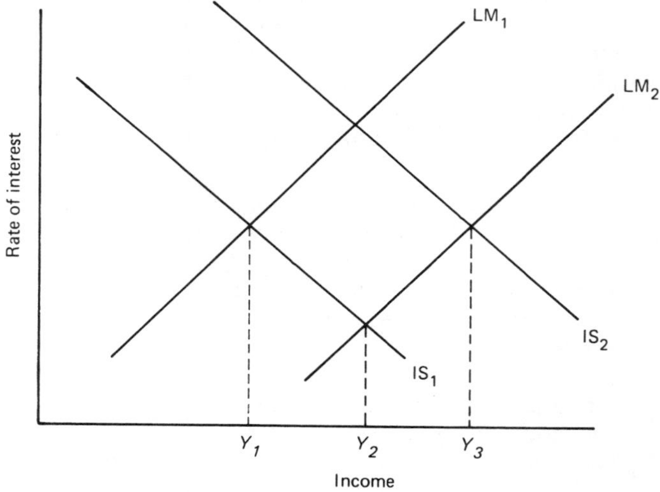

Figure 3.2 Bond and money-financed deficits

Bond-financed spending shifts the IS curve so the economy moves from Y_1 to Y_2. Money-financed deficits also shift the LM curve so the level of income rises to Y_3. Y_3 is necessarily larger than Y_2 unless the IS curve is perfectly inelastic or the LM curve is perfectly elastic. The budget constraint writers accept this as a short-run result but argue that it will be reversed in the longer term. Their argument assumes that neither currency nor bank claims on the public sector pay interest and that there will be no subsequent changes in tax rates or government spending. In this case, the money-financed government spending will leave the level of income at Y_3. Bond-finance, however, means that the government will pay interest to bond-holders in the following year. They will spend some of this, shifting the IS curve to the right. Indeed, the government will have to sell more bonds in order to finance the interest. In year 3, the interest payment will be larger and the IS curve will shift again. This process will continue until the level of income exceeds Y_3; in the long run bond-finance is more expansionary. This result can be assailed on pragmatic grounds – the long run might be several hundred years. Moreover, it has been challenged on theoretical grounds. The rise in interest rates (which are higher with bond-finance, r_2, than with money-finance, r_3) will reduce the value of existing bonds (the 'Keynes effect') and of wealth in general and thus shift the IS curve to the left. In addition, the change in wealth could shift the LM curve so as to reduce the expansiveness of public spending financed by bond sales to the non-bank private sector. Some budget constrait writers have argued that only a balanced budget can be consistent with equilibrium – otherwise changes in the money stock or interest payments must have some effect.

The budget constraint literature highlights some crucial policy issues.

(1) Has the government a PSBR target? If it has, as was the case with both Labour and Conservative governments, the result described above does not apply. Instead, however, government spending must be reduced or taxes raised to finance interest payments.

(2) Does the government pay interest on its borrowing from banks? If yes, then bank profits will raise shareholders' income and spending and so influence the IS curve.

(3) How does the government borrow? For example, if the government borrows by means of irredeemable stock, such as Consols, bond prices will alter when interest rates change, and wealth effects will be generated, but interest payments are fixed for ever when the government borrows. If the government borrows through a liquid asset whose interest rate is market determined (e.g. Treasury bills or NSB accounts), the reverse is true; there are now wealth effects but interest payments on past debt vary with current rates. The effect of government spending is greater in the second case. Thus, yet another factor 'matters'.

In general, the budget constraint model has incorporated flow-of-funds analysis into mainstream macroeconomic theory and in doing so

(1) highlights some policy problems;
(2) makes it clear that models must be dynamic because policy decisions in one period have implications for the future; and
(3) long-run results may differ from short-run ones.

3.5 THE NEW CAMBRIDGE SCHOOL

The 'New Cambridge School' is another offshoot of Keynesianism which reverses orthodoxy by producing 'elegant paradoxes' as two 'old Cambridge' writers, Kahn and Posner, described it[3]. The New Cambridge model has many virtues besides its inherent intrinsic interest. It is a useful teaching device with which to test understanding of the basic Keynesian model and illustrates the scope of this model, and so of 'A'-level economics, for policy analysis. The 'New Cambridge' approach shows how elementary economics can be applied to economic policy and how the difference in view between, say, Mrs Williams and Mr Benn is related to this basic model. By showing how different assumptions produce different results, it illustrates the methodology of economics and the reasons why economists disagree. It also shows the value of econometrics as a potential means of solving the disputes that divide economists. However, the New Cambridge School's major influence has been in stressing the macroeconomic case for import controls. It has played a large role in the emergence of this issue as a major one, especially through its influence on the Tribune group and, to a lesser extent, the TUC. More fundamentally, the New Cambridge group has stressed that macroeconomic policy is the principal determinant of the balance of payments and that the domestic effect of import controls and exchange rates is more important than that on the balance of payments. 'New Cambridge' has not been alone in making either of these points but the group has certainly done more than anyone else to destroy an artificial assignment of monetary and fiscal policy to prices and employment and exchange rates etc. to the balance of payments.

The formal model can be derived by starting from either flow-of-funds identities or national income ones. However, for this purpose sales of existing real assets have to be treated as current transactions, e.g. sales of council houses, or the Kuwaiti purchase of properties such as St Martin's. These are so small that the distinction is unimportant. However, if one starts with the basic Keynesian identity expressed in *current* prices; (all variables defined in key, p. 73):

$$X + G + I \equiv M + S + T \qquad (3.5)$$

Therefore,

$$(S - I) + (T - G) + (M - X) \equiv 0 \tag{3.6}$$

Defined in this way, $(S - I)$ is the private sector's financial surplus, and $(T - G)$ and $(M - X)$ the public and overseas sector's financial surpluses respectively. So, one could have written (3.6) as the flow-of-funds identity instead. The public sector financial deficit (i.e. $G - T$) is not quite the same as the PSBR because the PSFD is a net figure after deducting public sector loans to the private sector. So if the PSFD were £10 bn and the public sector loaned £2 bn to the private sector, the PSBR would be £12 bn.

If one knows that $A + B + C = 0$ and the value of A and B, C is determined. The New Cambridge School determines the balance of payments in this way:

$S - I$ is assumed to be a constant, independent of income

so

$$S - I = k$$

In 'A'-level economics, where I is usually taken to be fixed, exogenous, this assumption would be equivalent to S being independent of income, i.e. an *MPS* of 0, or an *MPC* of 1. A minor complication is that, strictly, the model says that the net level of $I - S$ can be predicted on 1 January without knowing income (that is, it is exogenous) although it can be influenced by credit policy.

The next assumption is to say that the government can behave as if it can fix $(T - G)$ independently of income. This is justified by the 'par tax' system even though Godley and his colleagues accept the usual endogenous influences on the PSBR: the yield of both expenditure and income tax rises with income and so do social security contributions and nationalized industry profits whereas unemployment pay falls as income rises. The government is assumed to fix its deficit at B:

$$T - G = -B,$$

so

$$M - X = B - k.$$

By varying B, the government can determine the balance of payments deficit directly. It is both a necessary and sufficient method of altering the balance of payments, i.e. the only way and an effective method.

KEY

X = exports at current prices
M = imports at current prices
T = taxation, net of transfers, at current prices
G = government expenditure on goods and services at current prices
I = private sector investment at current prices
S = saving at current prices
k = a constant
B = budget deficit
Y = national income (current prices)
P = price level
P_m = price imports
m = marginal propensity to import
Q_m = volume of imports
Q = volume of national income = output

Normally, an equilibrium level of income is determined by finding two formulae for a variable and calculating the value of Y that satisfies both, e.g.

$$S = I \qquad I = 20$$
$$S = 0.2Y$$
$$Y = 100$$

The New Cambridge models does the same, by using two formulae for $X - M$.

X is determined by world trade, relative prices and other 'exogenous trade factors' so $X = \bar{X}$, the bar representing the fact that X is determined outside the model.

The New Cambridge model assumes that the value of imports is a constant fraction of real GDP, i.e. that the import function has an income elasticity of 1 and a price elasticity of 0. Accordingly,

$$Q_m = mQ$$

(where m = marginal propensity to import – here also equal to the average propensity). The model is in current price terms which means that it is necessary to find the value of imports (M) – i.e. the volume of (Q_m) times price (P_m)

$$M = Q_m P_m = mQ_m P_m.$$

Moreover, as $Y = PQ$, $Q = \dfrac{Y}{P}$

$$M = \frac{m\,Y\,P_m}{P}.$$

(P_m/P thus captures the rise in the value of imports when overseas prices change and is equal to the terms of trade.)

Therefore,

$$M - X = \frac{mY\,P_m}{P} - \bar{X}$$

and

$$= B - k$$

Therefore

$$Y = \frac{B - k + \bar{X}}{m} \cdot \frac{P_m}{P}$$

This strange-looking equation is the multiplier equation in an unfamiliar form:

$$Y = \frac{\text{Net injections}}{\text{Marginal propensity to withdraw} - \text{Marginal propensity to inject}}$$

Since $MPS = MPI$, $MPG = MPT$ (because $S - I = k$ and $G - T = B$) and $MPX = 0$ (because exports are exogenous), the denominator collapses to m.

The model accordingly incorporates a 'paradox of imports' in that the import propensities determine the level of income and not the level of imports. This is exactly akin to Keynes's 'paradox of thrift'. As it is usually presented, an attempt to save more leaves saving unchanged but income lower. For example, if investment is 20 and saving = $0.1Y$, the equilibrium level of income is 200, at which level saving = investment = 20. If the saving propensity doubles, to $0.2Y$, the equilibrium level of income will be 100, at which point saving is equal to 20. Investment determines the level of savings, thriftiness the level of income necessary to generate this volume of saving. Similarly, in the New Cambridge world, the level of imports is determined by the PSFD (i.e. government tax and expenditure decisions) and the exogenous level of exports. Import propensities determine the level of income. There is a third paradox, that tax rates determine the level of income not tax yields, which Keynes cited in 1932. He argued that the National government's tax increases would depress income so much that tax yields would actually fall.

From this 'paradox of imports', the case for import controls follows. If import controls can either reduce the marginal propensity to income or introduce a negative constant into the import function, income must rise. (Just as in the 'paradox of thrift' example, if saving became equal either to $0.05Y$ or to $0.1Y - 20$, the equilibrium level of income would be 400.) Moreover, since the level of imports will not be affected why should anyone retaliate? Unfortunately,

(1) overseas governments may not accept that the New Cambridge argument is correct;
(2) even if the aggregate level of imports is unchanged, their distribution will be affected and the losers may retaliate.

The paradox of the New Cambridge argument is that only the budget deficit influences the balance of payments whereas both import controls and the budget deficit influence income. Accordingly, like an 'O'-level comparative advantage question, the conclusion to be drawn is that import controls should be used to influence income and budgetary policy to influence the balance of payments. Hence in 1976, for example, the group's prescription was tax increases to eliminate the balance of payments deficit and import controls to reduce unemployment and prevent the tax increases from increasing it.

The 'New Cambridge' analysis also includes a structural analysis of the economy, and a 'frustration' model of inflation (see p. 111 below). Nevertheless, its agility in turning elementary macroeconomic theory upside down is probably its major contribution to economic policy in the 1970s and 1980s. Its conclusions are unassailable if its premises (about $I - S$ and the par tax system) are valid. This shifts the onus of the case to

(1) econometric estimation;
(2) the group's forecasting record, where its emphasis on the terms of trade has produced some spectacularly good results

> (e.g. in 1974), but where, on balance, its record is no better than that of other forecasters; the group has had some very large errors to offset against its successes.

However, an evaluation of its econometric and forecasting record is beyond the scope of this chapter. Finally, like the budget constraint, the New Cambridge group has shown the value of flow-of-funds equations and the additional rigour imposed on forecasters as a consequence.

3.6 BACON AND ELTIS

At about the same time as the New Cambridge economists first gained a large amount of attention from the media, two Oxford economists received widespread coverage for their views following a series of articles in 1975 in the *Sunday Times* later extended into book form (Bacon and Eltis, 1978). Their thesis was that Britain's economic problems, especially its low rate of growth, had been caused by excessive growth of employment in the non-market sector (more or less equivalent to the public sector).

It must be emphasized that neither their diagnosis that the problems of the British economy were caused by underinvestment, nor their policy recommendations, were either original or surprising. They recommended a combination of investment incentives in the short run, the most orthodox of all possibilities, cheap credit and either a cut in public spending or a reduction in middle class living standards especially by means of import controls in the medium term.

The original part of the articles consists of a hypothesis of recent British economic history in which over-expansion of manpower by the 'non-market sector' is *indirectly* responsible for the low level of investment in the market sector. This theory was reinforced by a detailed statistical analysis but, as they emphasized in response to their most thorough critics, Hadjimatheou and Skouras (1979), their case must stand or fall by their theory.

Their thesis depends on two assumptions about the economy:

(1) Output (and employment) in the market sector are determined by capital stock in this sector. Further, as they assumed that the observed productivity growth in the market sector was exogenous, employment was bound to fall in this sector unless the capital stock grew rapidly.

(2) Inflation is determined by the quantity of market goods consumed by employees in the market sector, a version of the frustration hypothesis discussed on p. 111 below.

Starting with their identity,

GDP = Market Goods (MG) + Non Market Goods (NM)
= MG consumed by Market sector workers + MG consumed by Non Market sector workers + MG invested + MG for (X less Imports) + NM

They postulate the following sequence of events:

(1) A recession.
(2) The government expands non-market (i.e. public sector) employment, i.e. NM rises.
(3) The newly-employed workers use their wages to purchase market goods, i.e. MG consumed by Non Market sector workers increases. This produces overheating and sucks in imports because the supply of market goods is less than the demand.
(4) The government responds by cutting all demand for market goods. Thus both 'investment' and 'market goods consumed by employees in the market sector' fall. This latter phenomenon leads to inflation, i.e. there is a fall in all of
   (a) MG consumed by market workers,
   (b) MG for investment,
   (c) MG for balance of payments.
(5) The higher inflation leads to lower profit.
(6) Margins (assisted by 'voluntary price restraint' and incomes policies) fall. This reinforces the fall in investment. Hence investment falls still further.
(7) The low level of investment ensures that employment in the market sector falls. This produces a recession and the process starts again. Ultimately, one finishes with (structural) mass unemployment and an ever-growing public sector.

This explanation of recent history is consistent with the facts, with the possible exception of (7), but so are other more widely-held theories. The model can produce weird results because of the definition of 'market'and 'non-market'. Public sector goods are market goods in so far as they are charged for. Thus, a rise in council house rents increases the output of market goods and reduces that of non market goods. An increase in council house rents would increase market goods consumed by those in the non market sector, so it would reduce the level of wage claims! However, this is more of a quirk than an inherent defect in the model.

Personally, I do not accept the historical theory of Bacon and Eltis because there are more orthodox explanations which seem more plausible, and because underinvestment *per se* does not seem to be the major problem facing British industry (see Gowland, 1979, Chapter 4). Nevertheless, Bacon and Eltis do seem to have made two important contributions:

(1) They put emphasis on the *composition* of output, a factor almost totally ignored in conventional macroeconomics.
(2) Like the Marxists and neo-Marxists but unlike orthodox economists, whether monetarist or Keynesian, they give considerable prominence to the squeeze on profits in the UK since the early 1950s which is paralleled in other countries to a lesser extent.

3.7 RATIONAL EXPECTATIONS

The remaining three issues in macroeconomics, rational expectations, 'the Ricardian doctrice', and supply side economics, are often grouped together as the 'New Classical Macroeconomics' or the American New Right (Gowland, 1979, Chapter 5, Appendix A; Buiter, 1980; Sargent, 1979). This group of economists campaigned vigorously for Proposition 13 in California in 1978 and has supported similar tax-cutting refenda and initiatives elsewhere. They have also been prominent amongst President Reagan's economic advisers but have tended to lose influence to conservative economists, i.e. followers of Friedman, such as Treasury Secretary Regan.

The main use of rational expectations in new classical models is to demonstrate the futility of government macroeconomic policy and that the aggregate supply curve is vertical. This is, however, not their only role. The basic idea underlying all rational expectations models is that all economic agents use all available information to forecast any economic variables whose outcome would affect current decisions. For example, agents will endeavour to forecast inflation so as to decide how much to save and in what form to hold their assets. All such forecasts must be 'rational' and 'efficient' in the technical sense of making optimal use of the information and of being consistent. Such forecasts, it is argued, cannot be systematically biased and, in particular, the average error must be zero. If agents systematically under or over-predicted, they could adjust their forecasts by adding (or subtracting) a constant from their original forecast. Hence, for example, if you always underpredict inflation by an average of 1% you can improve your forecast by adding 1% to the number produced by your original method. In statistical jargon, a rational forecast must be a best unbiased efficient estimator. The new classicists go on to argue that the agents forecast will be the actual outcome plus or minus a random variable. Models are usually constructed such that the agent's expectation of a variable is the actual outcome generated by the model. This is now an almost universal equilibrium condition: that agents forecast correctly the relevant economic variables. This has been challenged by Evans (1980) who argues that agents' most profitable forecasts need not be the underlying equilibrium. His model is a mathematical version of Keynes's comparison of such private forecasting with a newspaper contest in which the aim is to guess how other people will rank the attractiveness of bathing beauties, not to evaluate their beauty. It may be very dangerous to predict 'rationally' if you believe that other people will act irrationally. In other words, the new classicists have sought to revive their self-righting mechanism of the classical school against the onslaught of the *General Theory* (Keynes, 1936), especially Chapter 12. If agents predict correctly, the economy will move towards a unique full employment equilibrium. Agents will know the market clearing wage and will both offer and bid for labour at this price. Hence, it is argued, full employment will always exist. Thus, macroeconomic policy is unnecessary.

The defects of rational expectations models have been examined by Evans (1980) and Buiter (1980). In addition to the Evans-Keynes argument that rational individual forecasting may not guarantee equilibrium, the major problem of the 'rational' models is the assumption that there is a unique equilibrium and that this would be a full employment equilibrium. If there is not, no one would (rationally) expect it. Moreover, a best unbiased efficient forecast need not be correct: to quote Evans: '[even] when agents use an optimal learning policy monetary policy is able to influence real output in the short run and possibly in the long run', a view which summarizes the work of various authors.

As stated above, rational expectations models have frequently been used to argue that government stabilization policy will be either unnecessary, futile or counter-productive. The argument that it is unnecessary has been examined: intervention in a self-righting economy is unnecessary. The argument for the futility or counter-productivity of state intervention is intuitively more appealing. If governments do intervene, it is argued, agents will endeavour to predict state actions. The effectiveness of macroeconomic policy will be influenced by forecasts of state actions. Keynesians have often used similar arguments to support intervention, e.g. the argument that a commitment to full employment by the government will generate enough *private* investment to ensure full employment with minimal *actual* state intervention; the willingness to intervene is crucial – for a forthright statement of this view see Graham (1980). In fact, it is easy to see how private reaction to policy making could produce any of these results:

(a) *An ineffective policy*

If the authorities varied income tax so as to influence disposable income in an attempt to produce a fluctuating pattern of consumers' expenditure in order to offset fluctuations in export demand, private action would render this ineffective. The private sector would realize quickly what the authorities were doing and would finance higher tax payments by reducing saving when the government raised tax rates (and therefore not reduce spending). The savings would be rebuilt when tax rates were lowered and, again, the authorities attempt to vary spending would be frustrated. (Alternatively, the private sector would vary its borrowing, borrowing to pay higher taxes and repaying the loans when taxation was reduced, with the same effect on net saving as above.) The use of tax policy to produce a contra-cyclical variation in consumers' spending would be frustrated because the private sector could adjust its savings and borrowing to offset official actions and maintain a stable level of consumption. This is a good example of the sort of mechanism envisaged by rational new classicists.

(b) *Intervention might be counter-productive*

Friedman has argued that prices and incomes policy could increase inflationary expectations, and so inflation (see p. 102 below). If inflation were 10% and the authorities announced an 8% incomes policy, reaction might be: 'Oh, I was expecting inflation to continue at 10% but if the government is introducing a wages policy, they must expect inflation to accelerate. Say they expect

15% inflation. This policy might reduce it to 12% so that is my new forecast.' Other examples are possible but this one combines simplicity and the paradox that a belief in government renders its actions ineffective.

(c) Intervention could be reinforced or self-fulfilling

If the authorities introduced a tax-credit or other incentive to induce greater investment, a rational response would be: 'They are always changing these allowances. I had better take advantage as quickly as possible.' In this case, the contra-cyclical effect of a policy of varying investment incentives would be reinforced because it was believed to be temporary.

The rationalists have attempted to argue that responses like the third are impossible. In some models they are and in others, such beneficial intervention can work, so no final judgement is possible yet.

Rational expectations has had a greater influence on macroeconomic theory than any other development in the late 1970s. In the process, macroeconomic models have become far more complex. In return, there seem to be a number of gains:

(1) A recognition that companies and individuals are not dummies easily manipulated by governments; this had often been stated but rarely incorporated in formal theory.
(2) A recognition that the formation of expectations is crucial and cannot simply be added onto an existing model, as was done so often in the 1960s and 1970s.
(3) A recognition that consistency is necessary in model construction and that certain forms of consistency were not present in existing models.

3.8 THE 'RICARDIAN' DOCTRINE

This aspect of the new classical economics is the argument that the effect of public spending on the economy is independent of its method of finance, i.e. it does not matter whether it is money-financed, tax-financed or bond-financed. Moreover, its effect will be to cause inflation. The name was used by one of its leading exponents (Barro, 1974) although it is misleading as the name is also used to denote neo-marxist followers of Sraffa.

The doctrine is neither monetarist nor Keynesian since it combines extreme features of both and denies propositions that are central to both. It can be presented in various ways; the one used here is not normally used by advocates of the school.

(1) Government spending financed by taxation will lead to an increase in nominal income. This could be justified by the 'balanced budget' multiplier or by any other model except a pure monetarist one.
(2) As the aggregate supply curve is vertical, an increase in nominal income must cause a rise in prices (see p. 941).
(3) If, instead, the increase in spending were financed by the sale of bonds to non-bank private holders, the effect on the economy would be identical to (1) or (2). Current taxation would be lower but expected future taxation would be higher and so current expenditure and nominal income would be at the same level as in (1). This is the Chicago doctrine discussed on pp. 60–61.
(4) If the expenditure were money-financed, the effect would be the same if this were by the sale of bonds to the banks. If the finance were by the issue of currency, or non-interest-bearing securities to banks, the situation would differ in that although the principal has to be repaid, interest does not, so apparently nominal income would be higher. However, some of the group have argued that as the currency-deposit ratio and banks' portfolios are independent of official action, there would be the same increase in currency as in (1) or (3) and similarly for banks' holdings of non-interest-bearing securities once the system had adjusted.

This model denies both the key Keynesian proposition that tax rates can affect nominal income and the monetarist proposition that inducing a switch by the private sector from holding bonds to holding money will affect the economy. It has proved appealing to some politicians because of the obvious attractions to right-wingers of the suggestion that a reduction in both government spending and taxation will reduce inflation and even more that tax cuts need not cause inflation. Indeed, if it is government spending which causes inflation, life is much simpler than if it is the money supply or the PSBR. It is to the credit of both the Reagan and Thatcher administrations that they have not been seduced by these restraints. The doctrine was savaged by Tobin (1980). More significantly, even Sargent (1979) who was regarded as a leading member of the group said that it was only a special case. However, it may be that the group is right to say that excessive attention has been paid to the money or tax or bond-financed spending debate.

3.9 SUPPLY SIDE ECONOMICS

This final argument of the new classicists has received most attention from politicians and the media, especially the American magazines such as *Fortune, Time* and *Newsweek*, than from academics. Nevertheless, the basic proposition is undeniable: that conventional macroeconomics has ignored aggregate supply. Aggregate supply curves are 'assumed' or 'assumed to be shifted by' certain factors, as in Chapter 4. However, little attention has been paid to their origins or nature. New classicists have built models in which labour supply is derived as an optimal household decision jointly with consumers' expenditure (notably the Lucas –Rapping model, discussed in Sargent, 1979). These models are not perfect nor is the approach necessarily right but there is a problem.

One famous, or infamous, device of the supply side economists is the Laffer curve, of which the original was devised by Laffer in a Washington restaurant (see *Fortune*, 14 July 1980). This is illustrated in *Figure 3.3*. It is assumed that all taxes can be combined into an omnibus tax rate (t) equal to both the average and marginal rate of tax. This is measured on the horizontal axis as a percentage. Tax yields are measured on the vertical axis. The yield from taxation (T) is equal to tY (the rate times income). If income were independent of the tax rate, T would be a straight line with gradient 45°, *OA* in *Figure 3.3a* and *b*. However, because of incentive and disincentive effects, income will be influenced by the rate. If the slope of T is greater than 45°, tax yields are rising faster than tax rates so income must be rising, *OB* in *Figure 3.3a*, and taxation must be having an incentive effect. Contrawise, if the slope is less than 45°, *BC* in *Figure 3.3b*, (or is downward-sloping), tax yields are rising less than tax rates so income is falling, i.e. there are disincentive effects of taxation.

Laffer argued that tax yields would be zero if tax rates were either 0% or 100%, when effort would be zero. Further the curve would be continuous between these points. In consequence, there is a tax rate which yields maximum revenue, t', in *Figure 3.3c* which illustrates all aspects of Laffer's views. Finally Laffer argued that in both the UK and the US actual tax rates were higher than t', so a reduction in rates would increase yields.

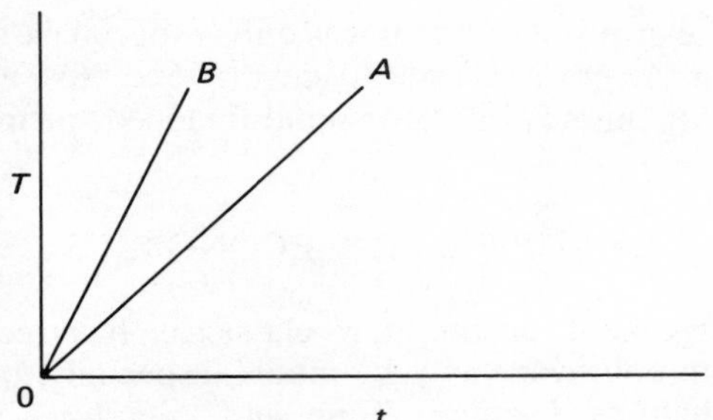

Figure 3.3a Laffer curve: incentive effect

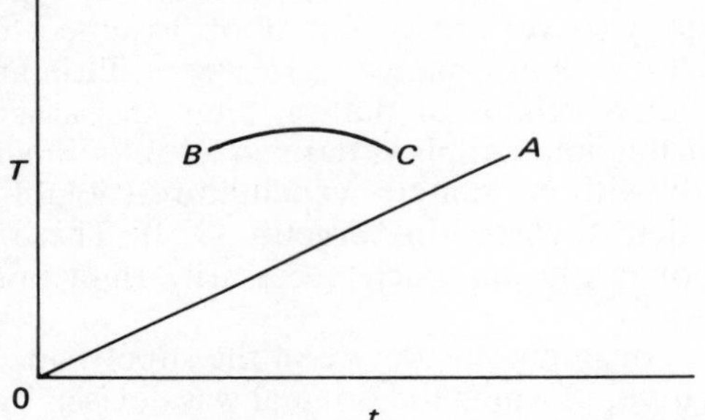

Figure 3.3b Laffer curve: disincentive effect

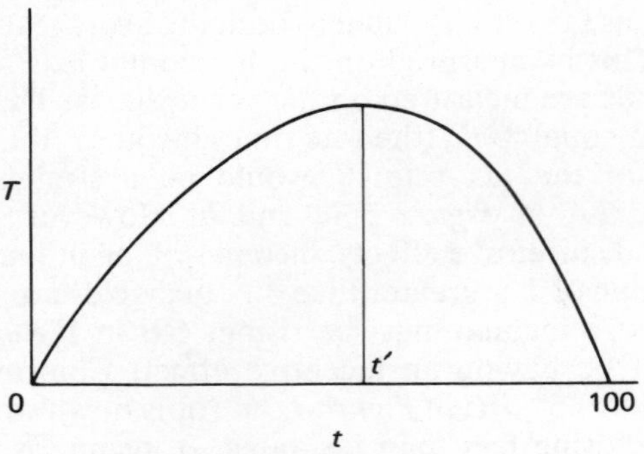

Figure 3.3c Laffer's own curve

It is not necessary to accept either part of Laffer's hypothesis to believe that the device is a very useful expository tool. This curve may be discontinuous, or meaningless at high rates. The US and UK economies may be below maximum yield, even if Laffer is right about the slope. All the same, the curve is a graphic illustration of incentives and disincentives and a fruitful framework for analysis. Other 'supply siders' have looked at tax incentives in more conventional frameworks and examined other schemes, for example announced but deferred tax reductions so that yields never fall (the incentive takes time to work through).

APPENDIX 3A

A specific example may help to illustrate Leijonhufvud's ideas. Imagine a 30 year old building worker who has a weekly income of £150, all of which he spends. A shock, such as bad weather, then reduces his earnings to £50 in one week. He would like to borrow £99.90 and repay the loan at 10p per week over the following 30 years. In this case his consumption would be £149.90 in each week. However, if he cannot borrow he is forced to reduce his consumption to £50; in Clower's terminology, his effective demand is £50 whereas his notional demand is £149.90. This undesired reduction in consumption is responsible for other workers losing their jobs.

Notes

1 For the monetarist-Keynesian debate, see Gowland (1979), Chapter 5.
2 For the IS–LM model, see also pp. 40–44 above, Gowland (1979), Chapter 5, Surrey (1976) and any macroeconomic textbook of which Laidler (1974) is the most useful as it includes both the algebraic and graphical versions of the model.
3 *The Times*, 17 March 1973: for the New Cambridge model see House of Commons Expenditure Committee (1974), Cripps and Godley (1976), all issues of *Cambridge Economic Policy Group Review*. For a critique, see Gowland (1979), Chapter 2, Appendix D: Crystal (1979); Cuthbertson (1979).

Guide to further reading

(1) For the mainstream debate prior to the reappraisal of Keynes: Metzler (1969); Patinkin (1969).
(2) For the reappraisal of Keynes: Weintraub (1979); Malinvaud (1977).
(3) For international monetarism: Frenkel and Johnson (1976), especially Chapters 1 (Frenkel and Johnson) and 6 (Johnson); Dornbusch (1980).

(4) On the budget constraing: Turnovsky (1977).
(5) On New Cambridge: Crystal (1979); Cuthbertson (1979).
(6) On Bacon and Eltis: Bacon and Eltis (1978).
(7) On rational expectations: Minford and Peel (1981); Sargent (1979), especially pp. 357ff.
(8) On 'Ricardians': Tobin (1980).
(9) On supply side economics: Eltis in IEA (1980).

More general background to the chapter can be found in Surrey (1976), Goodhart (1976), and Chick (1973).

Bibliography

BACON, R. and ELTIS, W. (1978), *Britain's Economic Problem: Too Few Producers* (2nd edn.), Macmillan; London

BARRO, R. J. (1974), 'Are Government Bonds Net Wealth?', *Journal of Political Economy*, Vol. 82, pp. 1095–1118

BARRO, R. J. and GROSSMAN, H. I. (1976), *Money, Employment and Inflation*, Cambridge University Press; Cambridge

BLINDER, A. S. and SOLOW, R. M. (1973), 'Does Fiscal Policy Matter?', *Journal of Public Economics*, Vol. 2, pp. 319–338

BUITER, W. H. (1980), 'The Macroeconomics of Dr Pangloss', *Economic Journal*, Vol. 90 (March), pp. 34–50

CHICK, V. (1973), *The Theory of Monetary Policy*, Gray Mills; London

CLOWER, R. W. (ed.) (1969), *Monetary Theory*, Penguin Modern Economics Readings, Penguin; Harmondsworth (includes his 1965 paper)

CRIPPS, T. F. and GODLEY, W. A. C. (1976), 'A FormalAnalysis of the CEPG Model', *Economica*, Vol. 43 (November)

CRYSTAL, K. A. (1979), *Controversies in British Macroeconomics*, Philip Allan; London

CUTHBERTSON, K. (1979), *Macroeconomic Policy*, Macmillan; London

DORNBUSCH, R. (1980), *Open Economy Macroeconomics*, Basic Books; New York

EVANS, G. (1980), *The Stability of Rational Expectations* (Discussion Paper No. 80), University of Stirling

FRENKEL, J. A. and JOHNSON, H. G. (1976), *The Monetary Approach to the Balance of Payments,* Allen & Unwin; London

GOODHART, C. A. E. (1976), *Money, Information and Uncertainty* (2nd edn.), Macmillan; London

GOWLAND, D. H. (ed.) (1979), *Modern Economic Analysis*, Butterworths; London

GRAHAM, A. W. M. (1980), 'Demand Management Policy in Changing Historical Circumstances', in CURRIE, D. A. and PETERS, W. (eds.), *Contemporary Economic Analysis*, Croom Helm; London

GURLEY, J. G. and SHAW, E. S. (1960), *Money in a Theory of Finance*, Brookings Institute; Washington D.C.

HADJIMATHEOU, G. and SKOURAS, A. (1979), 'Britain's Economic Problem: The Growth of the Non-Market Sector', *Economic Journal*, Vol. 89 (June), pp. 392–401

HANSEN, A. H. (1953), *A Guide to Keynes*, McGraw-Hill; New York

HICKS, J. R. (1937), 'Mr Keynes and the Classics', *Econometrica*, Vol. V (April)

HILLIER, B. (1977), 'Does Fiscal Policy Matter?', *Public Finance*, pp. 374–389

HOUSE OF COMMONS EXPENDITURE COMMITTEE (1974), *Public Expenditure, Inflation and the Balance of Payments*, HC 328, HMSO; London

IEA (1980), *Is Monetarism Enough?*, IEA Readings 24, IEA

KEYNES, J. M. (1936), *The General Theory of Employment, Interest and Money*, Macmillan; London (reprinted as Volume IX of Keynes's Collected Works, Royal Economic Society)

LAIDLER, D. E. W. (1974), *The Demand for Money* (2nd edn.), International Textbook Co.; Scranton, Pa.

LEIJONHUFVUD, A. (1968), *On Keynesian Economics and the Economics of Keynes*, Oxford University Press; New York

MALINVAUD, E. (1977), *The Theory of Unemployment Reconsidered*, Basil Blackwell; Oxford

METZLER, A. H. (1969), 'Money, Intermediation and Growth', *Journal of Economic Literature*, Vol. VII (March)

MINFORD, P. and PEEL, D. (1981), 'Is the Government's Economic Strategy on Course?', *Lloyds Bank Review*, No. 140 (April)

PATINKIN, D. (1956), *Money, Interest and Prices*, Harper and Row; Evanston, Ill.

PATINKIN, D. (1959), 'Keynesian Economics Rehabilitated: A Rejoinder to Professor Hicks', *Economic Journal*, Vol. XLI

PATINKIN, D. (1969), 'Money and Wealth', *Journal of Economic Literature*, Vol. VII (December)

PESEK, B. P. and SAVING, T. R. (1967), *Money, Wealth and Economic Theory*, Macmillan; New York

SARGENT, T. J. (1979), *Macroeconomic Theory*, Academic Press; London

SURREY, M. J. C. (1976), *Macroeconomic Themes*, Oxford University Press; Oxford

TOBIN, J. (1980), 'Government Deficits and Capital Accumulation', in CURRIE, D. A. and PETERS, W. (eds.), *Contemporary Economic Analysis*, Vol. 2, Croom Helm; London

TURNOVSKY, S. J. (1977), *Macroeconomic Analysis*, Cambridge University Press; Cambridge

WEINTRAUB, E. R. (1979), *Microfoundations*, Cambridge University Press; Cambridge

4
Inflation: some new perspectives

D. H. Gowland

4.1 INTRODUCTION

Conventional macroeconomic theory is a theory of the determination of nominal, or current price income[1]. This, often abbreviated as Y, is equal to price multiplied by output. Nominal income can change if output changes or if price changes or if both change. The Keynesian and monetarist models (at least in their strict sense) are equally restricted since both explain Y but do not offer an explanation of the breakdown into changes in the price level (P) and the aggregate output (Q). Sometimes an *ad hoc* addition is made to a model so that it can be presented as a model of either inflation or output and, so implicity, employment. In the 1960s many Keynesians assumed a fixed (exogenous) level of prices so that a theory of the determination of nominal income could be presented as a theory of output. Similarly, classical monetarists assumed a fixed level of output so that the quantity theory of money could be presented as a theory of the price level. Nevertheless, both theories were and are, essentially, theories of nominal income.

There are obvious limitations to the value of a theory which explains nominal income. To know that nominal income will rise by 10% is of little value unless one knows whether this is a 10% rise in output or a 10% rise in prices or a 3% rise in both. Moreover, it is possible that a 10% rise in nominal income could conceal a fall in real income together with a rise of more than 10%

in prices – as in the UK in 1980. It is the purpose of inflation theory to explain the breakdown of changes in nominal income into changes in price and changes in output (and employment).

Moreover, concentration on this ambiguity of conventional macroeconomics highlights the crucial problem of policy-making: can governments influence the division between price and output or must they accept whatever an apparently arbitrary fate determines? This issue provides one of the sharpest distinctions between the Labour government of 1974–1979 and the present (1982) Conservative government. The Labour government believed that it could influence the price/output split and, in particular, used incomes policies to try to achieve a higher level of output, and a lower level of prices, at each level of nominal income. Mrs Thatcher, on the other hand, believes that governments are powerless to influence the mix of price and output at each level of income at least in the short term.

The traditional theory of inflation is set out in section 4.2. The implication of this theory seems to be that governments face a choice between unemployment and inflation, the classic trade-off. Currently (1982), the Labour opposition accepts the existence of such a choice, whereas the Government denies it. This is the other crucial difference in economic theory underlying the contrasting approaches to economic policy of Mrs Thatcher and Mr Foot. The Government believes that the trade-off is, at best, a short-term phenomenon. *Accelerating* (not higher) inflation would be necessary to maintain a lower level of unemployment if the Government sought to reduce unemployment by demand management, Sir Geoffrey Howe's addictive drug (see p. xi). The reason for this belief is inherent in the modern, expectational theory of inflation discussed in section 4.3. The Government has gone further and argues that inflation in the short run causes unemployment in the longer term. This issue is also examined in section 4.3 and in Chapter 5.

To summarize, there are four critical issues in inflation theory and policy:

(1) What determines the level of price and output at each level of nominal income?
(2) Can governments influence the mix of price and output?
(3) Is there a choice between inflation and unemployment or does the one cause the other?
(4) What is the role of overseas factors in general and oil price increases in particular in the determination of inflation?

In this chapter, section 4.2 sets out the traditional theory and section 4.3 the modern (expectational) theory which is designed to remedy some defects in the conventional model. Together these comprise the standard economic approach to inflation, the successor to Samuelson's 'neo-classical synthesis'. Section 4.4 considers alternative approaches. Section 4.5 is devoted to overseas factors and, in particular, to the monetarist analysis of oil price increases. This is one of the more interesting and useful, but ignored, areas of monetarism. It denies that the OPEC price increases of 1973 and 1978 caused inflation. Section 4.6 presents some conclusions. Throughout the chapter, especial attention is paid to the scope of government policy in general and to the possible role of an incomes policy in particular.

4.2 THE TRADITIONAL MODELS

4.2.1 Some simple models: cost push, demand pull and all that

There are two solutions to the problem of determining the level of prices and of output. The first is to assume that prices are fixed, or at least exogenous, i.e. determined independently of income. The usual term applied to this approach is the 'cost push' theory of inflation. It is assumed that prices are fixed by cost factors, usually either import prices or wages, which are, in turn, often thought to be fixed by union behaviour. The rationale for this is some form of 'cost plus pricing' whereby firms determine prices by using a fixed mark-up over average cost at some normal level of output[2]. Whatever the merits of this approach to the analysis of firms' behaviour, its macroeconomic implications are clear. A change in the level of nominal income will mean that output has risen by the same amount.

Indeed, any cost push theory of inflation transforms the monetarist and Keynesian theories of the determination of nominal income into theories of output, as in 'French monetarism'. French monetarism is an amalgam of the quantity theory and of cost push inflation. Many self-styled 'Keynesian' models in the 1960s combined the determination of nominal income in a similar way, by injections and withdrawals with fixed prices, to produce a theory of output[3]. Within this model the role of incomes policy is both obvious and clear. Its aim is to reduce costs below the level at which they would otherwise have been and so ensure a lower price level. It is worth emphasizing that the theory of cost push inflation would also justify 'union-busting'. A South American dictator who tortured trade union leaders could appeal just as much to the cost push theory to justify his action as a pale pink advocate of incomes policy.

The other simplistic extreme theory is that output is fixed, or at least exogenous. Again, a theory of nominal income has been transformed into a theory of the price level. The best known of such theories is classical monetarism, a form of 'demand pull' inflation. This regards output as fixed in the short run at some full employment level. This level is determined by technological factors, available resources and other structural factors and is normally thought to rise over time. The microeconomic rationale of this theory is a special form of perfect competition.

There are a number of problems with both of these theories. One is that they are both extreme, simplistic and implausible. For example, there is considerable evidence that the mark-up varies according to the pressure of demand, so the simple cost push theory is hard to sustain. More seriously, the two theories are presented in a form which is not susceptible to analysis, still less to determining which is right. The art of the economist is to pose a question in such a way as to highlight the factors upon which the answer depends. Thus, it is necessary to put cost push and classical monetarist theory into some appropriate context. It seems that the most appropriate is the aggregate supply/aggregate demand model.

4.2.2 Aggregate supply and aggregate demand

The aggregate demand/aggregate supply model has many advantages as a framework within which to analyse the cost push –demand pull debate, and to try to resolve it. One of these is familiarity. The resolution of price and output is normally solved in economics by supply and demand analysis and exactly the same method can be used to analyse the aggregate price level and aggregate demand.

Monetarism and Keynesian nominal income analysis both determine the level of current price (or nominal) income, i.e. price (P) times output (Q). Thus, for a given money supply (and for given injections and withdrawals functions), $P{\cdot}Q$ is constant at the level derived by monetarist or Keynesian or IS–LM analysis. A constant level of $P{\cdot}Q$ is the definition of a unit-elastic demand curve. So, the aggregate demand curve is unit-elastic (i.e. a rectangular hyperbola) and shifts whenever the money supply and/or injections change, i.e. when nominal income changes. This is illustrated in *Figure 4.1*. AD_1 is the aggregate demand curve when the money supply is equal to M_A and government expenditure to G_A. If there were a higher (money-financed) level of government expenditure, the money supply would be M_B, government expenditure G_B and the aggregate demand curve AD_2. There are two further points about aggregate demand curves. One is that in some advanced macroeconomic models it is not necessarily unit-elastic, e.g. if

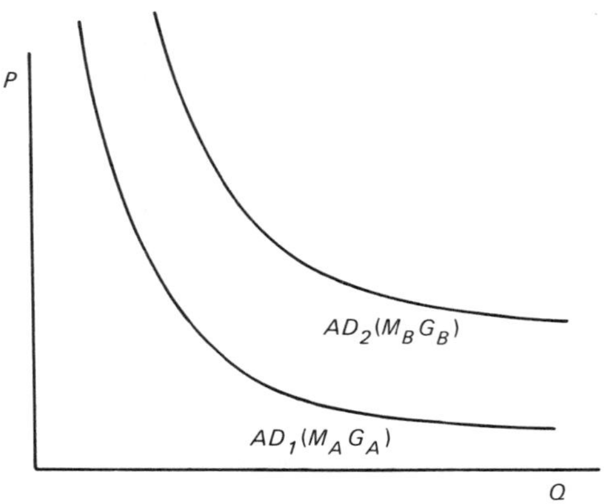

Figure 4.1 Aggregate demand

there are wealth effects, but it is in all the basic models (i.e. in IS–LM, quantity theory and elementary Keynesian). The other is that the authorities can determine the position of the aggregate demand curve. However, this does not say anything about where along the curve the economy will be. Mrs Thatcher's position could be reinterpreted as saying that she believes that she can determine aggregate demand but not aggregate supply. Mr Healey's position is that he can influence the point on the aggregate demand curve at which the economy will rest.

The determination of aggregate supply also follows classical microeconomic analysis. The cost push theory is that prices are determined by cost factors, irrespective of the level of nominal income, i.e. irrespective of the level of (aggregate) demand. Price does not change when the demand curve shifts. This is the definition of a perfectly elastic supply curve. Thus the cost push theory of inflation is that the aggregate supply curve is horizontal and shifts upwards when trade union pressure, corporate greed, or import prices so determine, as in *Figure 4.2*. The theory of demand pull inflation would, therefore, be equivalent to the proposition that aggregate supply curves are not perfectly elastic. For example, the classical argument, that output is exogenous, is equivalent to a perfectly inelastic supply curve, i.e. a fixed quantity.

The two theories discussed in section 4.2.1 have now been restated as two theories of the slope of the aggregate supply curve.

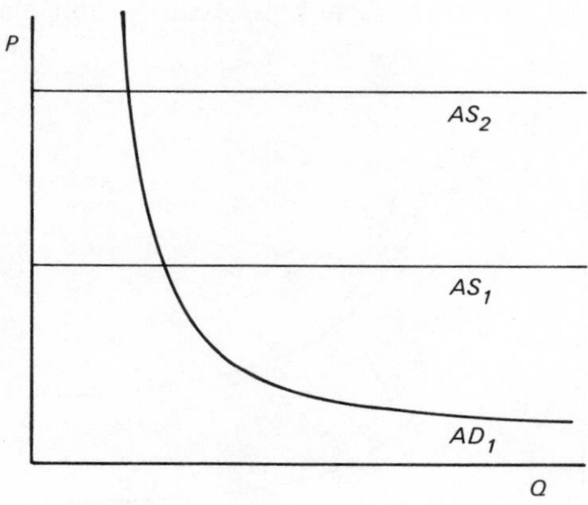

Figure 4.2 Cost push inflation

Their extreme nature is obvious and so is the fact that the aggregate supply curve can have other slopes. All possible slopes are discussed below and illustrated in *Figure 4.3*, but it is necessary first to discuss some features of the cost push model which were rightly stressed by Johnson in a number of crucial articles in the early 1960s[4]. The critical feature is illustrated in *Figure 4.2*. Cost factors can increase prices by shifting the *AS* curve upwards but there will be a fall in output, and so in employment, unless the authorities ratify inflation by shifting the aggregate demand curve. Unless there is a change in monetary and fiscal policy, cost push inflation will lead to ever rising unemployment. Johnson stressed both the role of government acquiescence in cost push inflation and the implausibility of prolonged cost push inflation, as an explanation of the 1950s. Accordingly, cost push inflation has been reinterpreted as inflation generated by a movement of the *AS* curve and demand pull as that generated by a movement of the *AD* curve (e.g. Curwen, 1976). However, it must be emphasized that, while such a definition may be useful, most of the basic textbooks' statements about cost plus inflation do not apply to this version. In particular, demand factors influence prices even when there is an exogenous shock to costs such as OPEC.

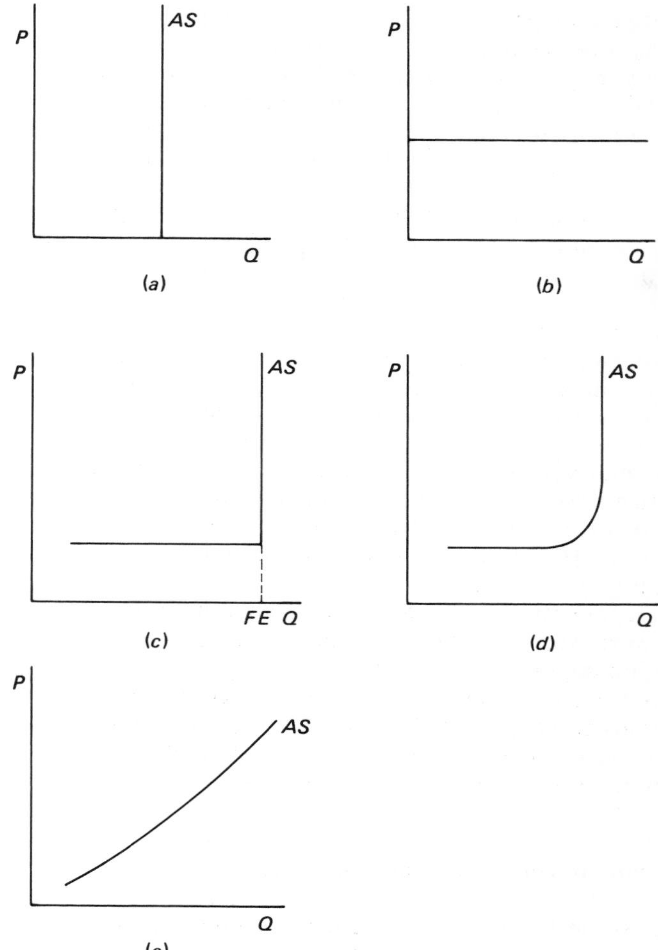

Figure 4.3 Aggregate supply curves (a) Classical; (b) Cost push; (c) Textbook; (d) Keynes; (e) Neoclassical

Many other aggregate supply curves are possible, besides the perfectly elastic and perfectly inelastic, because the consequence of changes in nominal income depends on many factors. An ubiquitous textbook theory starts with a full employment level of output. If actual output is less than this, an increase in nominal income will lead to an increase in output. If output is equal to the full employment level, an increase in nominal income will lead to an increase in prices. This hypothesis can be represented as a perfectly elastic supply curve up to full employment level and a perfectly inelastic one thereafter. This aggregate supply curve is a reversed 'L' with the kink at full employment output (*FE*) as shown in *Figure 4.3c*. This is sometimes called Keynesian but Keynes's own ideas seem to have been rather richer. He accepted a reversed 'L' at the level of the industry but believed that different industries hit full employment at different levels of aggregate output, 'bottlenecks' being the result. In consequence, the corner of the reversed 'L' is smoothed off as one enters a region where some industries increase price and others output. A neoclassical hardliner would say that Keynes has arrived at an upward sloping supply curve by a very tortuous route. The neoclassical proposition is that aggregate supply curves slope upwards because all supply curves are assumed to slope upwards unless there are strong arguments to the contrary. At the aggregate level, there are none. It is always possible to increase output – at a price. More and more unsuitable labour can be employed, the hours of work can be increased, the life of plant can be stretched and so on. Hence, the neoclassical supply curve slopes upwards over all relevant ranges.

Aggregate supply and aggregate demand analysis provides a framework within which to determine price and output. Different aggregate supply curves provide different predictions about the impact of monetary and fiscal policy. In section 4.2.3 an extension of the analysis is provided. This is followed by a discussion of the role of government policy (section 4.2.4) and a section (4.2.5) pointing out the limitations of the analysis.

4.2.3 Phillips curves and unemployment

It is possible to expand an aggregate supply/demand diagram to include unemployment as well as prices and output. this is done in *Figure 4.4*. Output is measured along the horizontal axis from left to right. As output rises, so does employment. Hence, employment is also measured on the horizontal axis, although not on the same scale as output. A 5% rise in output may require a 2% rise in employment at Q_1 and an 8% rise at Q_2. Thus the employment scale is non-linear. If the size of the labour force is marked on the horizontal axis, unemployment can be measured from right to left as the difference between employment and the labour force.

It is possible to redraw this diagram as in *Figure 4.4b* with unemployment measured from left to right and employment and

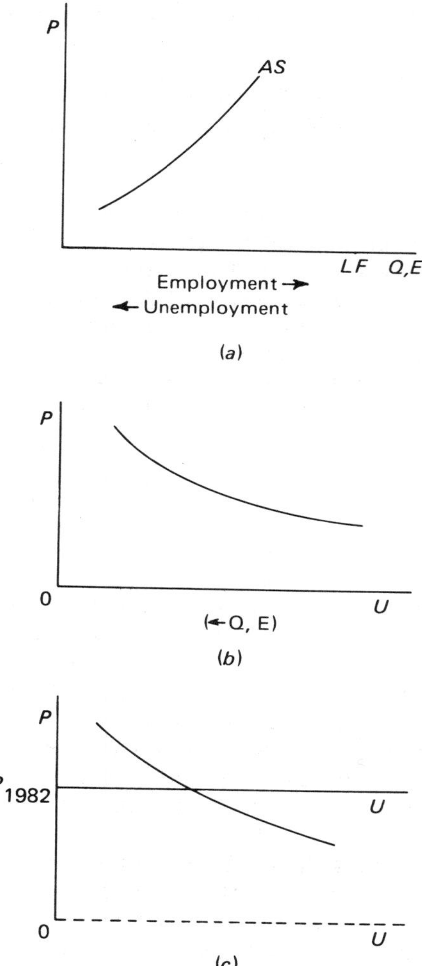

Figure 4.4 The derivation of the Phillips curve

output from right to left. This is one method of deriving a Phillips curve. Usually a Phillips curve shows the relationship between unemployment and the change in prices but this only involves moving the horizontal axis to the current level of prices and relabelling as in *Figure 4.4c*. This method of deriving Phillips curves has two features in common with the other (closely related) neoclassical approaches.

(1) The relationship is between a once and for all change in prices and unemployment (as in Lipsey's seminal work, 1960).
(2) The shape of the Phillips curve is ambiguous. Each aggregate supply curve implies a different slope of the Phillips curve.

This ambiguity is present in all derivations of the Phillips curve including those which are not neoclassical, e.g. those based on bargaining theory or utility maximizing unions.

Because there are so many alternative theoretical derivations of Phillips curves, no clear interpretations can be placed on them. For this and other reasons, some economists prefer to concentrate on aggregate supply and demand analysis and to relegate Phillips curves to the history of economic thought.

4.2.4 The role of government

One of the advantages of the aggregate supply–aggregate demand model is that it is easy to analyse the role of government. The authorities ought to be able to determine the aggregate demand curve, by monetary and fiscal policy. Unfortunately, manipulation of the level of aggregate demand produces the classic trade-off between unemployment and inflation. A higher level of output, and so lower unemployment, will almost inevitably imply a higher level of prices. Macroeconomic policy involves a choice of evils, or rather the choice of a mixture of evils. This dilemma could be avoided if the authorities could influence the aggregate supply curve (or, alternatively, the Phillips curve), either by shifting it or by changing its slope. If the authorities could cause the aggregate supply curve to shift outwards, they could have both a lower price level and more output, as shown in *Figure 4.5a*.

The $64 000 question is whether government can induce such a beneficial change, and, if so, how. Incomes policies, and price controls, have proved almost universally attractive to western governments as devices with which to endeavour to shift aggregate supply and Phillips curves. Indeed, in the 1960s, this was the standard rationale for incomes policy. It is worth making two comments about this argument. The first is that an incomes policy would probably pivot rather than shift the aggregate supply curve so that, at low levels of output, prices would be higher, and at high levels, lower, as in *Figure 4.5b*. The reason for this is that incomes policy necessarily weakens those market forces that tend to

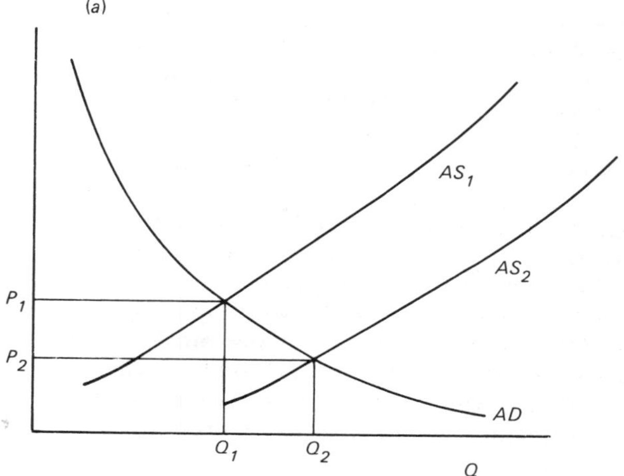

Figure 4.5a Incomes policy succeeds

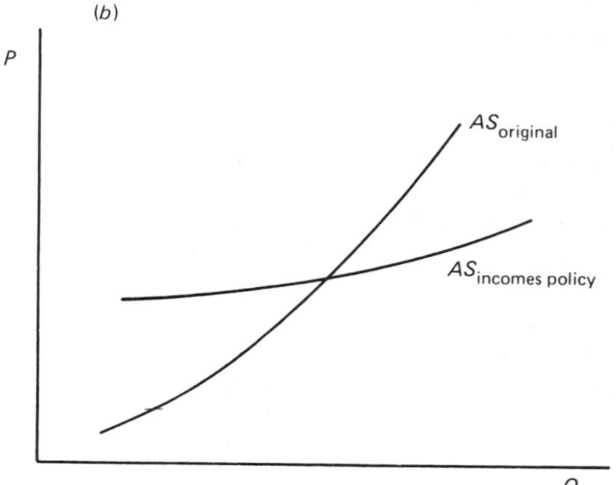

Figure 4.5b An ambiguous effect of incomes policy

produce upward sloping curves. The other is that no convincing evidence has been produced to show whether an incomes policy can, or cannot, have this effect[5]. In conclusion, the search for an incomes policy will continue because it seems to offer an escape from the bleak prospect presented by the opponents of incomes policy. In their world governments have not only to accept a lack of power but also to face an unpleasant choice.

Incomes policies are not the only means of shifting aggregate supply curves. Some of President Reagan's advisers have toyed with the old idea that a suitable tax policy might induce greater output (and so lower prices) at each output by providing incentives to work, save and invest. Supply side economics in general is discussed on p. 83 above. More importantly, it has been argued frequently that governments may inadvertently shift aggregate supply curves in a malevolent fashion, especially by over-generous unemployment pay and social security, such as the changes introduced in 1962 which included earnings-related supplements[6]. However, the theory is more widely applicable and includes a strongly argued view that it was a major problem in the 1930s, an opinion which most people find incredible[7]. Minford has argued that shifts of the aggregate supply curve are the major cause of increases in unemployment (e.g. in Minford and Peel, 1981).

In conclusion, one of the sharpest distinctions between the orthodox view of economic policy in the 1960s and Mrs Thatcher's approach is her belief that aggregate supply curves cannot be shifted by devices such as incomes policy. No evidence is available to determine who is right.

4.2.5 The limitations of the traditional approach

The traditional approach described in this chapter has two major defects. The first is that, in the 1970s, inflation and unemployment rose together, at least on a medium-term basis. The other is that the traditonal theory is really a theory of the price level, not of inflation. This is ironic as all textbooks have always emphasized that inflation is not just a once and for all rise in the price level but a persistent rise in prices:

> 'a process of continuously rising prices, or equivalently, of a continuously falling value of money. Its importance stems from the pervasive role played by money in a modern economy.'
>
> (Laidler and Parkin, 1975)

Neither cost push nor demand pull nor any of the other theories sketched above explains a process of continually rising prices. Some attempts have been made to produce a pseudo-dynamic model. The wage–price spiral is the best known of these models where, in a cost push model, a rise in prices generates a rise in wages and so a rise in costs, causing a rise in prices and so on *ad infinitum*. However, this is not satisfactory in itself. Firstly, both theory and evidence suggest that the rise in prices would be less than the rise in wages, even in a rigid mark-up model, because of imported raw materials. A rise in prices does not necessarily generate a *pari passu* rise in wages. Thus the spiral would produce decelerating inflation; using plausible values a 10% cost push would generate a 7% price increase and this, in turn would produce a 4% wage change, thus generating a 3% price change, etc.[8]. In other words, the spiral would quickly come to an end. The 'spiral', in its simple form, is probably better seen as a description of disequilibrium adjustment to a higher price level than as a theory of inflation. Moreover, the spiral should produce ever falling output and, so, ever rising unemployment, as in *Figure 4.6*.

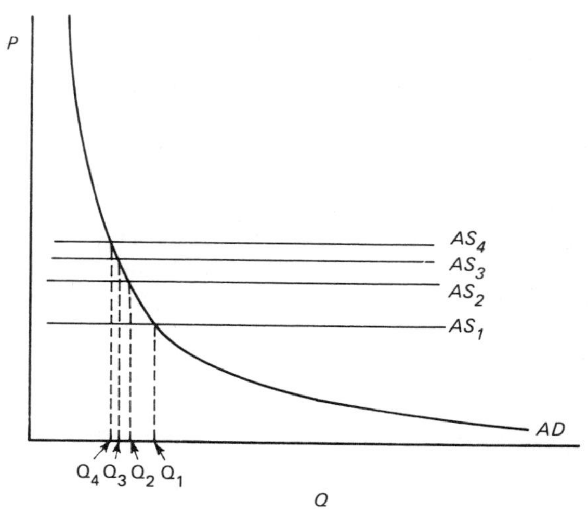

Figure 4.6 Cost-push inflation

The cost push explanation of the 1950s and 1960s was that a series of random shocks set off a series of spirals. In addition, the authorities at least partly ratified the change in prices by increasing aggregate demand so unemployment did not behave as the simple model would suggest. This explanation cannot be refuted but it is very *ad hoc* and again it is not an explanation of inflation as defined above. These two inadequacies of the conventional approach were solved by Friedman's expectational approach.

4.3 THE EXPECTATIONS MODEL

Whether they are monetarist, Keynesian, or neither, nearly all economists now base their theory of inflation on Friedman's insight that a change in the price level can be divided into two components (1968). The first is the expected change, the second the change predicted by the traditional theory, especially by demand factors.

Change in Price Level = Expected Change in Prices + Demand Effect (4.1)

Friedman's argument is that expectations change behaviour. To take a simple example assume that everyone believes that prices will be 10% higher today than they were yesterday: everyone entering a shop will be willing to pay more for a good than yesterday because they believe that the price of all other goods has risen 10%. This shift of the demand curve is foreseen and so prices have been marked up 10% by the shop. In the labour market, workers will demand wage increases which will be granted by profit-maximizing employers faced with a shift in the demand curve and a belief that other employers will pay more. Thus, everyone's behaviour changes in response to expectations, and it can be shown that the shifts in the supply and demand curves will be such as to generate the expected price change, *ceteris paribus*.

This theory can easily be used to procude a theory of inflation if the additionarl assumption is made that expectations of price changes are based on past price changes. In this case a change in prices generates expectations of further changes and so causes further changes and so on, i.e. a process of inflation. Therefore,

Inflation = Expected Inflation + Demand Inflation. (4.2)

Friedman also introduced another concept, namely the natural rate of unemployment. This is the rate of unemployment at which demand inflation is equal to zero, or inflation is equal to expected inflation – the two are equivalent (see equation 4.2 above). If there were perfect competition in all markets, the natural rate would be equal to frictional unemployment and would be 'ground out' by the 'Walrasian system', as Friedman put it (1968). Otherwise, the natural rate is not determined by adding up search unemployment etc., but, in principle, by observation of the relationship between expected and actual inflation. The natural rate is not necessarily constant from year to year; it may not even exist and is not 'natural' in the usual sense of the word.

The expectations model provides the best argument for an incomes policy. If an incomes policy reduces inflationary expectations, it will reduce inflation. Moreover, a short-term incomes policy may reduce inflation permanently by eliminating, or reducing inflationary expectations. If there is no subsequent demand inflation, a lower level of inflation will be permanent. This argument can be restated in terms of reducing the unemployment cost of lowering inflation, as Mr Healey argued so often during the period 1975–1979. If demand inflation is reduced, there is the cost to be paid in terms of unemployment, but if expectational inflation can be reduced, this cost is avoided. Finally, in these circumstances, an incomes policy can increase efficiency by reducing uncertainty and permitting the price system to work better (Friedman and Keynes have both argued that inflation makes it less likely that individuals would respond to price signals). In this way, an incomes policy could improve resource allocation rather than affect it adversely as is normally argued. This whole argument is crucially dependent upon an incomes policy which influences expectations favourably. The whole case for an incomes policy depends upon its impact on expectations and so will depend on circumstances. Hence, in 1970 Friedman accepted the case for an incomes policy, although he was worried abouts its effect on resource allocation. In 1974, he thought that incomes policy was futile because expectations would not be affected. By 1980, he thought that incomes policy would have the apparently perverse effect of increasing inflationary expectations. This can be justified either by popular scepticism about the success of official policy or by a belief that people will react to an incomes policy by regarding it as a sign that inflationary prospects are bad.

Incomes policies may be justified on expectational grounds sometimes, the case for them sounding like a refugee from a music hall with its reliance on official beliefs about private sector beliefs about official action. The argument is far stronger if expected inflation is determined by past inflation. If expected inflation is exactly equal to last year's inflation, an interesting special case arises for which three much-publicized propositions have been derived by Friedman.

4.3.1 Friedman's three propositions

Friedman derived three much publicized and enormously influential propositions about inflation and unemployment (1968). All three depend on the assumption that expected inflation is precisely equal to inflation in the previous period.

$$\text{Expected Inflation}_t = \text{Inflation}_{t-1} \quad (4.3)$$
$$[E(\Delta P)_t = \Delta P_{t-1}]$$

The three propositions are examined in this section and the modifications to the propositions, required when the special case is relaxed, are discussed.

Proposition 1: A higher rate of inflation will not reduce unemployment permanently; only accelerating inflation will achieve this.
This proposition is known also as the vertical Phillips curve hypothesis because it denies, in the long run, the Phillips trade-off between inflation and unemployment. Acceptance of this proposition by the present Government has created one of the sharpest distinctions between it and the Opposition. Sir Geoffrey Howe vividly made this theory a centrepiece of his Budget speech by comparing inflation to an addicitive drug, the more of which you had the more you needed, until the necessary dose destroyed you. The analogy was neat; more and more inflation is necessary to hold unemployment at a lower level, until, ultimately, the dose of inflation necessary has to be so high that it threatens social stability. On the other hand, the shadow chancellor, Mr Peter Shore, has made it clear that he does think that there is a trade-off between inflation and unemployment and would accept more inflation in order to reduce unemployment.

Friedman's proposition can be explained in various ways. The simplest uses his two basic relationships adding subscripts to denote time:

$$\text{Inflation}_t = \text{Expected Inflation}_t + \text{Demand Inflation} \quad (4.2)$$
$$\text{Expected Inflation}_t - \text{Inflation}_{t-1} \quad (4.3)$$

There is a negative relationship between demand inflation and unemployment. The government can utilize this in the short run to reduce unemployment at a cost in terms of demand inflation. This higher level of inflation increases inflationary expectations the following year so, with unchanged demand inflation and unemployment, inflation will be higher in the following year and so on. To take a simple example, suppose that inflation was originally stable and the government reduced unemployment at a cost of 2% demand inflation. In the first year, inflation would be 2% (0 expected inflation + 2% demand inflation). In year 2, inflationary expectations would have risen so that expected inflation = 2%, namely the inflation rate in year 1. The total inflation would be 4%

(2% expected inflation + 2% demand inflation). In the third year, inflation would be 6% because expected inflation was 4% and so on. A *constant* level of *demand* inflation would lead to an *acceleration* of *total* inflation by the amount of the demand inflation. A further, slightly more formal, example is given in the appendix which traces the path of an imaginary economy to illustrate Friedman's three propositions. One can summarize this approach to Friedman's first proposition by combining his two equations. Substituting (4.3) into (4.2)

$$\text{Inflation}_t = \text{Demand Inflation}_t + \text{Inflation}_{t-1} \tag{4.4}$$

An increase in demand inflation leads to a higher level of inflation which leads to a still higher level of inflation and so on *ad infinitum*.

An alternative approach uses a variant of the aggregate supply/aggregate demand model, in which, for convenience, the change in prices is shown on the vertical axis[9]. The crucial point of this analysis is that the aggregate supply curve shifts according to the level of expected inflation. A higher level of expected price induces a reduction in the quantity of goods offered for sale, since profit-maximizing behaviour dictates this (see p. 102 above). The effect of aggregate demand can be analysed as shown in *Figure 4.7*. The government increases its spending and the money supply so as to shift the aggregate demand curve from AD_1 to AD_2, as in *Figure 4.7a*. In the short run, this moves the economy from point 1 to point 2 and so increases output from Q_1 to Q_2, and consequently reduces unemployment. There is a rise in inflation to, say, 3%.

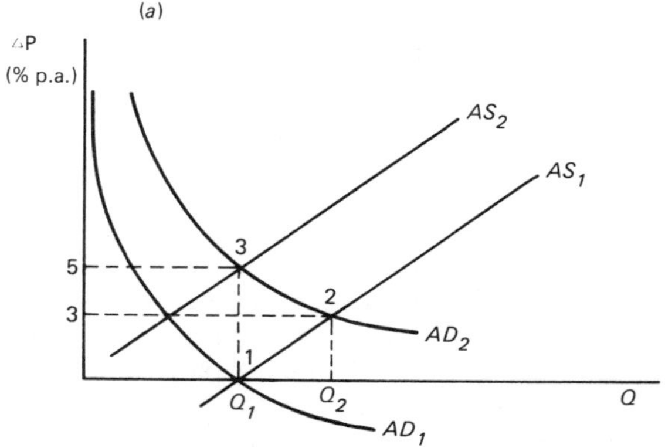

Figure 4.7 Friedman's first proposition

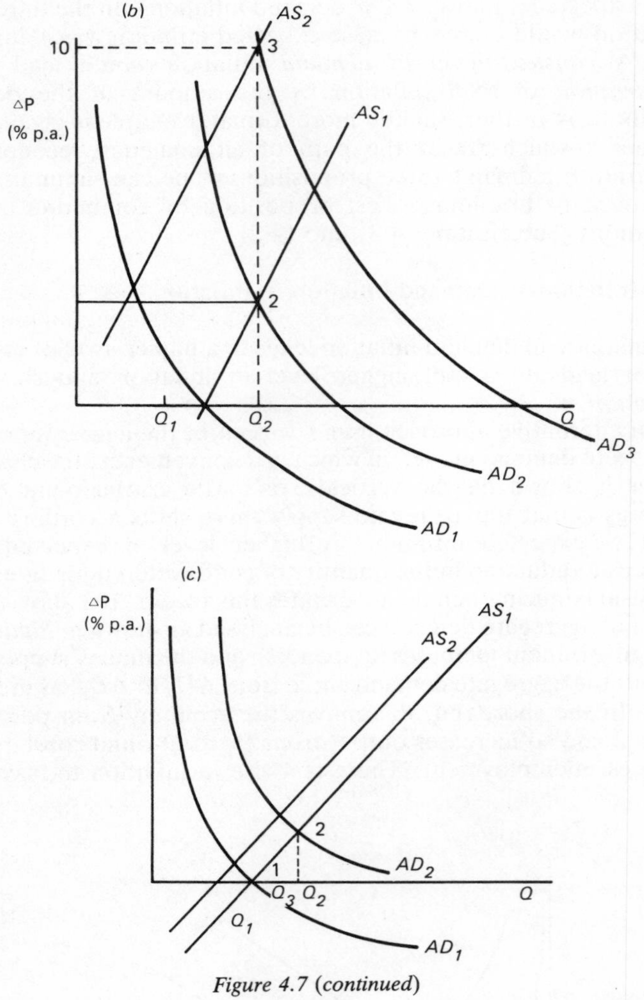

Figure 4.7 (continued)

This is the end of the story in the simple aggregate demand/aggregate supply model. In Friedman's model there is now a shift of the aggregate supply curve to AS_2, because the increase in inflation to 3% has increased inflationary expectations to 3% and so shifted the *AS* curve. This leaves the government with two choices, illustrated in *Figures 4.7a* and *4.7b*. In the first case (*Figure 4.7a*), the government leaves the aggregate demand curve at AD_2. The *AS* curve has shifted such that the new equilibrium eventually attained (point 3) is at the original level of output (Q_1), but both actual and expected inflation are at a higher level than initially, here equal to 5%. Higher inflation has only reduced unemployment in the short run. It is crucial to note that this is a special case, produced by Friedman's special assumption that expected inflation = inflation last year. This is necessary to show that the shift in the *AS* curve is exactly that which will leave the economy at point 3. Alternatively, as in *Figure 4.7b* the authorities can shift the *AD* curve again to AD_3 in order to maintain output at Q_2. In this case, inflation climbs to, say, 10%, and there is a further shift of the *AS* curve, so the same choice is faced again. Unemployment can only be reduced permanently by accelerating inflation.

Much empirical evidence suggests that expected inflation is not in fact equal to last year's inflation but to some proportion of it[10]. Parkin once justified this theoretically in the context of an open economy, by arguing that 0.7 was rational in the UK[11]. In this case, Friedman's propositions do not hold. Take the example in the appendix, but assume that expected inflation = 0.5 inflation in previous period. If demand inflation is constant, at 2% actual inflation is 2%, 3% (2% demand inflation + 1% expected inflation), 3½%, 3¾% and gradually approaches 4%. The calculation is set out in the appendix. In general, the long-run cost of reducing unemployment, measured in terms of inflation, is higher than the short-run cost but the trade-off exists. In terms of *Figure 4.7a*, the shift of the aggregate supply curve is not sufficient to reduce output to Q_1 again so the result shown in *Figure 4.2c* is the new equilibirum.

In general, Friedman's proposition is true if inflationary expectations are generated such that expected inflation is determined by past inflation, and if the coefficient on past inflation is equal to or greater than unity.

Proposition 2: To maintain a constant rate of inflation unemployment must equal the natural rate and if unemployment equals the natural rate inflation will be constant.

This proposition follows directly from Friedman's two basic assumptions:

$$\text{Inflation}_t = \text{Demand Inflation}_t + \text{Expected Inflation}_t\text{, and} \tag{4.2}$$

$$\text{Expected Inflation}_t = \text{Inflation}_{t-1}; \tag{4.3}$$

so,

$$\text{Inflation}_t = \text{Inflation}_{t-1} + \text{Demand Inflation}_t \tag{4.4}$$

If unemployment is at the natural rate, demand inflation is equal to zero by definition. Hence, inflation is equal to inflation in the previous year, i.e. it is constant. Similarly, if inflation is constant, demand inflation must be zero, and, hence, by definition, unemployment is at the natural rate. This proposition is also illustrated in the appendix, section A.

If the coefficient on past inflation is not unity, the proposition does not hold. If the coefficient is less than unity, i.e. if expected inflation is less than previous inflation, then when demand inflation is zero, inflation will obviously decelerate. If the coefficient is greater than unity, inflation will accelerate even if demand inflation is zero because expected inflation is greater than last year's inflation.

Proposition 3: To reduce inflation, it is necessary and sufficient for unemployment to exceed the natural rate.
This third proposition follows from Friedman's two basic assumptions, combined in (3) above:

$$\text{Inflation}_t = \text{Inflation}_{t-1} + \text{Demand Inflation}_t \tag{4.4}$$

If inflation is to fall, i.e. be less than in the previous year ($t-1$), demand inflation must be negative. Since, by definition, this means that unemployment must be above the natural rate, it is essential for a reduction in inflation that unemployment exceeds the natural rate. Similarly, by definition, if unemployment is above the natural rate, demand inflation will be negative, and so inflation will be less than in the previous year, i.e. the condition is sufficient for a reduction in inflation. This proposition is illustrated in the appendix (section A).

If the coefficient is less than unity, inflation will decelerate when demand inflation is zero – as explained above expected inflation being less than in the previous year: zero demand inflation is sufficient for a reduction in inflation. Thus unemployment need not rise above the natural level in order to produce a fall in inflation, i.e. it is not a necessary condition. If the coefficient is greater than unity, it is no longer sufficient for a fall in inflation that unemployment exceed the natural rate (see appendix, section C). The amount by which expected inflation exceeds last year's inflation may be greater than the fall in prices accompanying the unemployment. If expected inflation is twice last year's inflation and last year's inflation was 15%, expected inflation will be 30%. Thus, demand inflation must be greater than minus 15 (ignoring sign), if inflation is to fall. If demand inflation is −10% unemployment exceeds the natural rate, by definition, but actual inflation will be 20% (30% expected inflation less 10% demand inflation), a rise of 5% over the preceding year.

4.3.2 Explaining the 1970s and some conclusions

It is one of the principal merits of the expectational model that it can explain easily a simultaneous rise in unemployment and inflation. *Demand* inflation is negatively related to unemployment but unemployment is not necessarily negatively related to total inflation. If demand inflation falls but by less than the increase in expected inflation, both unemployment and inflation will increase. This can occur within Friedman's special case, as illustrated in the appendix. However, the effect is longer-lasting and there are more dramatic rises both in unemployment and inflation, if expected inflation is greater than last year's inflation. The example in Appendix C illustrates this. Expected inflation is taken to be twice the level in the previous year. The initial sequence is as in appendix. The government seeks to cut unemployment by tolerating more (demand) inflation. However, the acceleration in inflation is more pronounced. The difference becomes sharper when demand inflation is eliminated and unemployment is at the natural level; inflation (and unemployment) continues to rise. Increasing unemployment to twice or even three times the natural level does not stop the acceleration in inflation. Within this example, the proposition that unemployment has been caused by past inflation is easy to accept. The case against demand inflation as a means of reducing unemployment is equally obvious. On the other hand, the same applies to incomes policy – or any other device – used to break the fatal link between expected inflation and past inflation. This sort of model (with a coefficient of about 1.2 instead of 2 in the example in the appendix) works very well to explain the 1970s in the UK. The validity of this explanation is discussed below.

Thus, all the major policy questions concerning inflation and unemployment depend upon the nature of inflationary expectations.

(1) Is there a trade-off between inflation and unemployment, or is inflation an addictive drug?

This depends upon whether the influence of past inflation on current inflation has a coefficient of one or more than one, which supports the addictive drug theory, or of less than one.

This, in turn, answers, at least in part:

(2) Can inflation cause unemployment? and
(3) Is demand expansion a desirable method of reducing unemployment?
(4) Is incomes policy desirable?

This depends upon whether incomes policy can influence inflationary expectations in a (desirable!) manner.

(5) What else might influence inflationary expectations?

It has been argued that there may be other 'shocks' to the economic system that increase inflationary expectations. Parkin believed the 1967 devaluation to be one such shock (Laidler and Parkin, 1975). The OPEC price increase of 1973 might have been another. Finally, the foolishness of the 1979 VAT increase is shown very clearly within this model so long as observed price increases cause an increase in inflationary expectations.

In order either to understand the working of the UK economy or to determine optimal economic policy it is vital to know what determines inflationary expectations. At this point, the wise economist should mumble something about econometricians and hide, since, unfortunately, attempts to measure inflationary expectations have proved virtually impossible[12]. To explain something which cannot be measured involves practical as well as epistemological problems. Nevertheless, many people have tried. The main result for the UK seems to be that the coefficient on past inflation is less than unity[13].

This econometric evidence might seem to settle the issue and to suggest that Mr Shore is right to believe in a trade-off and Mrs Thatcher wrong. Unfortunately, this evidence is not conclusive. First of all, the econometric work suffers from a number of technical defects. Secondly, there is still no satisfactory method of measuring inflationary expectations. Finally, theory and plausibility suggest that the results cannot be valid. One reason for this is that the trend as well as the level of inflation might be examined; that is to say, if inflation had been 2%, 4%, and 6% over the past three years, your expectations would be different from those than if it had been 10%, 8%, and 6%. This is consistent with the econometric results. However, such a highly plausible method would produce inflationary expectations greater than last year's inflation – the crux of Mrs Thatcher's case. Friedman and others have argued that, in equilibrium, inflation must be constant and must equal expected inflation, since if expectations are not fulfilled, the economy cannot be in equilibrium. No rational person would forecast 2% inflation if, year after year, the outturn were 4%. This is an example of rational expectations (see p. 78 above).

4.4 SOME ALTERNATIVE THEORIES

Orthodox economic explanations of inflation all depend upon some form of inflationary expectations mechanism. There are alternatives to this, sometimes lumped together as 'sociological theories'. This characteristic is misleading as most of them incorporate some form of economic analysis. One theory, however, is purely sociological. This is the argument that inflation is a 'disease of western civilization', a phrase used in this context by André Malraux, Nobel Laureate, de Gaulle's Minister of Culture. The hypothesis is that western civilization is in decline and that all declining civilizations suffer from prolonged and substantial inflation. The syllogism can be completed simply; therefore the western world will suffer from inflation. One can challenge the underlying historical theory; not all declining civilizations are bedevilled by chronic inflation – even if it is accepted that western civilization is doomed. Moreover, the hypothesis need not rule out any other theory, e.g. declining civilizations might all produce excessive monetary growth because their governments spend too much and are too weak to finance their spending by taxation. So, if Malraux were right, it would still be worth analysing *why* inflation is endemic. Finally, the theory leaves no apparent role for anti-inflation policy, a very unwelcome prospect. However, the real issue is methodological; is one's preference for a sweeping untestable theory or for a conventional economic theory?

A much publicized theory is the 'frustration hypothesis' accepted *inter alia* by the New Cambridge School and Bacon and Eltis, pp. 71 and 76 above respectively. The theory was first tested by Johnson and Trimball (1973). The basic notion is that if workers do not receive as big a *real* wage increase as they have hoped for, they (and their unions) will respond by making very high *nominal* wage demands. These are, more or less, acceded to, so there is a substantial rise in prices. This, in turn, means that real wages are unsatisfactory so the 'frustrated' workers put in very large nominal claims once more. There are variants of the theory:

for example, all workers, or only unionized workers or only workers in the market sector may be those whose 'frustrations' matter. Moreover, it may be a deficiency of real income, of real consumer expenditure or total consumption, including some 'social wage', which induces frustration. Some theorists incorporate a threshold, for example frustration is felt only if an expected wage rise of 3% is not achieved.

The theory of frustration suggests that some orthodox policy prescriptions may be wrong. For example, most orthodox economists consider an income tax increase anti-inflationary because it shifts the aggregate demand curve leftwards. However, since it reduced real personal disposable income, it increases 'frustration'; in orthodox terms, this shifts the aggregate supply curve and, as most believers in frustration believe in a very elastic aggregate supply curve, this effect dominates. This view was accepted by the Government in 1972, when income tax was reduced in order to try to buy off union wage claims. The results were disastrous and an incomes policy was introduced quickly. In fact, all major wage explosions have followed abnormally large increases in real PDI and consumer expenditure, namely 1969–1970, 1973–1975 and 1979–1981. The 'winter of discontent' in 1979–1980 followed the largest annual increase, 8%, in real consumer expenditure for 20 years. Hence it seems that 'frustration' cannot be the major cause of union wage claims.

Finally, there are a class or group of 'conflict' theories. These argue that society is riven by conflicts, between unionized and non-unionized workers, public and private sector workers, traded and non-traded goods sector workers, as well as the classic class struggle between capital and labour. Wage claims are the weapon used in these battles because there is no alternative method by which public sector workers can seek to make themselves better off in relation to private sector workers. This theory is interesting and plausible but untestable.

It would be rash to claim that economic models provide a complete explanation of inflation, although they perform surprisingly well when tested. Clearly, there are socio–political factors at work and, for example, a complete theory would need to explain union militancy. Nevertheless, the orthodox analysis seems superior to all alternatives.

4.5 THE ANALYSIS OF OIL PRICE INCREASES

It is conventional to attribute some of the acceleration in inflation to the OPEC oil price increase of 1973. In fact, some models of inflation ascribe considerable importance to the international transmission of cost increases. For example, in the two-sector Scandinavian model prices in the competitive traded goods sector are determined by world costs and prices in the sheltered sector by the increase in the competitive sector. Monetarism, on the other hand, has always denied that an increase in the price of one good could cause inflation, arguing that it would cause only a change in relative prices. This argument is as follows:

(1) The money supply determines nominal income, price (P) and output (Q). This is true either at world level or for a single economy.

$$M \Rightarrow P \cdot Q \qquad (4.5)$$

(2) Nominal income ($P \cdot Q$) may be divided into expenditure on oil (price of oil P_o) and quantity (Q_o)) and expenditure on everything else ($P_r Q_r$).

$$M \Rightarrow (P_o Q_o + P_r Q_r) \qquad (4.6)$$

(3) If oil prices rise, the effect depends on the price elasticity of demand for oil. If this is greater than one, expenditure on oil will be reduced and so, expenditure on other goods will rise so that the total $P \cdot Q$ is unchanged. If, as is usually assumed, the elasticity is less than one, expenditure on other goods will fall

$$\text{if } \varepsilon_{\text{oil}} < 1, Q_o P_o \uparrow \; \Rightarrow (P_r Q_r) \text{ falling.}$$

Hence, either the price or the output of other goods will be less than it would otherwise would be.

Thus the monetarist prediction of the effect of oil price increases is

(1) The effect on the aggregate price level is unclear. Oil prices are higher but other prices are lower.
(2) Output falls in the non-oil producing countries.

Therefore the effect of an oil price increase is felt on unemployment rather than on inflation. For completeness, it is necessary to add that oil price increases caused deficits in many countries' balance of payments. As these were not fully sterilized, their money supplies were reduced in comparison with the level at which they would otherwise have been. OPEC's money supply did not increase sufficiently to offset this so world monetary growth was lower. This was a further factor which was added to the forces working to reduce output and offsetting any inflationary pressure.

Monetarist analysis, therefore, suggests that the OPEC price increases of 1973 and 1978 did not cause an increase in inflation but led to an increase in unemployment instead. Some evidence supports this:

(1) World inflation was lower in 1974 than in 1973. This is also true if the price increase is measured from September 1973–September 1974 when inflation was less than in the previous twelve months.
(2) Profit margins were squeezed world-wide. This suggests that prices rose less than costs, i.e. that prices rose less than they would otherwise have done, because of demand pressures.

4.6 SOME CONCLUDING REMARKS

Considerable attention has been paid in this chapter to the analysis of incomes policy in inflation. Unfortunately, it is totally unclear what effect incomes policy has. On the one hand, it is clear that it is trite to say that incomes policy has failed. Even in 1978–1979, despite crass mishandling by the Government and a ludicrously inappropriate target of 5%, a workable policy was salvaged in the form of Clegg and 8%. Wages and earnings rose only 13.2% in the year to June 1979. The 1975–1979 policy was not a failure, and it is tempting to conclude that incomes policy can, at least, offset any other socio-political factors and ensure that the level of wage settlements implied by analysis of unemployment, past inflation, corporate liquidity and so on will occur. On the other hand, there is no evidence to sustain this view. Incomes policies may not have failed but they have not succeeded either, except in the short term. The temptation to rely upon them as a (dangerous) form of escapism which will remove unpleasant options is as foolish as it would be to rule out their use permanently.

APPENDIX 4A: INFLATION, EXPECTED INFLATION AND UNEMPLOYMENT: FRIEDMAN'S THREE RULES

These are based on the special case, in which expected inflation equals inflation in the previous year. The example uses a short-run Phillips curve in which inflation + unemployment = 5, so natural rate = 5.

Proposition 1
Higher inflation will not reduce unemployment permanently, only accelerating inflation will (sometimes called the vertical long-run Phillips curve)

Year	*Expected inflation*	*Demand inflation*	*Unemployment*	*Inflation*
1	0	0	5	0
2	0	2	3	2
3	2	2	3	4
4	4	2	3	6
5	6	2	3	8

The government manipulates aggregate demand so as to maintain a constant level of unemployment below 5 (and demand inflation). In consequence expected and actual inflation accelerate.

Proposition 2
To maintain a constant rate of inflation, unemployment must equal natural rate.

Year	*Expected inflation*	*Demand inflation*	*Unemployment*	*Inflation*
6	8	1	4	9
7	9	0	5	9
8	9	0	5	9
9	9	0	5	9
10	9	0	5	9

Higher unemployment in year 6 fails to curb acceleration in inflation; increasing unemployment to natural rate stops inflation accelerating from year 7.

Proposition 3
To reduce inflation unemployment must rise above natural level.

Year	*Expected inflation*	*Demand inflation*	*Unemployment*	*Inflation*
11	9	–2	7	7
12	7	–2	7	5
13	5	–2	7	3

APPENDIX 4B: EXPECTED INFLATION LESS THAN LAST YEAR'S INFLATION

In this example expected inflation = 0.5 last period's.

Year	*Expected inflation*	*Demand inflation*	*Unemployment*	*Inflation*
1	0	0	5	0
2	0	2	3	2
3	1	2	3	3
4	1½	2	3	3½
n (long run)	2	2	3	4

The unemployment/inflation trade-off survives even though the long term cost is higher than the short.

n+1	2	0	5	2
n+2	1	0	5	1
n+3	½	0	5	½
n+n (long-run)	0	0	5	0

Inflation can be eliminated even though unemployment never exceeds the natural rate.

APPENDIX 4C: EXPECTED INFLATION EXCEEDS LAST YEAR'S INFLATION

In this example expected inflation = 2 inflation last year

Year	*Expected inflation*	*Demand inflation*	*Unemployment*	*Inflation*
1	0	0	5	0
2	0	2	3	2
3	4	2	3	6
4	12	0	5	12
5	24	0	5	24
6	48	–5	10	43
7	48	–10	15	76

Year 1: as before, government seeks to cut unemployment
Year 4: it gets worried and reduces employment to natural rate
Year 6: it lets unemployment rise to a very high level – but inflation continues to accelerate.

Notes

1 See Brittan (1981) who argues that insufficient emphasis on this point is responsible for most of the confusion in the monetarist –Keynesian debate, a point also made in Gowland (1979), Chapter 5.
2 See Godley, Coutts and Nordhaus (1978) or Brunner and Andrews (1975) for a justification of this model of pricing.
3 This model was also styled 'Keynesian' by Friedman in his reconciliation of monetarist and Keynesian (Friedman in Gordon, 1974).
4 See Johnson (1973) and the references cited therein.
5 See, for example, Laidler and Parkin's survey (1975).
6 See the discussion in Davies (in Gowland, 1979) and the references cited therein.
7 Benjamin and Kochin (1979).
8 These are based on the Treasury model of about 1975 when it incorporated this mechanism.
9 For a derivation of the one from the other see Dornbusch and Fischer (1981)
10 See, for example, Laidler and Parkin (1975).
11 This is summarized in the 1975 survey article by Laidler and Parkin (1975).
12 See the summary in Laidler and Parkin (1975) of Parkin and Carlson's work in this area.
13 See Davies (in Gowland, 1979). The best survey is still Laidler and Parkin (1975).

Guide to further reading

This chapter is intended to be a bridge between the demand pull/cost-push analysis of the elementary textbook and more sophisticated writing. Davies (1979) provides a summary of more advanced work, both theoretical and empirical. Thereafter Flemming (1976) and Curwen (1976) are probably the most useful.

Bibliography

BENJAMIN, D. K. and KOCHIN, L. A. (1979), 'Search for an explanation of unemployment in inter-war Britain', *Journal of Political Economy*, Vol. 81, No. 3 (June), p. 441

BRITTAN, S. (1981), *How to end the monetarist controversy*, Hobart Paper 90, Institute of Economic Affairs, London

BRUNNER, E. and ANDREWS, P. W. S. (1975), *Studies in Pricing*, Macmillan; London

CURWEN, P. J. (1976), *Inflation*, Macmillan; London

DORNBUSCH, R. and FISCHER, S. (1981), *Macroeconomics*, (2nd edn.), McGraw Hill; New York

FLEMMING, J. S. (1976), *Inflation*, Oxford University Press; Oxford

FRIEDMAN, M. (1968), 'The Role of Monetary Policy', *American Economic Review*, Vol. 58 (March)

GODLEY, W., COUTTS, K., and NORDHAUS, W. D. (1978), *Industrial Pricing in the UK*, Cambridge University Press; Cambridge

GORDON, R. J. (ed.) (1974), *Milton Friedman's Theoretical Framework*, University of Chicago Press; Chicago (papers by Friedman, Tobin, Patinkin, Davidson and Brunner and Meltzer)

GOWLAND, D. H. (1979), (ed.), *Modern Economic Analysis*, Butterworths; London

JOHNSON, H. G. (1973), *Macroeconomics and Monetary Theory*, Gray Mills; London

JOHNSON, J. and TRIMBELL, J. C. (1973), 'A Bargaining Theory of Wage Determination', *Manchester School*, Vol. XLI (June), p. 141

LAIDLER, D. E. W. and PARKIN, J. M. (1975), 'Inflation – a Survey', *Economic Journal*, Vol. 85 (December)

LIPSEY, R. G. (1960), 'The Relationship between Unemployment and the Rate of Change of Money Wage Rates in the UK, 1862–1957: A Further Analysis', *Economica*, Vol. 27 (February)

MINFORD, P. and PEEL, D. (1981), 'Is the Government's Economic Strategy on Course?', *Lloyds Bank Review*, No. 140 (April)

THE SCRIPT SYSTEM IS A LONG RUN PLAN. WE CAN LOCK PRICES AND SUBSIDISE THEM DOWN AND THEN SUBSIDISE FULL EMPLOYMENT. WE CAN INTRODUCE RIGHTS AND IF PEOPLE HAVE A ONE CHILD FAMILY FOR 5 GENERATIONS THE POPULATION WILL FALL TO 3½ MILLION WITHIN 150 YEARS AND WE CAN BUILD EVERYBODY BUCKINGHAM PALACE EACH. THERE ARE NO FASHION MODELS IN THE SCHOOLS AND THE STATE PLAN IS POOR.

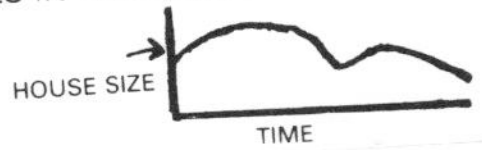

HOUSE SIZE

TIME

5

Consumption, Saving and Inflation

D. H. GOWLAND

5.1 INTRODUCTION

In the 1960s and 1970s, many economic 'popularizers' argued that a rise in the rate of inflation would make people less willing to save, as 'it would not be worthwhile'. Accordingly, they believed that if inflation rose there would be a fall in the savings ratio, that is to say saving as a percentage of personal disposable (i.e. after tax) income. More rigorous economic theorists disagreed and argued that an increase in inflation would almost certainly lead to an increase in the savings ratio, although strictly the result was ambiguous. Events in the UK have shown the theorists to be right, a reassuring result! The relationship between inflation and the savings ratio in the UK is a strongly positive one. Of especial interest is the 50% rise in the savings rate from 9 to 14½% in the early 1970s while inflation trebled. The sharp rise in inflation in 1979–1980 also produced a very sharp rise in saving, the ratio exceeding 20% in one quarter.

This positive relationship between inflation and saving is one of the brute facts facing economic policy-makers in the 1980s. Indeed it is one of the linchpins of Mrs Thatcher's economic strategy. One of her major propositions is that inflation causes unemployment and that a reduction in inflation is both necessary and sufficient for a reduction in unemployment. This point was emphasized by Sir Geoffrey Howe in his post-Budget TV broadcast in 1981 (see p.

109 above). One reason for this belief is the expectational argument discussed on p. vi above. Another stems from the relationship between saving and inflation: a reduction in inflation will increase consumers' spending and so pull the economy out of the current depression.

In the context of most elementary economic textbooks this chapter is an argument for a change of emphasis. It is conventional to consider the relationship between income and saving and consumption and then consider other factors that may influence consumption. It is usually argued that these are interesting but unimportant. However, the evidence of the 1970s suggests that they are in fact critical. Section 5.2 of this chapter outlines the development of the theory of consumption and saving. As saving is defined as income less consumers' expenditure, a theory of consumption is a theory of saving. In section 5.3 all the reasons why saving is related to inflation are considered. In section 5.4 a few complications are considered notably those stemming from Friedman's point that expenditure on consumer durables is a form of saving. The final section summarizes the implications of the analysis.

5.2 THE THEORY OF CONSUMTPION AND SAVING

The modern theory of consumption was pioneered by Keynes in the *General Theory*, (1936). His basic argument was that consumption depended only on current income and a number of unchanging psychological attitudes[1]. Changes in consumption and saving would occur only when income changed. Moreover any change would be predictable, the stability of the relationship being embodied in the concept of the marginal propensity to consume. This Keynesian or absolute income hypothesis is embodied in the familiar

$$C = \text{a} + \text{b}Y$$

where a is a constant and b is equal to the marginal propensity to consume.

It is perhaps worth emphasizing that the consumption function is expressed in this way in order to incorporate Keynes's 'fundamental psychological law' that the average propensity to consume is greater than the marginal. The inclusion of a constant term ensures this. The relationship is supposed to be valid only over relevant ranges of income and cannot sensibly be extrapolated back to zero income.

The constant is not included as the 'minimum level of consumption', i.e. it cannot be interpreted as an estimate of what consumption would be if income were equal to zero.

The first challenge to the Keynesian consumption function came from Duesenberry (1949). He suggested an alternative relationship between consumption and income and called it the 'Relative Income Hypothesis'. His work was inspired by an examination of the American national income data produced by Kuznets. In particular, he observed that in cross-sectional studies the average propensity to consume declined and the savings ratio rose with income, i.e. as suggested by Keynes' theory. On the other hand, the aggregate savings ratio was constant over time. If the average propensity to save, and to consume, are constant when income varies then, by definition, the average and marginal propensities to consume are equal. To reconcile this apparently conflicting data, Duesenberry suggested that a person's consumptions depends on other people's consumption and on his past consumption. The relatively poor consumed a higher percentage of their income than did the richer classes in an attempt to 'keep up with the Joneses'. However, if everyone became richer, everyone's saving ratio (APS) would remain unchanged. As further evidence, Duesenberry cited the higher savings at each level of income by black Americans. He argued that this reflected the fact that black consumption was not influenced by the richer whites whereas white consumption at an equivalent income was. The implications of Duesenberry's analysis were:

(1) The more equally distributed income was, the lower savings would be.
(2) Any attempt to redistribute income in any direction would reduce saving because the losers would not reduce spending by as much as the gainers would increase theirs.
(3) In a downturn savings ratios would fall thus acting to stabilize the economy.

The next major contribution to the consumption function was made by Friedman (1957). He distinguished sharply between consumers' expenditure and consumption whereas earlier writers had blurred the distinction. The major difference arises with consumer durables. A durable appears as part of consumers' expenditure only when it is purchased, but it yields a flow of services which are consumed over a period of years. If a television is purchased in 1981 for £250 and lasts 10 years, consumers' expenduture is £250 in 1981 and 0 thereafter. On the other hand, consumption may be 300 hours per year (of declining quality) which might be valued at £50 in 1981, £45 in 1982 and so on. Friedman sought to explain consumption, not consumers' expenditure. He argued that consumption should depend only on wealth and the liquidity of wealth. Wealth should include human wealth, that is to say the net present value of (expected) future income. Freidman stressed that consumption depends upon all one's resources, not just upon current income. However, wealth in the form of money will be spent more readily and easily than wealth in the form of land and both more than wealth in the form of future income. Friedman's next step was to consider how human wealth might be estimated. He suggested that 'permanent income' might be the best method of measuring human wealth, hence the term 'Permanent Income Hypothesis' for his theory. Permanent income is the income a person expects to go on receiving rather than any transitory or windfall element. In practice permanent income is measured as some weighted average of past income. Hence, Friedman suggested that consumption would depend on wealth, liquidity and permanent income.

Friedman's theory has two major features which are an improvement on Keynes, or at least on the textbook version of Keynes. The first is the emphasis on expectations, in particular on the expected level of future income. This is of crucial theoretical importance but, in practice, has to be measured by current and past income. The other is that it sharply distinguishes between short and long-run marginal propensities to consume. For a permanent change in income, the MPC equals the APC and may be very close to unity. For transitory income, the MPC is equal to zero. Hence the short-run observed aggregate MPC will be much less than the APC since some changes in income will be transitory. Moreover even permanent changes may not be viewed as permanent in the short run; an individual who has just seen his income rise may not know if this is temporary or permanent, so he will not increase his consumption by as much as he will when he knows the increase is permanent. This would explain the paradox noted by Duesenberry.

The principal practical merit of the permanent income hypothesis is not that it explains the behaviour of most consumers better than a Keynesian consumption function since for most consumers expected, present and past income are closely related. It is that it is significantly better at explaining the behaviour of the small minority who are both hardest to predict and most crucial to any successful prediction of consumers' expenditure. This is the small minority who do most of the discretionary saving in contrast to contractual saving such as pension contributions, life assurance, and the like. Of income recipients, 5%, not the richest 5%, are responsible for more than half of the changes in discretionary saving. This group includes many of the self-employed and others with fluctuating incomes. Undoubtedly these groups do maintain long-term consumption patterns and have a very low short-run marginal propensity to consume.

Friedman's theory has implications for fiscal policy which are radically different from Keynes's. The lower MPC in itself reduces the value of the multiplier and so the scope of fiscal policy. More importantly, many fiscal actions will not boost permanent income and will leave consumption unchanged. For example, a tax rebate is normally welcomed by Keynesians as a quick acting boost to the economy. As a transitory windfall, it has little effect on the size of permanent income and in itself is useless as an expansionary device (i.e. unless it increases the money supply). Nevertheless, the difference between Friedman and Keynes is not as great as it seems in this respect because Friedman sought to explain consumption, not consumers' expenditure as Keynes did. If transitory income is spent on consumer durables both theories may be right. Consumers' expenditure does increase substantially when income changes but consumption changes little. In other words consumers may have an uneven expenditure path, as Keynes argued, but a smooth consumption path as Friedman argued.

The next development in the consumption function literature was an elaboration of Friedman's model that produced a more rigorous, if less plausible, model. This was the 'Life Cycle Hypothesis' of Ando and Modigliani (1963). They postulated that an individual, or household, would determine its optimal lifetime consumption path in the light of the available resources, the receipts of income at different periods. Borrowing and lending, dissaving and saving, would then be used to adjust the income path to match the desired consumption path. In any period in which income exceeded optimal consumption, the excess would be invested and in any period in which planned expenditure exceeded income the deficit would be borrowed. Interest would be received or paid on these funds and this would affect the amount available for consumption in other years. In consequence the real rate of interest became a principal determinant of the consumption opportunities facing consumers, in other words their budget line. (This analysis is described on p. 39 above and used on p. 131ff, section 5.3.7 below). The life cycle hypothesis, in other words, set the consumption–saving decision up as a classic microeconomic theoretic choice problem involving the choice between consumption at different periods. This was analysed using the tools developed to analyse choice between different goods in the same period. Many other writers have followed this approach. These models of optimization have grown ever more complex (see, for example, Mussa, 1977). The models are most plausible for the salaried middle classes with predictable changes in income, but even here the models are not operational. Instead their role is to point out a number of aspects of the savings decision not explicitly captured in the other analyses.

The first of these factors is the role of age. Ando and Modigliani suggested that individuals were likely to receive a steadily rising income, say from 20 to 60, followed by a sharp drop on retirement. On the other hand, they would have to incur heavy expenditure when setting up a home (and perhaps having children) early in life. Thus expenditure would be heaviest between perhaps, 20 and 40. No one would wish to see a sharp drop in living standards on retirement. Therefore, the analysis hypothesized that individuals would be net borrowers in the first phase of their working lives. Then they would be heavy net savers, say from age 40 to 60, both to pay off the debts incurred earlier and to build up assets to dissave and so finance consumption during retirement. Similar life cycle models had earlier been applied to poverty, see Maynard (in Gowland, 1979), but neither rigorously nor to saving decisions.

One implication of this was that the age-structure of the population could affect saving. Another was that a large part of observed differences in wealth holdings might be a result of differences[2]. The notion that inequality in wealth is because the middle aged are rich and the young poor is more attractive to some than others. A lively debate has ensued to see how much wealth inequality is attributable to this factor. One the whole it seems that, to quote Atkinson (1975), ‘the distribution of wealth cannot be attributed simply to age differences’ (p.142), a conclusion endorsed by Flemming and Little (1974).

A variant of the life cycle model is Samuelson’s (1968) loan-consumption model (see Dixit, 1976, pp. 116–122). This was used to demonstrate the superiority of non-market to market as the means of providing for expenditure when the beneficiary receives no income. In particular, Samuelson argued that the family is a more *efficient* means of providing for one’s expenditure during childhood than either a hypothetical market in which children borrow against future income or slavery. Similarly, a state-financed system of pensions is more efficient than market provision.

Another implication of the life cycle model is that the growth of real incomes is likely to be a major determinant of saving. The argument is that net saving is equal to saving by the young less dissaving by the old. With growth, the young receive higher incomes than the old did when they were young, so net saving is higher as a percentage of income than in a static society.

Another consequence of the Ando–Modigliani model concerned the role of fiscal policy. No *anticiapted* change in income affected planned consumption at all. Hence the role of fiscal policy had to be either direct or to arise through causing unexpected changes in income. Even an unanticipated change in income will lead to a very small change in consumption as it will be smoothed over all future years. Hence the MPC in this model is virtually zero.

A necessary corrective to the optimization models was administered in the late 1960s by various economists, notably Clower and Leijonhufvud. They sought to justify the Keynesian consumption function as aprt of the reappraisal of Keynes[3]. In particular they argued that the optimization procedure only determined what an individual would like to do, that is Clower's notional demand. His actual spending, effective demand, might be very different. Institutional arrangements and limits to borrowing might make actual, or realized, income a binding constraint on spending. Clower made realized income constraints the centrepiece of his neo-Keynesian models. Leijonhufvud went further. He argued that 'the multiplier was an illiquidity phenomenon', that the downward spiral of contraction in income caused by an initial shock was caused by the forced reduction in consumption by the initially unemployed. If they had been able to borrow in unlimited amounts against future income, or sell labour forward, then there would be no slumps. A market in human capital is illegal and it is very easy to see why no one would lend to the unemployed in the necessary amount. Virtually every form of market failure is present in this market.

Econometric studies had helped to produce a consensus in the late 1960s. Variables other than income did not seem to be a significant influence on expenditure in the short term in the UK, in part because the crucial variables were almost constant[4]. Permanent income had to be measured by past income. Any model that explained consumers' expenditure by current and past income was consistent with Friedman's model, at least while wealth and liquidity were constant. The results could equally well be explained as an absolute income model with lagged values. The econometric models relying on such a consumption function proved inadequate in the UK in the 1970s as saving and inflation developed a symbiotic relationship.

5.3 SAVING AND INFLATION

It became clear in the 1970s that in the UK saving and inflation were strongly and positively related. The various possible reasons for this are analysed in this section. More than one may be right but it is crucial which matter and which do not. This is because they concentrate on different aspects of inflation, some on the price level and some on the rate of inflation, some on anticipated inflation, some on unexpected inflation, some on the level of inflation, others on changes in the rate. These differences are important analytically. They are crucial to the effect of falling inflation, or a stable price level, on saving. Some of the theories predict results very different from others and so have very different implications for the success of Mrs Thatcher's policy.

Before considering these explanations it is vital to emphasize the nature of saving and the savings ratio, or APS. Saving is defined as a residual, as income less consumers' expenditure. Hence if consumers' expenditure falls, *ceteris paribus*, observed saving rises. A reason for a fall in the ratio of consumers' expenditure to income (the APC) is *necessarily* a reason for a rise in the savings ratio. Some popularizers seem to have ignored this point.

5.3.1 Wealth effects

It is generally accepted that the wealthier a person is the more he will spend at each level of income, whether one uses Keynes's or Friedman's model. Hence the wealthier a person is, the less he will save at each level of income. Thus a reduction in wealth holding with income constant would cause a fall in consumption and a rise in observed saving. Hence the savings ratio (APS) will rise when the value of wealth falls. A fall in the value of wealth is precisely what inflation causes. Much of the personal sector's wealth is in money-dominated forms, especially bank deposits, gilt-edged securities and national savings (for building society deposits, see section 5.3.2 below and for housing and equities, see section 5.4). A rise in the price level reduces the real value of these assets. Thus wealth is less and so consumers' expenditure lower and saving higher (this is sometimes called the real balance effect or Pigou effect). The effect of inflation on the real value of money-denominated assets is dramatic – the fall was 50% in 1974–1975.

Thus even a small wealth effect, as a proportion of wealth, multiplied by an enormous change in wealth would lead to a large absolute change in consumers' expenditure and a dramatic effect on saving, as Townend pointed out (1976). This wealth effect was publicized in the UK by Forsyth of Morgan Grenfell (1975). He argued for a special form of the hypothesis with an optimal liquid assets to income ratio (about 87% on his definition). Consumers would alter consumption dramatically to re-attain equilibrium if the actual value of their holdings deviated from the optimal level. In this form the theory is akin to a version of the quantity theory with a very wide definition of money.

In summary, wealth is agreed to be a major determinant of consumers' spending and *ipso facto* of saving. Changes in the price level have a dramatic effect on the real value of personal sector wealth.

5.3.2 Liquidity

It is generally agreed that, if wealth and income are held constant, the more liquid a person's wealth the higher his spending will be. The theme is as central to modern Keynesianism of either the Tobin or the Clower variety as it is to monetarism, whose emphasis is on the money–non-money distinction. This proposition is that the higher liquidity is (wealth and income being constant), the lower the level of savings and thus the APS or savings ratio. In general there is a negative relationship between saving and liquidity.

There is an equally clear relationship between inflation and liquidity. A high level of prices in itself does not change the total net value of assets, but it redistributes wealth by reducing the value of both assets and liabilities denominated in money terms. Sometimes, as demonstrated in section 5.3.1 above this reduces personal sector wealth, when the counterpart liability which is reduced is a public, corporate or overseas one – for instance, the case of government bonds. Sometimes, it redistributes wealth within the personal sector. The most obvious example of this is building society mortgagees who gain at the expense of depositors and shareholders. Redistribution will have some effect in itself (section 5.3.3) but more importantly liquidity is reduced by the simultaneous destruction of both asset and liability. This can be seen in the following example. Imagine a representative individual with a mortgage of £10 000 and building society deposits of £10 000. If inflation reduces the value of both, perhaps by 50% as in 1973–1975, then his net worth is unaltered but his stock of liquid assets falls. By definition, his liquidity is less. Thus his spending will fall and in consequence there will be a rise in his saving, the residual between income and spending. At an aggregate level, personal sector liquidity falls with inflation, i.e. the higher price level, so there is a reduction in spending and measured saving increases.

5.3.3 Redistribution of wealth and income

As argued above, inflation effected a large redistribution of wealth in the UK in the 1970s. Leijonhufvud (1968) argued that one of the main faults in conventional economic analysis is that it ignores such effects. He is right inasmuch as such a major redistribution could have large effects. However, conventional analyses explain the 1970s satisfactorily without reference to distributional effects and, moreover, it is difficult to see how a redistribution could have led to more saving.

Just as inflation redistributes wealth in a capricious and unjust fashion so does it redistribute income. To some extent, this is systematic, e.g. away from fixed-income groups. To a large extent it is purely arbitrary depending on such whims of fate as one's place in the wage round. The redistribution effected in the 1970s was very large but, again, there seems no evidence that it led to more saving. Indeed, at the level of casual empiricism, the most obvious gainers came from traditional low saving groups, e.g. miners, and the losers from higher saving strata. Thus while redistribution of wealth and income *could* have led to an increase (or fall) in the savings ratio, there is no evidence that it did.

5.3.4 Inflation and high nominal rates

It might be argued that there is a logical flaw in the arguments in sections 5.3.1–5.3.3 above in that in all of them it was implicitly assumed that the change in the price level is unexpected. Instead, if it were anticipated, then wealth-holders should have received compensation in the form of higher nominal interest payments. This counter-argument is not convincing but even if it were the effect is to strengthen the underlying theses. It does not seem that much of the surges in inflation in 1974–1975 and 1979–1980 was anticipated, certainly not more than a few months in advance. Even in so far as it was expected, nominal interest rates did and do not adjust sufficiently to compensate for inflation for a variety of reasons which are discussed in Chapter 2. Moreover, recipients of interest payments may not distinguish appropriately between income and compensation. Nevertheless, it is the case that some part of interest payments in an inflationary age are disguised repayments of capital. It may be, in fact probably is, that as inflation rises, the amount of compensation rises even if by an inadequate extent. This compensation would not be regarded as income by a rational individual but is treated as such in the national accounts (and by the Inland Revenue). Thus it might be reasonable to save the whole of this increase in compensation for inflation. In this case the observed savings ratio and APS both necessarily rise.

5.3.5 Inflation and cash flows

The effect of inflation on nominal interest rates was the basis of an interesting theory put forward by the OECD. Their argument was that inflation leads to a lower level of borrowing and so a lower level of spending. Given that the savings ratio is both a residual and a net (of dissaving) variable, it was presented as an argument that higher (expected) inflation leads to more saving. Their thesis seemed to be applicable to those continental countries that experienced a similar positive relationship between saving and inflation in the mid 1970s but not to the UK.

The argument starts with the truism that a high nominal rate of interest acts as a form of compulsory repayment. To borrow at 10% interest when inflation is 25% is to borrow at a real rate of −15%. However, it is not the same as borrowing at an interest rate of −15% when inflation is zero even though the real interest rate is identical. Instead it is the same as borrowing at −15% together with an obligation to repay 10% of the loan each year (you pay £10 and the real value of the debt falls 25%, so it is the same as repaying £10 and 'gaining' 15% interest. The OECD argument is that this compulsory repayment causes cash flow problems which deter borrowing. This would be so unless it were both possible and acceptable to borrow to pay interest. This OECD theory is probably more applicable to corporate than individual borrowers in the UK[5].

However, a wider version of this cash flow problem may have some relevance. This concerns mortgagees who in 1972–1973 and 1978–1980 saw substantial rises in (nominal) mortgage rates. At the time with accelerating inflation and soaring house prices, mortgagees' real wealth was rising very rapidly. Nevertheless few mortgagees rejoiced at the consequences of a replay of Barberism in a minor key. Instead of focusing on the increase in wealth, they, not unreasonably, felt the cash flow constraint. If mortgagees' spending fell, observed saving would rise unless depositors increased theirs (in fact, as argued above, they cut theirs). This may have been a minor factor in the rise in saving.

5.3.6 Uncertainty

The arguments presented in the first two sub-sections, concerning wealth and liquidity, involved changes in the level of prices. The next argument concerning redistribution and expected inflation involved both the level of prices and inflation, usually assumed to be anticipated. In this section and the next attention is paid to both the level of inflation and its acceleration. It is explicitly assumed that inflation cannot be predicted accurately.

The first of these arguments seems to have originated with Juster and Wachtel (1972). This is that one of the major motives for saving is uncertainty, especially uncertainty about future real income and future real commitments. The more uncertain the future is, the higher the level of saving. Both of these propositions are undeniably unless some unusual assumption such as risk-lovingness is assumed. Juster and Wachtel argued that both higher inflation and accelerating inflation made it harder to estimate its future level. In other words the future level of inflation is more uncertain. Hence also uncertain are the future level of real income and the expected real cost of unknown contingencies (such as medical bills or roof repairs). Thus people will save more because inflation is higher or accelerating. An even simpler argument is that more inflation means more uncertainty in general (Keynes and Friedman have both endorsed this view) and so more saving.

5.3.7 Money illusion

Another reason why higher and/or accelerating inflation may lead to an increase in saving was advanced by Deaton (1977). This argument involves a version of money illusion. The argument is that individuals mistake a change in absolute prices (i.e. inflation) for a change in relative prices. To take an example, an individual goes shopping to supermarket *A* and finds baked beans are more expensive than he had expected because of unanticipated inflation. Therefore he decides to buy them at supermarket *B* later in the week or to buy fresh vegetables when he passes the greengrocer's instead. On arrival in supermarket *B* he finds its price is also at the higher level. He may then buy his baked beans but may also find some other good to be more expensive, and again delays his purchase. Some purchasers are continually delayed (not always the same one, of course) so spending is always below the expected level so observed saving is higher.

This hypothesis is obviously more relevant to some purchasers than others. It is probably more applicable to one-off purchasers (search goods) than repeated ones (experience goods). Nevertheless it seems, to me at least, implausible that it will be a major explanation of a *large, prolonged* increase in saving as experienced in the 1970s and 1980s.

(1) As both Keynes and Friedman argued, inflation may lead to relative price changes being mistaken for absolute ones (our hypothetical shopper notices that tomatoes are more expensive than expected in supermarket *A* but assumes, wrongly, that they will have gone up everywhere else and buys some anyway).
(2) One might expect search activity to increase for goods (in practice durables) expensive enough to justify prolonged search rather than see purchases deferred.

In brief Deaton's theory is important in stressing the role of accelerating inflation, and of the distinction between expected and unanticipated inflation. His model is probably important on occasions as a very short-run phenomenon but as Townend (1976) put it,'[the nature of this hypothesis] makes robust econometric results extremely hard to obtain' (p. 72).

5.3.8 The popularizers refuted: income and substitution effects

Finally, in this section, the popularizers' argument is analysed and its inadequacies explained. The argument is that people will save less because it is not as worthwhile to save. This can be restated by saying that the opportunity cost of present in terms of future consumption has fallen so present consumption will rise. In other words, the issue is a problem of choice (between present and future consumption) when relative prices change. Accordingly the problems can be set up and analysed within the conventional microeconomic framework.

This analysis is presented in *Figure 5.1*. It illustrates the case of an individual who receives income in one period but spends it in two. This is chosen in part for simplification, the analysis can easily be extended to incorporate receiving income in both periods, borrowing, and more than two periods[6]. However, it can be argued that most saving is for retirement and so this is the most

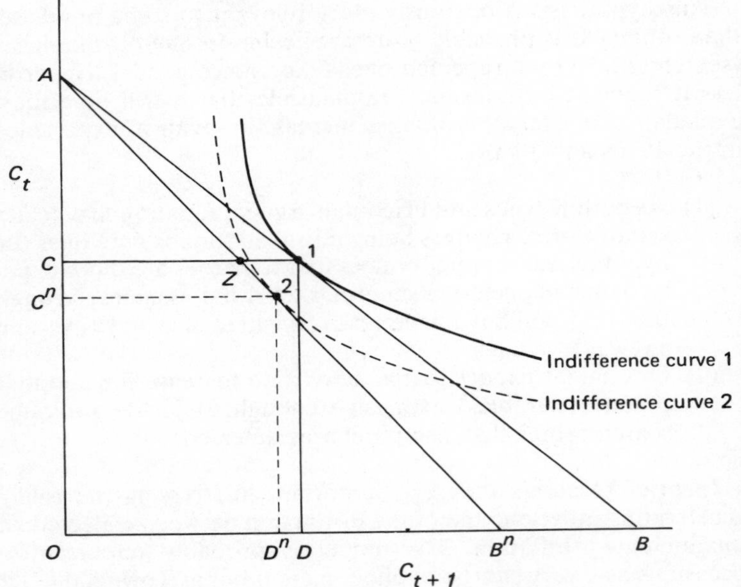

Figure 5.1 Popularizers refuted

interesting case where period 1 is one's working life and period 2 the period of retirement. The axes show consumption in the first period (C_t) and in the second period (C_{t+1}). To explain the individual's choice it is first necessary to draw the budget line; this shows the boundary of his consumption opportunities. The most he can consume in the first period is his income (Y_t). This is *OA*. The most he can consume in period 2 is his income, plus the interest he receives less the effect of inflation on its purchasing power. This is

$$\text{Maximum } C_{t-1} = Y_t \{(1 + i)/(1 - p)\} = Y_t (1 + r)$$

where *i* is the nominal rate of interest, *p* the rate of inflation and *r* the real rate of interest.

This maximum is drawn as *OB* and the budget line is the line joining these two maxima, *A* and *B*. Its slope is the relative price of future in terms of present consumption (and is a straight line because the individual cannot influence either inflation or interest rates). The individual then selects his optimal level of consumption in each period: this is shown as 1 and is where the budget line is tangential to indifference curve 1. He consumes *OC* in period 1 and *OD* in period 2. More significantly as $OA = Y_t$ and $OC = C_t$, then *AC* is his saving.

$$\begin{aligned} S_t &= Y_t - C_t \\ &= OA - OC \\ &= AC \end{aligned}$$

The effect of changes in inflation, or interest rates, on consumption and saving can now be calculated. So long as *OA* is held constant, the change in saving is above the change in the savings ratio (or APS). (If not the calculation of the APS is simple.)

In particular, it is possible to see what happens when either (expected) inflation or interest rates change, i.e. when the real rate of interest varies. Hence it is possible to analyse rigorously the thesis that people cease to save 'when it isn't worthwhile', in other words when a higher expected level of prices increases the opportunity cost of future consumption in terms of present consumption. This is represented as a pivot of the budget line from AB to AB^n. Maximum present consumption *OA* is unchanged but maximum future consumption (AB^n) is reduced. The individual's new optimal position is where an indifference curve is tangential to the new budget line. In *Figure 5.1*, the example makes the standard assumption of unitary income elasticity, homothetic tastes, and consequently indifference curves are parallel. The new equilibrium is represented by point 2 where the dotted indifference curve 2 is tangential to the new budget line. Present consumption is OC^n and future consumption OD^n. The new level of saving (S_t^n) *is* $Y_t - C_t^n = OA - OC^n = AC^n$ (see *Table 5.1*). Saving is higher despite the highr price of future consumption. In fact the 'income effect' has outweighed 'the substitution effect', as can be demonstrated by the actual method of drawing a budget line parallel to AB^n tangential to indifference curve 1.

The reader may have seen the same diagram used to illustrate the ambiguous effect of income tax changes on work effort (Brown, 1980). As in that case, the effect is ambiguous, as either the substitution or the income effect may be larger. To use the diagram of *Figure 5.1* if the relevant indifference curve is tangential to AB^n along *AZ*, the substitution effect is larger and saving

TABLE 5.1
THE IMPACT OF INFLATION ON SAVING

Original level of inflation					
Income	Y_t	:		OA	
Consumption	C_t	:		OC	
Saving	S_t	=	Y_t	–	C_t
		=	OA	–	OC
		=	AC		
New level of inflation					
Income	Y_t	:		OA	
Consumption	C_t^n	=		OA^n	
Saving	S_t^n	=	Y_t	–	C_t^n
		=	OA	–	OC^n
		=	AC^n		
Δ Saving		=	S_t	–	S_t^n
		=	AC	–	AC^n
		=	OC^n		

falls. If the tangency is at Z, the two effects exactly balance and the savings ratio is unchanged. If the tangency is between A and B^n saving and inflation are positively related.

This ambiguity is useful in explaining the divergence between UK and US behaviour. In the US, there is almost as strong a negative relationship between saving and inflation, as there is a positive one in the UK. Formally, this suggests that the substitution effect is much stronger relative to the income effect in the US. In an indifference map this implies that the slope of US indifference curves is much closer to the NW–SE straight line (which implies perfect substitutability) and the UK ones to the L-shape of perfect complementarity. This may be related to the different mixes of consumer goods in the two countries, in particular American expenditure on pure consumption goods is much lower.

5.3.9 Saving and inflation: some conclusions

It would seem that in the UK the positive relationship between saving and inflation is mainly the result of

(1) The wealth effect.
(2) The liquidity effect.
(3) The real interest rate effect.

Two problems remain. The first is to which assets does a wealth effect apply and to which a liquidity effect, i.e. which are 'inside' and which 'outside' assets (see p. 60 above). As far as the personal sector is concerned, it seems reasonable to assume that all outside assets comprise

(1) All claims on the public sector, including currency.
(2) All claims on the corporate sector and the overseas sector in sterling.
(3) That part of bank deposits matched by bank loans to the public and corporate sector.
(4) Claim on other financial institutions (building societies in particular) matched by claims on the public sector.

The final puzzle concerns the implicit assumption made throughout this analysis. It has been assumed that the private sector saves only in money-denominated assets. This is true, except for durables including housing. It is not obvious why this is so, a problem discussed in the next section.

5.4 THE ANALYSIS EXTENDED

Two questions are left unanswered by the analysis presented above. The first is why do savers invest so heavily in money-denominated assets rather than in real assets. The other is how are the conclusions reached above affected by the investment in real assets which does take place, especially houses and consumer durables (see Taylor and Threadgold, 1980).

There are a number of overlapping reasons why savers hold monetary assets on such a large scale:

(1) There are few alternatives – even the assets touted as hedges against inflation have not proved very effective in this role, especially equities. The one exception is property.
(2) Management and transmission costs on real assets are high. Whether one examines auctioneers' fees or dealers' margins, the cost of investing in antiques or art are very large. Commodities such as copper are cheaper but storage costs are enormous. Property is the most attractive real investment but when not owner-occupied, there are substantial problems of management ranging from rent control to defaulting tenants.

(3) Real assets are available only in, for most individuals, very large units. It is difficult to think of a real asset for which an investment of less than £10 000 is possible, or, at least, where the risks are not extremely high.
(4) Because real investments are often risky. Paintings, stamps and coins have risen in value and more than kept pace with inflation since 1960 but many individual paintings etc. have fallen in value.
(5) Real investments are illiquid, almost by definition.
(6) The generality of money, the lack of commitment to any real asset or spending plan, discussed above (p. 64), remains immensely attractive despite inflation.

In brief, investment in real assets is not really a practicable proposition for most savers. One reason why inflation is so unfair is that only the wealthy can insure against it. This is one of the many arguments for indexation at last conceded in the 1982 budget.

In fact, the only real assets which have proved attractive to most savers are those that yield services directly to the holder, namely consumer durables and housing. The analysis presented above only explained consumption and it is necessary to expand the model to include assets which yield services over many periods. The above analysis is maintained intact as an explanation of consumption. However, a second stage is added – what assets does the individual hold and what does he choose to consume. Durables and houses whose return is fixed in real terms become more attractive relative to other assets when inflation rises (unless nominal rates rise to compensate the lenders). Hence, more wealth will be held as durables and housing and less as other assets. This is reinforced by resale considerations, especially in the case of housing. This is matched by a switch in relative prices, e.g. television services become cheaper relative to attending cinemas. For example, £500 could be invested in a building society and the interest used to purchase cinema seats every year or to buy a colour television. Inflation will reduce the seats purchased at the cinema but leave the real television services unchanged. Indeed, one can generalize: services from durables will be consumed less because of the income effect (total consumption is reduced) and more because of the substitution effect (they are cheaper). This is most marked in housing where services are often available at a negative price if one allows for the resale opportunity.

It is possible to leave this rather abstract analysis and present some conclusions about the effect of inflation:

(1) Consumption will almost certainly fall when inflation rises;
(2) Consumption on non-durables will fall as a percentage of consumption;
(3) From (1) and (2), expenditure on non-durables will fall as a percentage of PDI (personal disposable income);
(4) Expenditure on durable goods, as a percentage of PDI, could either rise or fall (in the UK it has remained unchanged, it seems);
(5) Saving is likely to rise as a percentage of income but need not do so;
(6) Expenditure on housing, not part of consumers' expenditure, will rise. The enormous level of expenditure on housing investment in the UK is almost certainly as attributable to inflation as to the tax system (see Chapter 10).

5.5 SOME CONCLUSIONS

It is no longer true 'that short-period changes in consumption largely depend on changes in the rate at which income [measured in wage units] is being earned and not on changes in the propensity to consume out of a given income' (Keynes, 1936). Both theorists and policy-makers have to note the other influences on consumption.

Further, it seems to be the case that in the UK there is strong support for the view that a reduction in inflation is necessary (if not sufficient) for sustained expansion because otherwise saving would rise to wipe out the impact of government spending. Inflation may not have caused unemployment but it may well be that there is no possibility of reducing unemployment by accepting a higher rate of inflation.

Guide to further reading

On consumption theories see Surrey (1976). On Samuelson's loan–consumption model see Dixit (1976). And on saving and inflation see Townsend (1976) and Dorrance (1980).

Notes

1 See Keynes (1936), Chapters 8 and 9, including the famous list of motives for saving: precaution, foresight, calculation, improvement, independence, enterprise, pride and avarice.

2 See Atkinson (1975) which summarizes both his 1971 research paper and the debate.
3 Leijonhufvud's and Clower's arguments are reproduced in Surrey (1976), but Leijonhufvud (1968) is one of the classics.
4 See e.g. the 1972 version of the *Treasury Macroeconomic Model* or Surrey's article in Hilton and Heathfield (1970).
5 See Gowland (1979), Chapter 4 'U.K. Financial Institutions: Have They Failed the Nation?', for a fuller presentation of this argument in the context of corporate borrowing.
6 It is also assumed that the individual is certain about the rate of inflation, for a relaxation of this, see Hey (1979).

Bibliography

ANDO, A. and MODIGLIANI, F. (1963), 'The Life Cycle Hypothesis of Saving', *American Economic Review*, Vol. 55 (June)

ATKINSON, A. B. (1975), *The Economics of Inequality*, Oxford University Press; Oxford

BROWN, C. V. (1980), *Taxation and the Incentive to Work*, Oxford University Press; Oxford

DEATON, A. S. (1977), 'Involuntary Saving through Unanticipated Inflation', *American Economic Review*, Vol. 67, pp. 889–910

DIXIT, A. K. (1976), *The Theory of Equilibrium Growth*, Oxford University Press; Oxford

DORRANCE, G. (1980), Saving in the 1970s, in *Lloyds Bank Review*, No. 138 (October), p. 12

DUESENBERRY, J. S. (1949), *Income, Saving and the Theory of Consumer Behaviour*, Harvard Economic Study 87 (reprinted in 1967 by Oxford University Press)

FLEMMING, J. S. and LITTLE, I. M. D. (1974), *Why We Need a Wealth Tax*, Methuen; London

FRIEDMAN, M. (1957), *A Theory of the Consumption Function*, Princeton University Press; Princeton, NJ. for National Bureau of Economic Research

GOWLAND, D. H. (ed.) (1979), *Modern Economic Analysis*, Butterworths; London

HEY, J. D. (1979), *Uncertainty in Microeconomics*, Martin Robertson; London

HILTON, K. and HEATHFIELD, D. F. (1970), *The Econometric Study of the UK*, Macmillan; London

JUSTER, F. T. and WACHTEL, J. T. (9172), 'A Note on Inflation and the Saving Rate', *Brookings Papers on Economic Activity*, Vol. 3, pp. 765–768

KEYNES, J. M. (1936), *The General Theory of Employment, Interest and Money*, Macmillan; London (also in Vol. VII of his *Collected Works*)

LEIJONHUFVUD, A. (1968), *On Keynesian Economics and the Economics of Keynes*, Oxford University Press; New York

MORGAN GRENFELL (1975), 'A New Analysis of the Savings Ratio', *Morgan Grenfell Economic Review*, (September)

MUSSA, M. (1977), *A Study in Macroeconomics*, North Holland; Amsterdam

SAMUELSON, P. A. (1968), 'An exact consumption loan model of interest with or without the Social Contrivance of Money', *Journal of Political Economy*, Vol. 66, pp. 467–482

SURREY, M. J. C. (1976), *Macroeconomic Themes*, Oxford University Press; Oxford

TAYLOR, C. T. and THREADGOLD, A. R. (1980), 'Real National Saving and Its Sectoral Composition', *Bank of England Discussion Paper No. 6* (October)

TOWNEND, J. C. (1976), 'The Personal Savings Ratio', *Bank of England Quarterly Bulletin*, Vol. 16, No. 1 (March), pp. 53–73

6
The Economics of Industrial Relations and Strikes

N. Jennett

6.1 INTRODUCTION

Economists usually feel safely within their own territory when analysing the questions of inflation, unemployment and many of the other issues conventionally deemed within the ambit of economic analysis. Criticized for failing to 'solve the problem' they may be, but hardly for not having tried! Curiously, however, they are rarely charged with failing to suggest policies to deal with the 'problem' of strikes. This is probably because it is usually assumed that the phenomenon of the strike is not something which readily lends itself to economic analysis. After all, doesn't economics have something to do with 'rational' choice? Far removed, it would seem, from the bloody mindedness of the British industrial workforce, diagnosed as the British disease, for which the only known cure is to stand up to overmighty trade unions and bring them within the law.

So, from the outset, economists choosing to analyse strikes may be called upon to justify their exertions. This I would like to try to do by showing:

(1) Why economists have something to say about strikes. This will involve considering the nature of bargaining power and wage determination, and examining one of the best known of economists' collective bargaining models.

(2) What economists have said about strikes, and in particular how they have tried to explain variations in strike frequency[1].
(3) The implications for policy suggested by an economic analysis of strikes.

6.1.1 Strikes in Britain

Initially, it is important to be aware of the features of strike behaviour which economists attempt to explain. In Britain there are a number of marked characteristics.

(1) In the post-war period strike frequency in Britain has been generally rising. Fluctuations around this upward trend appear to be related to a number of economic indicators, a phenomenon further examined in section 4.1.
(2) Strikes are concentrated predominantly among male, manual workers in a relatively few industries. The contribution to overall strike frequency of the coal-mining industry, engineering and shipbuilding, vehicle manufacture, iron and steel and the docks, in the post-war period has been disproportionate in comparison with their contribution to total national employment[2].
(3) Strikes are concentrated in a few industrial plants, in particular, the very largest[3]. Obviously, it is to be expected that there will be more strikes in larger plants, but Prais (1978) found that strike frequency (i.e. strikes per worker) varies in Britain in almost direct proportion to size of plant, measured by number of workers employed. Strike incidence is even more highly concentrated in the largest plants, but for a number of reasons strike frequency is a more appropriate measure of strike activity for the purposes of economic analysis[4].
(4) The majority of strikes appear to be broadly concerned with questions of pay, although a perhaps surprising number are reported to be caused by other issues, such as manning levels or working conditions.

6.2 WHY DO STRIKES OCCUR?

Economists have generally analysed the strike as a breakdown in the bargaining process. The bargaining process with which we shall be particularly concerned here is that which goes on between trade unions and employers or managers, usually known as collective bargaining. Unions bargain, on behalf of their members, with managements over a whole range of issues, of which questions of pay are among the most important. Basically, this is a means by which the price of labour is determined by negotiation between two parties and so economists have generally employed a bilateral monopoly model of price determination to analyse wage determination under collective bargaining. The bilateral monopoly model has a number of weaknesses, some of the assumptions may seem unduly restrictive, but the model does capture a number of important features of this type of wage determination. Of particular importance is the prediction from economic theory of an indeterminate price under bilateral monopoly.

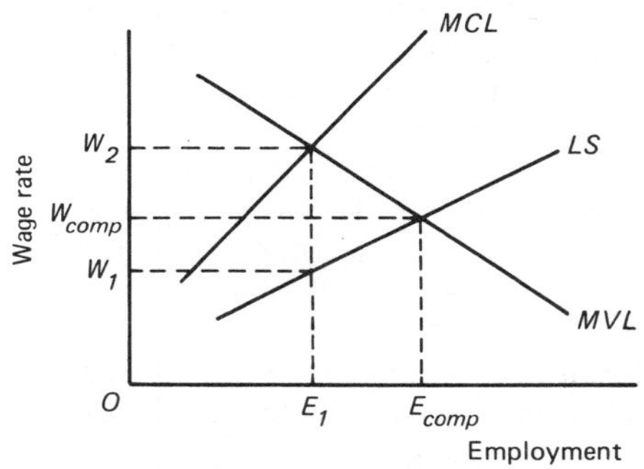

Figure 6.1 A union and a monopsony

The monopsonist (in this case the firm as a single buyer of labour) in an otherwise competitive market faces an upward sloping supply curve of labour (LS) (see also p. 184 below). To attract an additional worker, it must increase wages. Assuming that all employees are paid the same rate, therefore, the marginal cost of employing an extra worker is greater than that individual's supply price. A profit-maximizing monopsonist will attempt to equate the marginal cost of labour with marginal benefit from an extra worker employed. In other words, the monopsonist's preferred employment level is E_1, shown above where the marginal cost of labour curve (MCL) intersects the marginal valuation of labour (MVL) curve. The wage the monopsonist must pay to secure E_1 employment is W_1.

This is straightforward enough, but the entry of a monopolist (here a trade union) makes matters rather more complex. The firm and its management, we assume, act to maximize profits, but the union is unlikely to have a single maximand. For example, it is unlikely that a union would wish to maximize the wage-rate paid to its employed members, as with a conventional downward-sloping demand curve for union labour, this would mean having only one member employed. Unions are more likely to have both wage and employment goals and, in some way, trade these off against one another. *Figure 6.1* illustrates the wage–employment options available to the union. A monopoly union in an otherwise competitive labour market can impose a perfectly elastic labour supply curve at its preferred wage rate and so, in effect, choose its preferred employment level. Here bargaining is unnecessary, except within the union itself over the form of its wage–employment trade-off. However, under bilateral monopoly this behaviour is precluded. The union is no more able to enforce its preferred wage-rate than is the firm. The major effect of bilateral monopoly in labour markets is to prevent either party exercising monopoly power, hence the need for bargaining, absent under simple monopoly or monopsony.

What, then, will be the final wage outcome? As presented here, the model is indeterminate. The final agreement will involve the payment of a wage-rate somewhere between the two parties' preferred positions. Clearly, both parties would like to exercise monopoly power and so if, for simplicity, we assume that the union seeks the highest wage attainable consistent with employment of not less than E_1, then its preferred wage rate is W_2. The preferred wage solution for the maximizing monopsonist is W_1. The final settlement wage-rate will lie between W_1 and W_2, but the bilateral monopoly model can take us no further. It is the bargaining power of the parties which will determine whether the final solution lies closer to the preferred position of the firm or of the union. Only a bargaining model taking explicit account of the power of the two parties can give further insights.

6.2.1 Bargaining power

The key to the concept of bargaining power usually employed by economists is the recognition that over any issue contended by managements and unions there are costs to both of failing to agree and of agreeing. The relative size of these costs determines bargaining power. This notion of bargaining power would seem to be the only one applicable to the circumstances of industrial conflict. For example, most 'common-sense' notions of power would almost certainly suggest that the Ford Motor Company was somewhat more powerful than 187 Dagenham sewing machinists, who were, moreover, striking for the first time, in summer 1968[5]. In this particular dispute the costs of agreement were relatively high for both parties. The Company felt its new wage structure to be at stake; the strikers felt undervalued in the new grading. The costs of disagreement, however, proved considerably higher for management as national production began to be affected and the Company was lambasted for an alleged discriminatory attitude to its female workers. Under these particular circumstances, at this particular time, the sewing machinists proved to be the more powerful.

So, in general a union's bargaining power will be defined by

$$\frac{\text{Costs of disagreeing with management}^{6}}{\text{Costs of agreeing with management}}$$

and for management bargaining power is given by the relative size of the costs of agreeing and disagreeing with the union's demand.

The costs of agreeing will be positive for the union when it accepts a smaller wage increase than it had otherwise wished to do and managements suffer agreement costs when conceding larger wage increases than had been their intention. The costs of failure to agree are the respective costs to the parties of strikes. Union members lose wages during the dispute and firms may lose both short and long-run profits.

It is sometimes argued that a certain level of strike activity is central to the whole process of bargaining, simply to retain a credible threat and maintain an opponent's expected costs of disagreement. This may provide one answer to the question of why (although not how many) strikes may occur. The problem with this as an explanation is that it does not show why threats remain credible longer in some industries than others or under what circumstances credibility is likely to wane. As with all such costly deterrents, skilful bargaining to convince an opponent that the sanction might be used is far preferable, if it is possible.

6.3 HICKS'S THEORY OF INDUSTRIAL DISPUTES[7]

A more interesting answer to the question of why strikes take place is to be found in an interpretation of Hicks's theory of industrial disputes. The theory is basically a simple bargaining model which, using an economic concept of bargaining power can suggest some important conclusions about the nature of strikes.

Hicks describes a situation in which a trade union claims a wage rate (W_u) higher than that which management may wish to offer (W_f). Management may either pay the higher wage or refuse to do so and risk suffering a direct cost from a strike. In both cases the employer will be worse off than had W_f been accepted. In settling at any wage rate above W_f management suffer costs of agreement but a failure to settle imposes costs of disagreement. When costs of disagreement are directly related to the duration of a strike, then the longer management expect a dispute to last, the greater the concession on wage-rates they will be prepared to make to avoid a strike. Hicks constructs an employer's concession curve (*ECC*) showing the wage-rates management would be prepared to pay in order to avert a costly stoppage of an expected length shown on the horizontal axis. In the complete absence of a plausible strike threat from the union, management would pay W_f, but where a plausible strike threat exists the employer's concession curve slopes upwards from left to right.

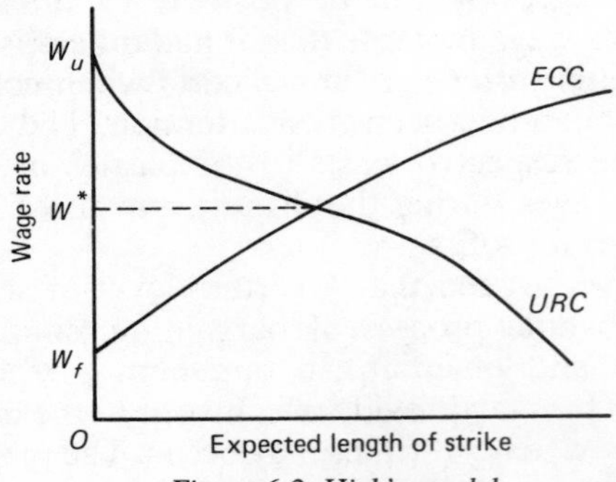

Figure 6.2 Hick's model

The union's resistance curve (*URC*) slopes down from left to right. The wage-employment trade-off places an upper limit of W_u on the union's demand. It will seek a wage increase of W_u where this can be achieved costlessly, that is, without resort to a strike. Strikes are costly to union members, so the union will be prepared to accept a lower settlement from a firm it believes to be willing and able to take a long strike than from one it believes is not. Once again, the longer the strike, the higher the cost and so Hicks's union resistance curve slopes down to show the settlements the union would be prepared to accept rather than suffer a strike of an expected duration shown on the horizontal axis.

The bargaining power of the two parties is obviously important in determining the position of the concession and resistance curves. The higher is the cost of disagreement relative to agreement, the more steeply will the employer's curve slope upwards and the union's curve slope downwards. So, for example, it might be expected that the higher is the level of inventories held by a firm, other things being equal, the less costly is a strike likely to be and the less steeply will the concession curve slope upwards. A number of other factors may influence the relative costs of disagreement at the various levels of wage demand. In some industries, output lost as a result of a strike can, to some extent, be made up later by more intensive working. In this case the major cost might come from the changed timing of sales revenues and wages. Thus, the lower the discount rate applied by a party to future 'returns', the greater its relative bargaining power. Alternative sources of income available to strikers during a stoppage are also important. These include union strike pay, supplementary benefits payable to strikers' families and even earnings from work taken on a temporary basis during the strike. Should one of these become no longer available, the costs of disagreement relative to agreement would rise and workers' bargaining power would be reduced. The resistance curve, as in *Figure 6.3*, would slope down more steeply and it would intersect the employer's concession curve at a point further to the left.

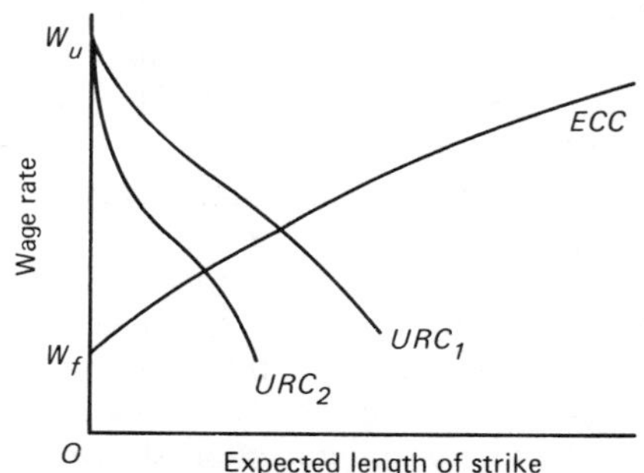

Figure 6.3 The impact of reducing bargaining power

But, it is the existence of this intersection of the resistance and concession curves which poses the Hicks model something of a dilemma. Both parties know that whatever wage is fixed after a strike, it would have benefited both of them to have agreed the same settlement before the strike. The bargaining power approach of Hicks's analysis suggests that both parties would gain by settling immediately at a wage rate of W^* (*Figure 6.2*) and avoiding the costs of a strike. This highlights the bargaining model dilemma. If models suggest the existence of a mutually beneficial settlement point, available to the parties in advance, then why do strikes take place at all? On the other hand if the model does not suggest a single point, it fails to predict a solution to the indeterminacy of the bilateral monopoly model and is therefore inadequate[8].

6.4 THE APPLICATION OF HICKS'S MODEL

But strikes do occur, and Hicks's determinate bargaining analysis suggests two reasons why.

(1) Strikers are irrational

This seems to have an immediate appeal, in certain quarters at least. Managements and unions have been told countless times that 'no one wins from strikes'. This may well be the case, but of itself does not suggest that strikers are acting irrationally[9]. Certainly in purely financial terms had the parties to a dispute accepted the post-conflict settlement prior to the stoppage, a Pareto improvement would have been possible. However, if workers or managers place a value greater than zero on the non-pecuniary benefits of striking (break from routine, the excitement of defiance or whatever), then even under conditions of complete certainty, the involvement in a certain level of strike activity is perfectly rational.

This could be a point of some significance. In analysing the distribution of costs and benefits to the parties to strikes, Fisher (1973) suggested that from experience workers and managers come to expect a certain annual level of strike activity in their industries. This level of strike activity involves lost wages and profits, but these expected costs are adjusted for in the labour supply decisions of the individuals involved. In particular, workers seek employment in industries where net returns are the highest available. Fisher shows, therefore, that unexpected strikes and their resulting costs, cause workers to redistribute labour away from their firm or industry. The important point here concerns the characteristics of the workers who will be first to quit. Imagine two workers with similar earnings prospects outside the strike-hit industry, where both expect the same annual level of strike activity, but where one has a zero and the other a positive valuation of the non-pecuniary benefits of striking. If they prove to have underestimated strikes in a given period, it is to be expected that the worker with the zero intrinsic valuation of striking will be the first to leave the industry. So, there could be mutually reinforcing tendencies for workers and managers with the highest valuation of striking, *per se*, to become crowded into strike-prone industries. This hardly involves irrationality on the strikers' part; indeed, it represents a least cost solution! But, putting this possibility aside, Hicks's theory suggests a second explanation for strikes.

(2) Strikes result from uncertainty and bargainers' mistakes

It seems that the major conclusion of Hicks's model is that strikes are a result of miscalculations[10]. Initially, this may seem rather unsatisfactory, but in fact, Hicks's insight is of great significance. Hicks's contribution is in showing that under conditions of perfect certainty, unions and managements bargaining over a particular issue could (where their respective utility functions do not include a positive value for the act of striking itself) settle without a strike, at a wage rate indicated by W^* in *Figure 6.2* above, to their mutual benefit. But misjudgements and uncertainties about the positions of concession and resistance curves might preclude this solution. So, it is to be expected that conditions likely to increase the scope for uncertainty between the parties will tend to increase strike frequency. Moreover, the model implies that it is usually optimal to suggest that *ECC* is lower and *URC* higher than is really the case. These insights could provide a theoretical base for a great deal of the econometric work explaining variations in strike frequency over time and between industries. Strike frequency is expected to increase in conditions where the parties to a dispute find greater difficulty in assessing their relative bargaining power. This might be because

(1) The parties are receiving different information.
(2) The parties are receiving less information.
(3) They are incorrectly interpreting information.
(4) Both sides may believe they have an increased incentive or opportunity to cheat[11].

The implications for the type of explanations of strike frequency offered by economists can be examined in three general areas.

6.4.1 Economic activity

The relationship between strikes and cyclical fluctuations has been accepted for many years. In the United States, Rees (1952) found that strike frequency tends to increase in periods of cyclical upturn, although the strike peak is reached before the cyclical peak. Rees shows that the strike peak corresponds with the point of maximum divergence of expectations between the parties and, so, greatest uncertainty. Unions and managements, he argues, may be receiving different information. For example, unions will pay particular attention to employment which may still be rising while, say, investment spending has begun to fall away. In this way, the two sides may form different impressions of short-term economic prospects, making misjudgement of the position of concession and resistance curves the more likely.

Unemployment is found to have a dampening effect on strike frequency in a number of British studies (Pencavel, 1970). Increasing unemployment will tend to narrow the bargaining range and give less scope for uncertainty. The information available to both sides has increased (for example, on the constraints of the market environment on what firms can pay) and the interpretation (unions' increased sensitivity to the employment effects of their wage policies) is relatively unambiguous. A given reduction in union member employment is clearly proportionately more significant the fewer union members in total there are employed.

Some studies have suggested the price level as an appropriate determinant of strike frequency (see Cronin, 1979, pp.74–92 for a summary). More usually the lagged rate of change of prices (Davies, 1979) and wages (Pencavel, 1970) have been found to be significant, although in opposite directions.

Not surprisingly, the rate of change of prices seems to have a positive effect on strike frequency. The same information is available to both sides, but the influence of the past rate of change of prices on, for example, inflationary expectations is notoriously difficult to interpret. Both sides will be increasingly uncertain of the future real value of wages and profits. The negative relationship between strike frequency and the previous rate of increase of real wages might seem to be more surprising. Why should it be that when real wages are rising more quickly, the parties are clearer about each other's intentions? The dual nature of union goals, for both employment and wages, might suggest one explanation. The more slowly have wages been rising, the less that can be discerned about the state of the union's wage–employment trade-off. It may be that previous settlements indicate the union's true preference, but, as other things being equal unions seek a higher settlement and managements a lower one, it may be that relatively unfavourable bargaining power has constrained the union's choice. In other words, a relatively low level of past real

wage growth may say something about union objectives or relative bargaining power. But, the higher the past rate of increase of wages, the more likely we are to be able to say something about bargaining power *and* the union's wage–employment trade-off. Managers have a single objective, but the fact that unions have two means more information is discernible in periods in which wages are rising relatively fast.

6.4.2 Structural factors

Plant size has consistently been found important in determining strike frequency[12]. Increasing plant size brings a number of problems, among them strained communications, more indirect representation and a hierarchy of authority relationships more conducive to misrepresentation and misunderstanding than more simplified channels of control in smaller plants. Payment systems, in particular the proportion of workers involved in payment by results schemes (Shorey, 1976), seem to affect inter-industry strike frequencies. Piecework, as a far more complex method of pay determination than time-based schemes, generally yields greater fluctuations in per period earnings and involves a greater exposure to bargaining and so increased potential for misunderstanding. The slightest change in working practices may disrupt established pay relationships, threaten workers' earnings potential and thus become subject to negotiation. Technical change generally appears to have similar effects (Shorey, 1976). Changes breed uncertainty and altered work practices and so, it is to be expected, increase strike frequency.

6.4.3 The role of the state

Finally, Hicks's model suggests some interesting implications for the extent to which governments can and can not influence strike frequency. The effect of incomes policy on stoppages over pay was examined by Davies (1979). He suggests that a major aim of policies has been to narrow the range within which managements and unions can settle pay negotiations. The important point here is that the policy communicates information to the two sides and so Davies's conclusion that strike frequency is reduced while the policy is being supported by managements and unions should come as no surprise. However in what Davies terms the 're-entry' period when incomes policies break down, as over time in Britain they have tended to do, the effect on strikes seems to be perverse.

Once again this is hardly surprising. The breakdown of an incomes policy is always likely to be a turbulent period for collective bargaining. This is particularly likely in the case of 'voluntary' policies when governments have threatened management and tried to appeal to workers over the heads of their trade union representatives – hardly conducive to confidence on either side.

The Hicks analysis shows that through a successful incomes policy governments may be able to influence strike frequency. It also demonstrates that by reducing welfare payments to strikers' families, governments can not[13]. The so-called 'state subsidy' theory of strikes has never enjoyed widespread academic support and empirical tests of some of its implications have met with little success[14]. Nevertheless it appears, at times, to have had some influence on policy-makers. The 'theory' recognizes that the cost to strikers of withdrawing their labour consists of wages forgone throughout the period of the dispute. This cost can be offset to some extent by other forms of income available only during a strike. In particular it is argued that the payment of supplementary benefits to strikers' families lowers the cost of stoppages and so increases the number of strikes. Hicks demonstrates that this result is unlikely. Obviously such payments reduce the cost to strikers of disagreeing with management and unions' bargaining power is increased, but more strikes would ensue only if management failed to recognize the improved position of unions. Otherwise, as Addison and Siebert (1979) point out, the outcome would be higher equilibrium wage settlements, not more stoppages. An analogous situation would be that in which firms take out strike insurance. This might increase their bargaining power, but strike frequency would be unaffected.

6.5 CONCLUSIONS: IMPLICATIONS FOR POLICY

To an extent the economic analysis of collective bargaining can explain some features of British strike activity, for example why strikes vary with economic conditions and are concentrated in a few industries and a few plants. The major policy implication is that circumstances under which there is likely to be greater uncertainty in bargaining and the parties find it more difficult to gauge their opponents' attitude, will be those in which strike frequency will increase. In some cases a fluctuating strike frequency will simply be the result of a dynamic economy and the changed wage differentials and new technology which go with economic growth. For this reason, if for no other, from a policy point of view, it would seem that the optimum number of strikes is most unlikely to be zero. In fact the optimum number of disputes will be dependent upon their external costs. The internal costs of disputes (that is, those to the parties concerned) have in general proved very difficult to estimate in any meaningful way, and it would seem that the calculation of external costs would be almost impossible. Nevertheless, over a number of years British governments seem to have believed that the strike 'problem' was placing a constraint upon the achievement of other goals of economic policy[15] and have sought to reduce strike frequency and its attendant costs. An economic analysis of strikes suggests a number of implications.

(1) Policies designed simply to reduce the bargaining power of one of the parties to industrial disputes may affect the level of wage settlement but are unlikely to reduce strike frequency. Of course the level of wage settlements may have been the objective of policy.

(2) There may, however, be effects on strike frequency from successful incomes policies or controls on industrial concentration.

(3) Although this represents a somewhat unconventional argument for 'industrial democracy', institutional changes such as the election of trade union members to boards of directors might reduce strike frequency by improving both the availability and interpretation of information. To the extent that such developments took place outside traditional trade union channels, this effect might be reduced.

(4) Governments are concerned to regulate the external costs of industrial disputes, which may well explain their encouraging unions to hold ballots before calling strikes. Were strike patterns more predictable, then consumers, producers and workers could adjust their behaviour to mitigate both external and internal costs of disputes.

(5) Finally, the analysis appears to suggest that a change in the legal framework within which industrial relations in Britain operate might reduce uncertainties in some areas of collective bargaining. In particular, collective agreements might be made legally enforceable or so called 'cooling-off' periods prior to strike action might be legislated for in certain circumstances[16]. Traditionally in Britain, however, both managements and unions have preferred to regulate their relations without threat of interference from the

courts. For this reason, the consequences for strike frequency of new restrictive labour legislation are by no means clear. History seems to suggest that few developments are likely to cause greater uncertainty than attempts to force unwelcomed innovations on to a system generally so resistant to change.

In conclusion, then, it is not surprising that economists do have something to say about strikes and have made useful contributions to an understanding of strike frequency in Britain. For this reason, they can also produce and evaluate policies designed to reduce strike frequency. But, of course, the question of whether, in fact, strikes *do* produce the alleged externalities that perhaps society would do well to control, is quite another issue.

Notes

1 Strike frequency is defined by the Department of Employment as the number of strikes per year per 100 000 workers employed. Strike incidence refers to working days lost per year per 1000 employed.

2 See Smith *et al.* (1978) and Department of Employment *Gazette* annual strike reviews.

3 Smith *et al.* (1978) reported that during 1971–1973 only 2% of manufacturing plants were affected by stoppages, but these employed 20% of the total manufacturing workforce (p. 63).

4 Annual working days lost are unduly affected by a few very large disputes. In 1979 16 million, of a post-war record of 29.1 million working days were lost in a series of engineering workers' strikes.

5 This admittedly dated example has been chosen with some care:

(1) A lucid account and analysis of the strike has recently appeared in Friedman and Meredeen (1980).

(2) Almost certainly the strike was a result of a gross miscalculation of the relative costs of agreement and disagreement on the part of the company at least.

6 See Cartter (1959), pp. 116–121. Cartter defines this as a measure of a party's 'bargaining attitude' with bargaining power being 'a function of the propensity to withhold agreement plus the ability to reduce an opponent's propensity to

fight'. The important point remains that if costs of disagreement increase relative to those of agreement, bargaining power, however defined, will be reduced.

7 Hicks (1963), pp. 136–158.

8 The same problem is encountered in most bargaining models. A possible exception is that of Ashenfelter and Johnson (1969) which 'solves' the indeterminacy problem by making the decision on whether or not a strike takes place purely the firm's. See Vanderkamp (1970). Addison and Siebert (1979) suggest many of the points in the text in connection with the somewhat more complex model of Zeuthen (1930).

9 As Farber (1978) comments: 'It is probably true that strikers are rarely net monetary gainers from work stoppages and, hence, they are not acting rationally when they strike.' (p. 262).

10 Addison and Siebert (1981) develop this conclusion further. They produce a sophisticated 'accident model' of strikes, some of the implications of which can be derived directly from an interpretation of Hicks.

11 The existence of an incentive to cheat in a two-player bargaining situation is well-established in the game theory literature. See, for example, Hirshleifer (1980), Chapter 13.

12 Prais (1978) suggests the most persuasive explanation.

13 See the discussion of the implications of Zeuthen's model in Addison and Siebert (1979).

14 Tests were attempted by Durcan and McCarthy (1974). See also the criticism of their approach by Hunter (1974).

15 Encouraged, no doubt, by assertions along these lines contained in the Donovan Report (1968).

16 Certain provisions of this kind were made available in the Industrial Relations Act 1971.

Guide to further reading

Monthly strike data are collected by the Department of Employment and published in the *Gazette*, with an annual review of stoppages, usually in the summer. A comprehensive review of British experience in the early 1970s is provided in Smith *et al.* (1978). Bargaining models, including those of Hicks, Zeuthen and Cross (1965) are surveyed in Mayhew (1979); for non-econometricians, the strike frequency models of Shorey, Pencavel and others are summarized in Cronin (1979). For the overall contribution economists have made to the study of strikes, see Addison and Siebert (1979) and (1981).

Bibliography

ADDISON, J. T. and SIEBERT, W. S. (1979), *The Market for Labor: An Analytical Treatment*, Goodyear Publishing Company; Santa Monica, Cal.

ADDISON, J. T. and SIEBERT, W. S. (1981), 'Are Strikes Accidental?', *Economic Journal*, Vol. 91 (June)

ASHENFELTER, O. and JOHNSON, G. E. (1969), 'Bargaining Theory, Trade Unions and Industrial Strike Activity', *American Economic Review*, Vol. 59

CARTTER, A. M. (1959), *Theory of Wages and Employment*, Irwin; Homewood, Ill.

CRONIN, J. E. (1979), *Industrial Conflict in Modern Britain*, Croom Helm; London

CROSS, J. G. (1965), 'A Theory of the Bargaining Process', *American Economic Review*, Vol. 55

DAVIES, R. J. (1979), 'Economic Activity, Incomes Policy and Strikes – A Quantitative Analysis', *British Journal of Industrial Relations*, Vol. 17

DONOVAN (1968), *Report of the Royal Commission on Trade Unions and Employers' Associations*, Cmnd 3623, HMSO; London

DURCAN, J. W. and McCARTHY, W. E. J. (1974), 'The State Subsidy Theory of Strikes: An Examination of Statistical Data for the Period 1956–70', *British Journal of Industrial Relations*, Vol. 12

FARBER, H. S. (1978), 'Bargaining Theory, Wage Outcomes and the Occurrence of Strikes: An Econometric Analysis', *American Economic Review*, Vol. 68

FISHER, M. R. (1973), *Measurement of Labour Disputes and Their Economic Impact*, OECD; Paris

FRIEDMAN, H. and MEREDEEN, S. (1980), *The Dynamics of Industrial Conflict. Lessons from Ford*, Croom Helm; London

HICKS, J. R. (1963), *The Theory of Wages*, Macmillan; London

HIRSHLEIFER, J. (1980), *Price Theory and Applications*, Prentice-Hall International; London

HUNTER, L. C. (1974), 'The State Subsidy Theory of Strikes – A Reconsideration', *British Journal of Industrial Relations*, Vol. 12

MAYHEW, K. (1979), 'Economists and Strikes', *Oxford Bulletin of Economics and Statistics*, Vol. 41

PENCAVEL, J. H. (1970), 'An Investigation into Industrial Strike Activity in Britain', *Economica*, Vol. 37

PRAIS, S. J. (1978), 'The Strike Proneness of Large Plants in Britain', *Journal of the Royal Statistical Society* (Series A), Vol. 141

REES, A. (1952), 'Industrial Conflict and Business Fluctuations', *Journal of Political Economy*, Vol. 60

SHOREY, J. (1976), 'An Inter Industry Analysis of Strike Frequency', *Economica*, Vol. 43

SMITH, C. T. B., CLIFTON, R., MAKEHAM, P., CREIGH, S. W. and BURN, R. V. (1978), *Strikes in Britain*, Manpower Paper 15, HMSO; London

VANDERKAMP, J. (1970), 'Economic Activity and Strikes in Canada', *Industrial Relations* (Berkeley), Vol. 9

ZEUTHEN, F. (1930), *Problems of Monopoly and Economic Welfare*, Routledge and Kegan Paul; London

7
The Theory of the Firm

Mark Austin

7.1 INTRODUCTION

This chapter presents an analysis of the criticisms of the conventional or neoclassical approach to firm behaviour and considers some of the alternative models that have been proposed. By 'neoclassical' is meant those models that take as their starting point the assumption that the firm can be treated as a single decision-making unit which has the maximization of profit as its sole objective. The caricature is of the owner-entrepreneur who is the personification of the firm and who seeks to maximize his wealth which is naturally reflected in the profit goal for the firm. The fact that most firms have some form of complex organizational structure is seen as relatively unimportant. Further assumptions are often added such as that the firm operates with perfect information and that the 'long run' is comprised of a succession of identical 'short-run' periods. This last assumption ensures that the maximization of short-run profits implies the maximization of long-run profits, so that there is no problem of a trade-off between profits 'today' and profits 'tomorrow'.

On this basis the behaviour of the firm in a variety of industrial contexts is analysed. The most successful of these models are undoubtedly the extreme market forms of perfect competition and monopoly. Both of these models enable unambiguous predictions to be made concerning the firm's reaction to, say, the imposition of a tax. In the case of perfect competition it is also possible to construct the market supply curve which is crucial to supply and demand analysis.

The models of industrial structures that lie somewhere between the two extremes are less successful. Traditional models of monopolistic competition and oligopoly can only generate determinate solutions by assuming that the firm can ignore the behaviour of its rivals[1]. It is extremely unlikely that firms can safely do this. One immediate source of criticism then, is that neoclassical theory is unable to deal adequately with those market structures that are empirically the most important. As will be seen, however, the alternatives fare little better in dealing with the problem that with a number of important firms in a market, no one firm can act independently – it must consider the reactions of its rivals. An approach that tries to tackle this problem head on, but which will not be discussed here, is the theory of games[2].

7.2 CRITICISMS OF NEOCLASSICAL THEORY

Criticisms of the neoclassical approach go back at least as far as the 1930s. An important study was that undertaken by Hall and Hitch (1939) which was an empirical investigation into industrial pricing policies. Their evidence consisted of questionnaires completed by 38 'efficiently managed enterprises'. They concluded that firms did not attempt to maximize profits by using the familiar marginal cost equals marginal revenue rule, and also that profit was not the sole objective of the firm. Prices were set, they found, on what is called the 'full cost' principle. Because businessmen were interested in 'fair' profits, but also in goodwill and the stability of the market, prices were set by calculating the full average cost of production and adding a conventional mark-up.

An immediate implication of this evidence was taken to be that a theory that relies heavily on marginal principles cannot be satisfactory if firms do not actually take decisions with reference to marginal considerations. However, full cost pricing does not, by itself, imply that firms are not aiming to maximize profits. As long as the mark-up varies (which Hall and Hitch found it did) then this pricing rule can be consistent with any objective including profit maximization. In fact, Machlup (1967) has argued that as long as firms are aiming to maximize profits prices will be set where marginal cost equals marginal revenue despite the fact that firms use the administratively simpler full cost pricing rule.

Perhaps the most important conclusion to come from the Hall and Hitch study is that firms may well have multiple goals. The implications of this are considered in section 7.4.

The assumption of profit maximization is defensible as long as the firm is run by its owners. However, the evidence presented by Berle and Means (1932) and Larner (1966) purported to show that, with the growth of the joint stock company, this was no longer the case for the largest and most important companies. The owners of the joint stock company are its shareholders but, it is argued, they are such a large and disparate group that effective control has passed into the hands of professional managers who usually own very few shares in the company. The managers' power comes from their intimate knowledge of the workings of the firm and of the markets in which it operates. Shareholders are inevitably less well-informed and have to rely heavily on the managers' advice. As long as the firm is performing reasonably well there is no reason why shareholders should do anything but accept the managers' policies. However, as managers are not owners, they cannot be expected to pursue policies that are in the best interests of owners. The basis of the 'managerial' theories of the firm is that managers will have objectives other than profit and that the separation of ownership from control gives them the opportunity to strive for these objectives. Managerial models are discussed in section 7.3.

The evidence presented by Berle and Means and by Larner is summarized in *Table 7.1*. Their method was to analyse the pattern of share ownership in the 200 largest non-financial US corporations and use this to classify them by 'type of control'. If they were able to find an individual or a well-defined group that held a

TABLE 7.1
CONTROL OF THE LARGEST 200 NON-FINANCIAL US CORPORATIONS
1929 and 1963

S (%)	*Type of control*	*1929 (%)*	*1963 (%)*
$S \geqq 80$	Private	6	0
$50 \leqq S < 80$	Majority	5	2.5
$10 \leqq S < 50$	Minority	23	9
	Legal device	21	4
$S < 10$	Management	44	84.5

S = Percentage of shares held by largest well-defined group.

Source: Derived from Berle and Means (1932) and Larner (1966)

significant proportion of shares (10% or more), then they classified the firm as under the effective control of this group, despite the fact that the group may not have had an absolute majority holding. If they could find no such group, then they classified the firm as under 'management control'. As can be seen from the table, 84.5% of the firms were classified in this way for 1963.

This evidence has not, however, gone unchallenged. The pattern of share ownership is extremely complicated and seemingly different concerns that own shares in a company may, in fact, be linked together. Banks appear to be particularly important in this respect, at least in the US, and the Patman Committee (1968) reported that 36 of the firms that Larner had classified as under management control were ultimately owned by two large banks. A more important problem is that share ownership, by itself, is a poor measure of control. For example, Kotz (1978) argues that 69 of the largest 200 US corporations were under 'financial control' in 1969, where this is measured by share ownership, representation on the board of directors, and source of funds for investment. Whether these particular measures are adequate is open to debate, but there are clearly several avenues along which control can be exercised[3].

Another important area of debate about the validity of the neoclassical approach concerns the role of the capital market. This is important because it is the market where company securities are traded and it is usually regarded as a competitive market. If it is such, then the price of a firm's shares will be a good indicator of profitability. If the firm is pursuing policies that reduce profits below potential this will cause a fall in share price. There is now an incentive for another organization to buy the shares (that is, to take over the firm) and turn it into a profit maximizer.

The mechanism invoked here is called 'economic natural selection'. The analogy is with the Darwinian principal of the survival of the fittest, with 'fittest' in this context being the most profitable. Even if product markets are not competitive so that firms are not forced to maximize profits, and even if managers have effective control and wish to pursue alternative objectives, the working of the capital market, in this view, will ensure that only profit maximizers survive. A theory based on the assumption of profit maximization will, in this case, be adequate, because in the long run firms that do not conform to behaviour consistent with this objective will disappear. For the natural selection mechanism to work, it is necessary that non-profit maximizing firms get taken over and that profit maximizers do not. The evidence on take-overs will be considered in section 7.5

7.3 MANAGERIAL THEORIES

The managerial theories of the firm have as their basis the separation of ownership from control and an imperfect discipline from both the product and capital markets. This imperfect discipline allows managers some discretion to pursue objectives other than profit and the problem becomes one of specifying what these alternatives will be. It has been suggested by Williamson (1964) that consideration should be given to the managerial utility function which would include such factors as power, prestige, security, salary and leisure. For simplicity these objectives are often encapsulated into one measure, such as size or growth, which is seen as reflecting the objectives of managers. A variety of models has been presented and just two examples will be taken here. It should be noted that all managerial theories retain the assumption of maximization, but often profit is a constraint rather than an objective.

7.3.1 Sales revenue maximization

One of the earliest managerial models was that presented by Baumol (1959). He suggested that managerial utility is best served by the pursuit of size (measured by turn-over) rather than profit. However, profits cannot be ignored because shareholders will demand some dividends on their investment in the firm, so the firm must earn sufficient profit to satisfy shareholders and to provide funds for investment. If profits fall below this minimum level the firm will be taken over and the management team will be replaced.

The theory can be illustrated on a diagram (see *Figure 7.1*) which plots costs, revenues and profits against output. The total revenue function (*TR*) is derived from the downward sloping demand function (in the imperfect product market) and this, combined with the total cost function (*TC*), gives the profit function (π). The profit-maximizing firm would clearly choose an output of Q_π where profits are at their greatest, but the sales revenue maximizer will choose either output Q_{S1} or an output such as Q_{S2}. Which is chosen will depend on the severity of the minimum profit constraint. With a weak profit constraint such as π min 1 the firm can maximize total revenue without profits becoming too low and will thus choose Q_{S1}. If the profit constraint is more severe (such as with π min 2) the firm can no longer choose Q_{S1} and the best it can do is choose Q_{S2} where the minimum profit

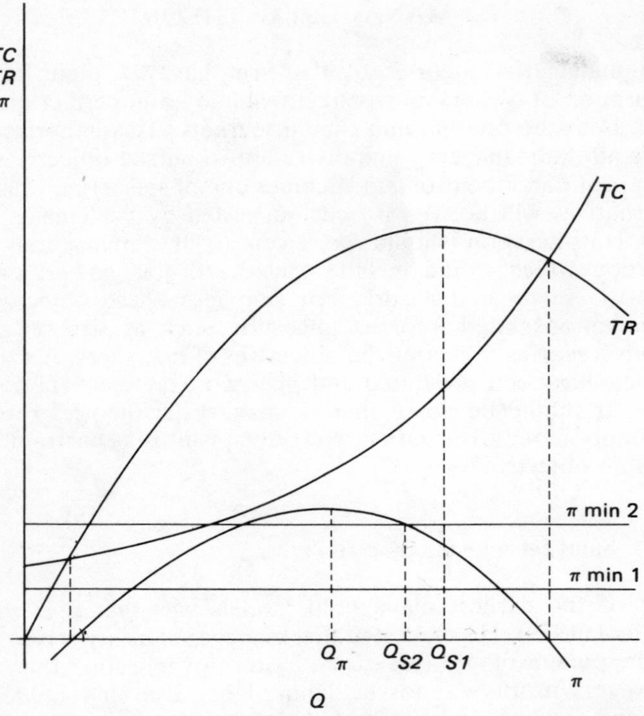

Figure 7.1 Sales revenue maximization

constraint is just satisfied[4]. In fact, Baumol argues that the firm will always choose the output where the constraint is just satisfied because if it is in a position such as Q_{S1} it has 'excess' profits which it can sacrifice in advertising expenditure. As long as advertising always adds to total revenue, it will always be in the managers' interests to use up profit in this way until the constraint is just met. Advertising expenditure is not usually analysed in the neoclassical theory of the firm, and recognition of its importance is a strength of Baumol's model. The profit-maximizing firm will, of course, only advertise until the marginal cost of advertising equals the marginal revenue generated by it.

It is clear from *Figure 7.1* that the sales revenue maximizing firm will always produce more than and earn less profits than the profit maximizing firm. This, however, is not sufficient to allow discrimination between the theories on empirical evidence because it is impossible to tell whether observed levels of profit are as great as they could be.

In principle, the theories can be tested by comparing the prediction they make about the firm's response to changed circumstances. One prediction on which Baumol places much emphasis is the response of the firm to an increase in fixed costs. Such an increase would cause a downward shift in the profits curve and this is illustrated in *Figure 7.2*.

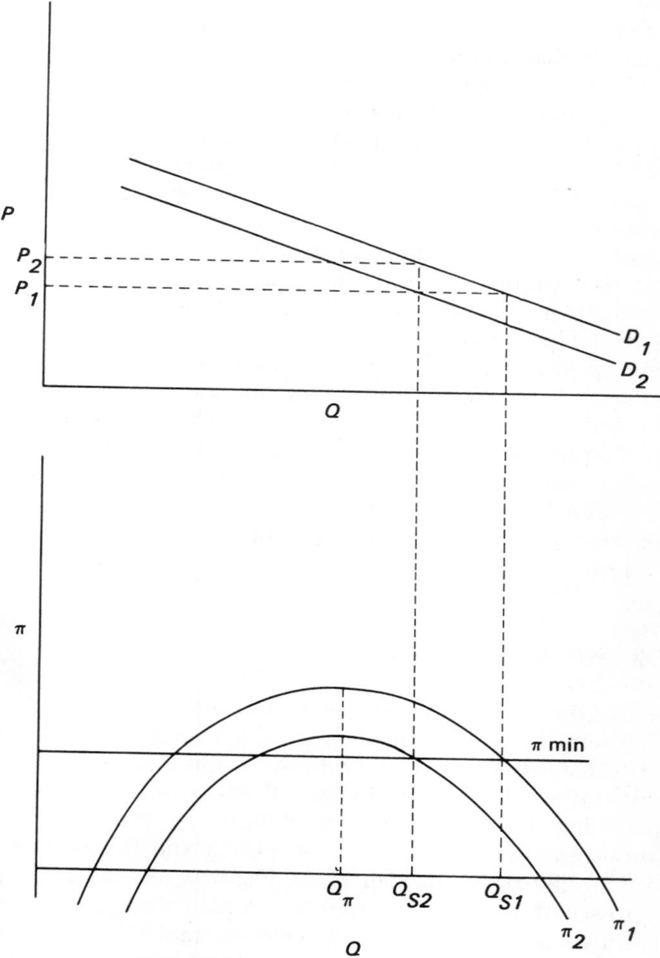

Figure 7.2 Response to an increase in fixed costs

The profit-maximizing firm would not change output (because fixed costs do not affect marginal costs), but the sales revenue maximizer will reduce output in order to maintain profits. Baumol argues further that a reduction in output will, via the demand curve, imply an increase in price from P_1 to P_2. Baumol uses evidence that firms do increase price in response to increased costs (such as the full cost pricing evidence) in support of his theory. However, reduced output will also mean reduced advertising expenditure which will tend to shift the demand curve to the left. If it shifts as far as D_2, then no price increase will occur, and the prediction that Baumol would like to make is not necessarily generated by his theory.

The theory does predict reduced output in this situation, whereas a profit maximizer would maintain output, and so, in principle, it would appear possible to discriminate between the theories on this basis. However, the theory does not allow for the operation of the firm over time and it is not clear that it will adequately reflect the behaviour of the managerial firm. In any event, the predictions that the theory generates are crucially dependent on the way in which the minimum profits constraint operates. The constraint acts very much like a switch: above or at minimum profits the management are completely free to pursue their own objectives, below minimum profits the firm will get taken over and the management will be replaced. It is unlikely that the constraint will operate in this way. Yarrow (1973) has argued that the constraint will be one of an increasing probability of take-over, the greater is the deviation from maximum profits. With this type of constraint many of the predictions of the Baumol model are changed.

7.3.2 Growth maximization

Marris (1964) suggests that managerial utility is best reflected in the growth rather than in the size of the firm. Considerations of growth make analysis very complicated and, in order to make the problem tractable, Marris assumes that the firm chooses a rate of growth that it will maintain indefinitely. He then describes two relationships between the rate of growth and the rate of profit. These are illustrated in *Figure 7.3*. The first relationship concerns the growth of demand for the firm's output. Marris argues that the only way to achieve permanently growing demand is by diversification – the introduction of new products. If the firm decides not to grow it will earn some rate of profit (marked *A*), but some low

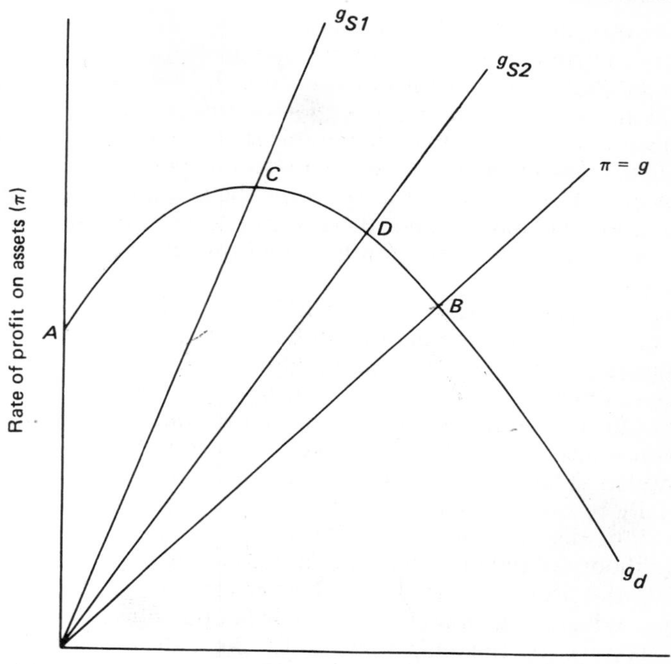

Figure 7.3 Growth maximization

rates of growth will enhance profitability because the firm is able to move into the most profitable new markets. If the firm wishes its demand to grow very fast, however, there will come a point where profitability will suffer as not all new products will be successful and there will be considerable disruption caused by rapid growth which will lead to inefficiency. The resulting relationship between profits and growth is labelled *gd*.

In order to be able to supply this growing demand the firm will need to increase its capital stock by investment and this has to be financed. Marris assumes for simplicity that all financing comes from retained profits[5] in which case the growth of supply will depend on the rate of profit and the proportion that is retained. If the firm paid out no dividends it would be able to grow, depending on its profits, at a rate along the ray where $\pi = g$ because, for example, a 10% rate of profit on assets could be converted into a 10% growth of assets. Given that the growth of supply must equal the growth of demand for the firm to be in equilibrium, the maximum possible rate of growth is given by the point *B*.

However, the firm will not retain all its profits, but will pay out some proportion as dividends to shareholders. If the firm aims to maximize its rate of profit it would choose the point C along g_{S1}[6]. If g_{S2} defines the maximum proportion of profits that the firm can retain without inducing an unfavourable shareholder reaction then the growth-maximizing firm will choose the point D. The constraint on the managerial firm concerns the proportion of profits paid out as dividends and not the absolute level of profits. This is clearly more realistic in the context of a firm with a growing level of profits.

It is clear that the growth-maximizing firm will grow faster and earn a lower profit rate than the profit maximizer. Again, however, this is insufficient to enable discrimination between the theories. Further, it has been shown by Solow (1971) that both types of firm will respond qualitatively in the same way to a change in, for instance, a tax rate. This makes direct comparisons between the models at an empirical level very difficult and economists have generally resorted to various sorts of indirect evidence. Some of this will be discussed in section 7.5.

The theory of the growth of the firm is clearly important in that it views the firm as concerned with such variables as investment, finance, advertising and research and development. However, like the sale revenue maximization model the industrial context in which the firm operates is given little consideration – the behaviour of rival firms is effectively ignored.

7.4 BEHAVIOURAL THEORY

Neoclassical theory treats the firm as if it were an individual with the single goal of profit maximization. Managerial theory treats the firm as being composed of two crucial groups, managers and shareholders, who have different objectives. Behavioural theory goes further and argues that the firm is composed of a large number of groups with different objectives. As such, they argue, it makes little sense to consider the objectives of 'the firm' because these will depend on the objectives and relative strengths of the groups within the firm. Because of the impossibility of considering a unique motivation behind the decisions of the firm, behavioural theory concentrates on the process of decision-making.

The major work in this area is that of Cyert and March (1963) who argue that because the objectives of the different groups within the firm (such as engineers, accountants and sales staff) are bound to conflict, and because the continued existence of the firm requires that this conflict be resolved, the notion of maximization must be abandoned.

Instead, the relevant concept is 'satisficing' introduced by Simon (1959). The difference between satisficing and maximizing is as follows. The satisficer sets a target value for a variable and strives only to improve performance if this target is not met. The maximizer will continue to search for improvement until no further gains are possible. Further, for the satisficer, the target is not fixed, but adjusts in the light of experience. The decision-making process considered appropriate is illustrated in *Figure 7.4*.

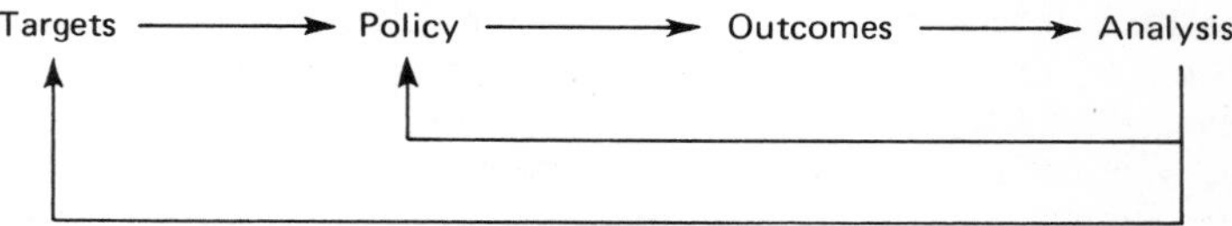

Figure 7.4 The decision-making process

The first stage is to set targets which for the firm may be sales, profits, market share and production, and these will be set in the light of recent experience. Alternative policies are considered sequentially and the first one that looks likely to achieve the objectives is chosen. The outcomes associated with this choice are monitored and analysed and, if the targets are achieved, the policy is maintained. If the targets are not achieved the first response is to change the policy in an attempt to improve performance. Persistent under-achievement will result in the targets being revised downwards.

The behavioural approach yields some useful insights into the internal operations of firms and into the process of decision-making, but its major weakness is that any behaviour is consistent with satisficing. Because the targets are not fixed, any observed choice may simply reflect a change in objectives. For this reason, the behavioural approach has had relatively little effect on mainstream economics.

7.5 EMPIRICAL EVIDENCE

Most of the empirical debate has surrounded the neoclassical and managerial theories. Because of the problems of generating direct tests, indirect evidence has mostly been used[7]. Two important areas concern managerial remuneration and the take-over mechanism.

If it is the case that managerial remuneration is closely associated with company profitability then it would be unlikely that there would be much divergence of objectives between owners and managers. It would in this case seem reasonable to maintain the profit-maximization assumption even if firms are under the control of managers. The evidence seems to be, however, that company size rather than profitability is the main determinant of managerial remuneration. There have been several studies in this area[8], one of the most thorough of which is by Cosh (1975). He looked at the relationship between the chief executives' compensation and company size and profitability for 1000 UK firms. The results showed that 49% of variation in compensation could be explained by size alone and that, with profitability added, the proportion rose to only 54%. From this evidence there would appear to be an incentive for managers to pursue size rather than profitability.

As far as take-overs are concerned the major work is that of Singh (1975). For the economic natural selection mechanism to work it is necessary that profitable firms do not get taken over and that unprofitable firms do. Singh found, however, that small but highly profitable firms are often taken over by larger but less profitable ones as a means of defending market position. Similarly, large firms, because of their sheer size, had a reduced chance of being taken over even if their profitability was poor. Singh also found that the best way for a firm to avoid being taken over was for it to grow rather than for it to become more profitable. From this evidence size would seem to have greater survival value than profitability.

7.6 CONCLUSIONS

The neoclassical theory of the firm has come under severe attack and a number of interesting alternatives have been suggested. The neoclassical theory has not, however, been replaced and this is partly because of the different theories being applicable to different types of firms, and partly because of the difficulty of constructing convincing empirical tests. The managerial and behavioural theories have broadened the scope of the theory of the firm and have yielded useful insights into the workings of the large modern corporation.

Notes

1 For a discussion of these models see, for example, Koutsoyiannis (1979), Chapters 8, 9, 10 and Sawyer, (1979) Chapters 3, 4.

2 For an introduction to this see Sawyer (1979), section 4.15 and Bacharach (1976), especially Chapter 4.
3 The evidence presented here is by no means the only available, and is chosen only as an example. For a summary of the available evidence see Scott (1979), Chapter 3.
4 Profit maximization can be seen as a limiting case of constrained sales revenue maximization where minimum acceptable profits equal maximum attainable profits.
5 Firms can, of course, finance investment by borrowing, but empirical evidence shows that the majority of investment is internally financed.
6 The maximization of the profit rate will not, in general, be in the best interests of the shareholders. Growth will lead to an increased share price and shareholders will prefer slightly more growth at a lower profit rate than at point *C*.
7 For an interesting attempt at a direct test see Herendeen and Scheckter (1977).
8 See, for example, McQuire *et al.* (1962) and Lewellyn (1968).

Guide to further reading

The best single text which covers all the theories (but none of the evidence) considered in this chapter is probably Sawyer (1979). A detailed discussion of the managerial theories is given in Wildsmith (1973). Much of the empirical evidence is summarized in Hay and Morris (1979).

Bibliography

BACHARACH, M. (1976), *Economics and the theory of Games*, Macmillan; London

BAUMOL, W. J. (1959), *Business Behaviour, Value and Growth*, Macmillan; New York

BERLE, A. A. and MEANS, G. C. (1932), *The Modern Corporation and Private Property*, Harcourt, Brace and World; New York

COSH, A. (1975), 'The Remuneration of Chief Executives in the United Kingdom', *Economic Journal*, Vol. 85 (March)

CYERT, R. M. and MARCH, J. G. (1963), *A Behavioural Theory of the Firm*, Prentice-Hall; Englewood Cliffs, N.J.

HALL, R. L. and HITCH, C. J. (1939), 'Price Theory and Business Behaviour', *Oxford Economic Papers*, Vol. 2 (May)

HAY, D. A. and MORRIS, D. J. (1979), *Industrial Economics – Theory and Evidence*, Oxford University Press; Oxford

HEREDEEN, J. and SCHECKTER, M. (1977), 'Alternative Models of the Corporate Enterprise: Growth Maximization and Value Maximization, An Empirical Test', *Southern Economic Journal*, Vol. 43 (April)

KOTZ, D. M. (1978), *Bank Control of Large Corporation in the United States*, University of California Press; California

KOUTSOYIANNIS, A. (1979), *Modern Microeconomics*, 2nd edn., Macmillan; London

LARNER, R. J. (1966), 'Ownership and Control in the 200 largest Non-Financial Corporations, 1929 and 1963', *American Economic Review*, Vol. 56 (September)

LEWELLYN, W. G. (1968), *Executive Compensation in Large Industrial Corporations*, National Bureau of Economic Research; New York

MACHLUP, F. (1967), 'Theories of the Firm: Marginalist, Behavioural, Managerial', *American Economic Review,* Vol. 57 (March)

MARRIS, R. L. (1964), *Economic Theory of 'Managerial' Capitalism*, Macmillan; London

McQUIRE, J., CHIU, I. S. Y. and ELBING, A. O. (1962), 'Executive Incomes, Sales and Profits', *American Economic Review*, Vol. 52 (September)

PATMAN, W. (1968), 'Commercial Banks and their Trust Activities', *US House of Representatives Sub-Committee of House Banking and Currency Committee*; Washington, DC

SAWYER, M. C. (1979), *Theories of the Firm*, Weidenfeld and Nicholson; London

SCOTT, J. (1979), *Corporations, Classes and Capitalism*, Hutchinson; London

SIMON, H. A. (1959), 'Theories of Decision Making in Economics and Behavioural Science', *American Economic Review*, Vol. 49 (June)

SINGH, A. (1975), 'Take-overs, Economic Natural Selection and the Theory of the Firm', *Economic Journal*, Vol. 85 (March)

SOLOW, R. M. (1971), 'Some Implications of Alternative Criteria for the Firm', in MARRIS, R. L. and WOOD, A. (eds.), *The Corporate Economy*, Macmillan; London

WILDSMITH, J. R. (1973), *Managerial Theories of the Firm*, Martin Robertson; London

WILLIAMSON, O. E. (1964), *The Economics of Discretionary Behaviour*, Prentice-Hall; Englewood Cliffs, NJ.

YARROW, G. K. (1973), 'Managerial Utility Maximization Under Uncertainty', *Economica*, New Series, Vol. 40 (May)

8

Market Failure and State Intervention

D. H. Gowland

8.1 INTRODUCTION

The analysis of market failure is an examination of the justification for state intervention. Under certain highly restrictive assumptions, allocation by price within a market produces a socially optimal outcome. When these conditions are not fulfilled, the market has 'failed' and so there is an economic case for intervention either to override or to improve the working of the market. The concept of 'market failure' provides a rigorous analytical framework within which the case for state invervention can be examined and its potential benefits assessed – and compared with the costs.

In this chapter, the *prima facie* case for the market system is set out (section 8.2). In the following section (8.3) the various forms of market failure are analysed. The next section 8.4, sets out the possible forms of state intervention and the advantages and disadvantages of these alternative methods of seeking to remove the consequences of market failure. Finally, some conclusions are drawn in section 8.5.

8.2 THE CASE FOR THE MARKET SYSTEM

Ever since Adam Smith, many economists have sought to defend the market system. Some of these advocates of the free market have concentrated on political arguments, for example that only free markets are compatible with a liberal society or that the market system promotes individual responsibility[1]. However, the orthodox argument for the market system is that it produces a socially optimal allocation of resources. The problem of allocation (what should be produced, how and by whom and to whom it should be distributed) has always been recognized as the critical problem of microeconomics and indeed figures in the best known of all definitions of economics – 'the allocation of scarce resources to unlimited wants' (Robbins, 1931).

The orthodox, neoclassical analysis has the aim of showing that the market system will produce an efficient or Pareto optimal outcome; that is no one can be made better off without someone else being made worse off nor can the output of any good be increased without reducing that of another nor can the quantity of any input be reduced without increasing the quantity of another. The proof of this proposition can be demonstrated in two ways. The first sets up the problem as the maximization of social welfare. In all cases, maximization of a variable requires that its marginal value should equal zero and that an appropriate supplementary (second order) condition be fulfilled. The best known example of this is profit maximization which requires both that marginal profit be equal to zero, i.e. marginal revenue be equal to marginal cost, and that marginal cost cuts marginal revenue from below or that at the output concerned the switch be from profits to losses.

Social welfare will be maximized when the marginal net social benefit is equal to zero, that is when marginal social benefit is equal to marginal social cost. One of the assumptions required to prove the optimality of markets is that only the buyers and sellers are affected by any transaction, so it will be sufficient if

$$\text{Marginal Benefit} = \text{Marginal Cost.} \tag{8.1}$$

In a market system in which producers maximize profit

$$\text{Marginal Revenue} = \text{Marginal Cost.} \tag{8.2}$$

Consumers are assumed to maximize utility in which case

$$\text{Marginal Benefit} = \text{Marginal Cost of Purchase.} \tag{8.3}$$

In a price takers' market, e.g. under perfect competition,

$$\text{Marginal Revenue} = \text{Price} = \text{Marginal Cost of Purchase.} \tag{8.4}$$

So

Marginal Cost = Price (from (8.2) and (8.4))

and

Marginal Benefit = Price (from (8.3) and (8.4))

Accordingly

Marginal Cost = Marginal Benefit – i.e. (8.1) has been proved.

Alternatively, the case for the market system of allocation starts by examining a conventional competitive supply and demand diagram, *Figure 8.1a*. It is crucial to note that the supply curve is

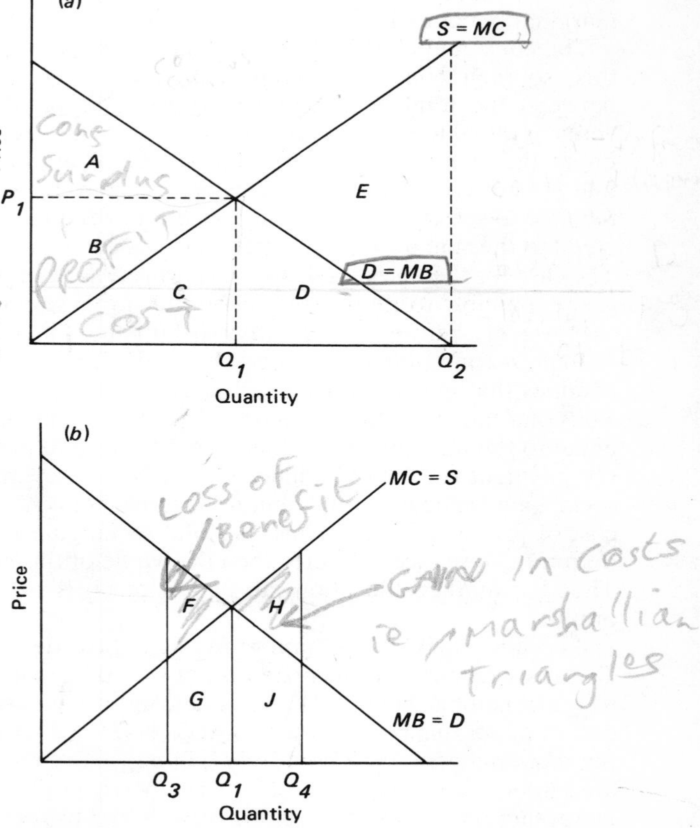

Figure 8.1 Optimality of market allocation

the marginal cost curve and the demand curve, the marginal benefit curve. This follows from the fact that suppliers will increase the quantity offered for sale so long as price exceeds marginal cost and will reduce it so long as price is less than marginal cost so the quantity they wish to supply at each price is that at which price equals marginal cost. Similarly, buyers would like to increase purchases if price is less than marginal benefit and reduce purchases if price exceeds marginal benefit. So, their desired purchases (the demand curve) at each price are those where price equals marginal benefit. In equilibrium price will be P_1 and output Q_1. Any total magnitude is equal to the area under the appropriate marginal curve, i.e. the sum of the marginal values over the relevant range so total benefit to consumers in equilibrium is equal to area $(A + B + C)$, which is the area under the marginal benefit (demand) curve.

The consumers pay Area $(B + C)$ – i.e. price × quantity – for this, so their consumers' surplus is equal to A, the difference between the total benefit and total expenditure. Producers' revenue is equal to $(B + C)$ and their costs to C, total cost is the area under the marginal cost curve. Hence profits are equal to B. No one but consumers and producers are affected, by assumption, so the gain to society from the market-determined price and output is equal to the sum of the consumers' surplus and profits, i.e. $A + B$. The case for the market allocation is proved if it can be shown that it is impossible to find an output at which this gain is exceeded.

However, before showing that social gain is at a maximum at output Q_1, one simplification can be made. The case for a market assumes that income distribution is irrelevant (see p. 190 below). Thus one can argue that the gain to society from an output of Q_1 is equal to the benefits to consumers less the cost of production, i.e. the payment for it can be ignored as an irrelevant transfer. Thus social gain is equal to total benefit to consumers $(A + B + C)$ less cost of production (C). Thus the total social gain is $(A + B)$. If output were reduced to zero, then the whole of this would be lost. Thus the market allocation, an output of Q_1 is preferable to no output.

Another possible allocation would be to provide the goods free. To satisfy demand at this price output would have to be increased to Q_2 (it can be shown that excess demand is never optimal). The cost of increasing output from Q_1 to Q_2 is $(D + E)$, the area under the marginal cost curve between Q_1 and Q_2. The benefit is D, the area under the marginal benefit curve between Q_1 and Q_2. Thus increasing output to Q_2 would involve a loss to society of E, i.e. society would be better off with production at Q_1 rather than Q_2 by an amount equal to E. Hence it has been demonstrated that Q_1 is preferable to either no output or the output at the level at which goods would be provided free. This argument is set out in tabular form in *Table 8.1*.

TABLE 8.1
OPTIMALITY OF MARKET DETERMINED OUTPUT

At output Q_1		
Consumers' surplus	=	Total Benefit − Total Outlay
	=	$(A + B + C) - (B + C)$
	=	A
Profit	=	Total Revenue − Total Cost
	=	$(B + C) - C$
	=	B
Social gain	=	Consumers' Surplus + Profit
	=	$A + B$
	or	
Social gain	=	Benefit to Consumers − Cost of Production
	=	$A + B + C - C$
	=	$A + B$
At output Q_2		
Social gain of increase in output	=	Benefit to Consumers − Cost of Production
	=	$D - (D + E)$
	=	$-E$
i.e. a social loss of E if output increased to Q_2		
At output Q_3		
Social gain of reducing output from Q_1 to Q_3	=	Reduction in Cost − Reduction in Benefit
	=	$G - (F + G)$
	=	$-$F
i.e. a social loss of F if output is reduced to Q_3		
At output Q_4		
Social gain in increase in output from Q_1 to Q_4	=	Increase in Benefit – Increase in Cost
	=	$H - (J + H)$
	=	$-J$
i.e. a social loss of J if output is increased from Q_1 to Q_4		

This argument can be extended, as in *Figure 8.1b*. Any reduction in output below Q_1 would involve a loss to society. If output were reduced to Q_3, then the reduction in costs would be equal to G. The reduction in benefits would be equal to $(F + G)$. Thus the social loss would be the reduction in benefits less the reduction in costs. This would be equal to $(F + G) - G$. Thus the social loss would be equal to F. For any increase in output, represented as Q_1 to Q_4, the extra cost of producing $(Q_4 - Q_1)$ is $(H + J)$ and the benefits are only J (area under the demand curve between Q_1 and Q_4). Thus the extra cost exceeds the extra benefit by H. In general any variation in output from Q_1 would cost society either F or H appropriately measured. These are sometimes called 'welfare triangles' or 'Marshallian triangles'.

To summarize, the market system ensures the production of the optimal level of output of every good, so long as various highly restrictive assumptions are satisfied. The case for markets is that they ensure the optimal level of output and its allocation to those who are prepared to pay most for it, who are those who value it most, or at least so the marketeer argues. The argument is that those who would *pay*, should consume the good, not that they should pay for it. However, no satisfactory alternative method of determining who would pay has been discovered, other than who does pay. The crucial feature of the argument is that price should equal marginal social cost. Given the assumptions, the market ensures this. Many forms of market failure occur when price does not or cannot equal marginal social cost.

8.3 MARKET FAILURE

8.3.1 Monopoly and monopsony

One of the assumptions necessary to show that market forces produced the optimal output of a good was that all producers and consumers were price takers. If this assumption is relaxed, two of the classic forms of market failure arise: monopoly and monopsony. It is one of the classic results of elementary economics that a monopolist reduces output below the competitive level so as to increase profits. Accordingly it is not surprising that monopoly is a form of market failure since output will not be at the competitive level so long as the monopolist maximizes profit.

It is possible to calculate the social cost of monopoly quite easily. In *Figure 8.2* the monopolist's equilibrium price and output are P_1 and Q_1, i.e. where marginal revenue is equal to marginal

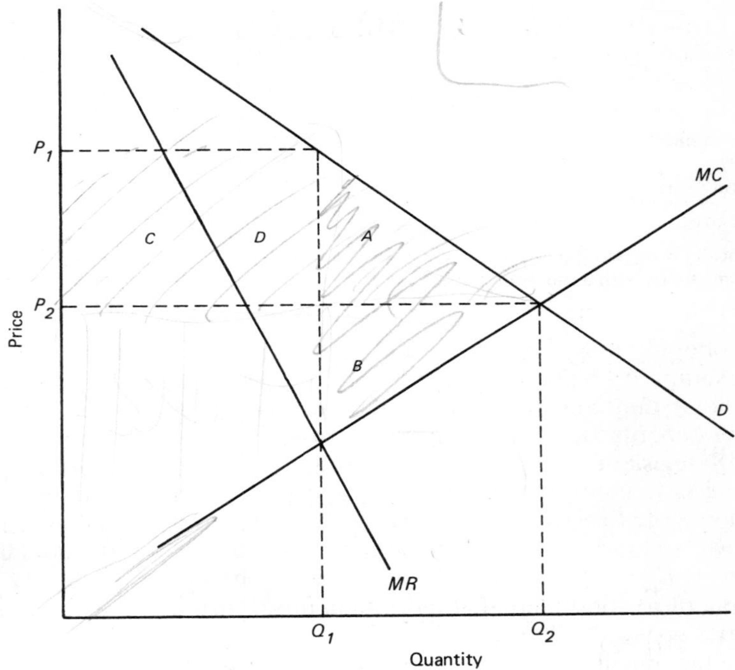

Figure 8.2 The social cost of monopoly

cost. This can be compared with the competitive equilibrium, when price is equal to marginal cost. This is, therefore, at a price of P_2 and an output of Q_2. The existence of the monopoly, *ceteris paribus*, reduces consumers' surplus by $A + D + C$. The monopolist's profits are $(C + D - B)$ greater than under perfect competition. B is the profit that would be earned by a competitive industry on the output $(Q_2 - Q_1)$, which is forgone by the monopolist. $C + D$ is the profit that arises because price is higher on the output Q_1 than it would be under perfect competition. These can be added and the social cost of monopoly calculated $(A + B)$: the calculation is set out in *Table 8.2*. $(C + D)$ has been transferred from consumers to producers but this transfer is neither a social gain nor a social loss. $(A + B)$ is, of course, a Marshallian triangle of the sort derived in section 8.1 above.

This analysis provided the intellectual underpinning of the 1948 Monopolies Act and much subsequent UK legislation (Hattersley, 1978). The 1948 Act required the Monopolies Commission to estimate $(A + B)$ and to compare this with any benefits that a

TABLE 8.2
THE SOCIAL COST OF MONOPOLY

	Gain (+) or Loss (−)	
Consumers	$-A-C-D$	
Producers		$C+D-B$
Society	$-A$	$-B$

Society is worse off by $(A + B)$ as a result of the existence of the monopoly in comparison with a situation where $P = MC$.

monopoly might produce – e.g. higher exports or dynamic gains resulting from greater expenditure on research and development. The assumption that social welfare can be derived by adding up the benefits and costs to different groups has been present in all UK legislation on monopolies, restrictive practices and related topics. In contrast the normal US approach has been to require a monopoly to show that its activities benefit consumers rather than society at large. The relevant area for a US district court would be $(A + D + C)$ not $(A + B)$ and it would be necessary to find a benefit to consumers that more than offset this, e.g. greater after sales service facilities.

One possible benefit of a monopoly would be lower costs resulting from economies of scale or better technology. This possibility was explicitly considered in the 1965 legislation that dealt with mergers (Hattersley, 1978). It was assumed that a merger would result in lower costs and the benefits of these had to be compared with the costs imposed by a monopoly. Before presenting the formal analysis embodied in the 1965 Act, there are a number of other important points concerning this legislation. The first is that the Act implied that when the comparison of costs and benefits was to be calculated there should be no prior presumption about which would be the greater. In 1978, it was stated by the authorities that the onus of proof had been in favour of a merger. Thus a merger was held to be desirable unless it could be proved otherwise (Hattersley, 1978). Indeed the consultative document suggested that it might be desirable to change to the arrangement which most observers had originally thought to be in the 1965 Act. The consultative document also provided information about the 'Mergers panel', a group of civil servants in the Department of Trade[2]. In effect this panel, rather than the Monopolies and Mergers Commission, was responsible for deciding which mergers should go ahead. Over the period 1965–1977, some 1900 mergers fell within the terms of the Act (Hattersley, 1978). All were initially considered by the panel. In all but 43 cases it gave its approval so the merger was not referred to the Commission. In the 43 remaining cases the merger rarely went ahead irrespective of the Commission's views. A referral to the Commission involved a six-month delay which led many ardent suitors to change their minds about the desirability of a merger. Thus, in effect, the panel decided virtually all merger cases.

The formal analysis of a merger is shown in *Figure 8.3*. For simplicity, the merger illustrated is that of all the firms in an

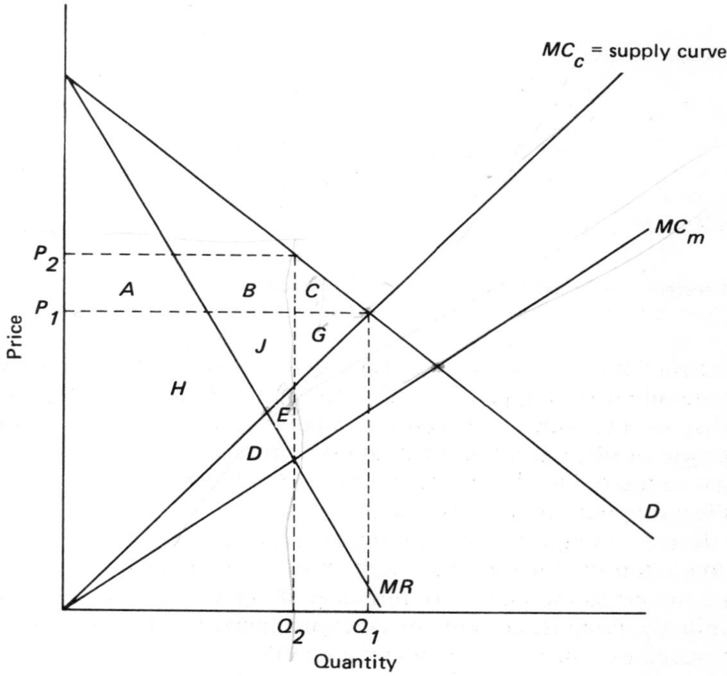

Figure 8.3 The desirability of a merger

industry. The merger lowers costs, represented by a rightward shift of the marginal cost curve from its competitive level (MC_c) where it is the supply curve, to MC_m. Society will lose because of the creation of a monopoly but will gain because of lower costs. It is necessary to balance these two to decide if a merger is in the public interest. Price rises from P_1 to P_2, and consumers thereby are worse off by $(A + B + C)$, their loss of consumers' surplus – *Table 8.3* shows the calculation. The combined profits of the industry would be $H + J + G$ before the merger, i.e. total revenue less total cost, the area under the marginal cost curve. The profits of the new firm should be $A + B + D + E + H + J$. Thus profits will rise by $(A + B + D + E - G)$. Society's gain can be calculated by adding the change in consumers' surplus to the change in

TABLE 8.3
THE DESIRABILITY OF A MERGER

			Gain (+),	Loss (−)
Consumers			$-A - B - C$	
Producers	Profits pre-merger	$G + H + J$		
	post-merger	$A + B + D + E + H + J$		
	Increase	$A + B + D + E - G$	$A + B$	$+ D + E - G$
Society			$- C + D + E - G$	
		i.e. $(D + E) -$		$(G + C)$

A merger is in the public interest if $(D + E)$ exceeds $(G + C)$

profits. This is $(D + E) - (G + C)$. In other words the merger will be justified so long as $(D + E)$ exceeds $(G + C)$. A final ironic twist to the issue is that the available evidence suggests that mergers lead to a *fall* in profitability[3]. In other words, it appears that mergers shift the marginal cost curve leftwards by enough to offset any extra monopoly profit.

If the assumption that all market agents are price takers is violated on the buyers' side then there is a monopsony, i.e. when the buyer has the power to influence the price paid. In this case, while the monopsonist equates marginal benefit with marginal cost of purchase, just as the price taker did, the marginal cost of purchase is now in excess of the price (which is, in fact, the average cost of purchase). Hence even if the price is equal to the marginal cost of the supplier, it is no longer equal to the marginal benefit to the consumer. This is illustrated in *Figure 8.4*. One can calculate the social cost of monopsony, which is the Marshallian triangle $(A + B)$. The detailed calculation is shown in *Table 8.4*.

The major examples of monopsonies are in the labour market. The government has major influence in many markets but does not use this in a monopsonistic fashion (Harley and Tisdell, 1981),

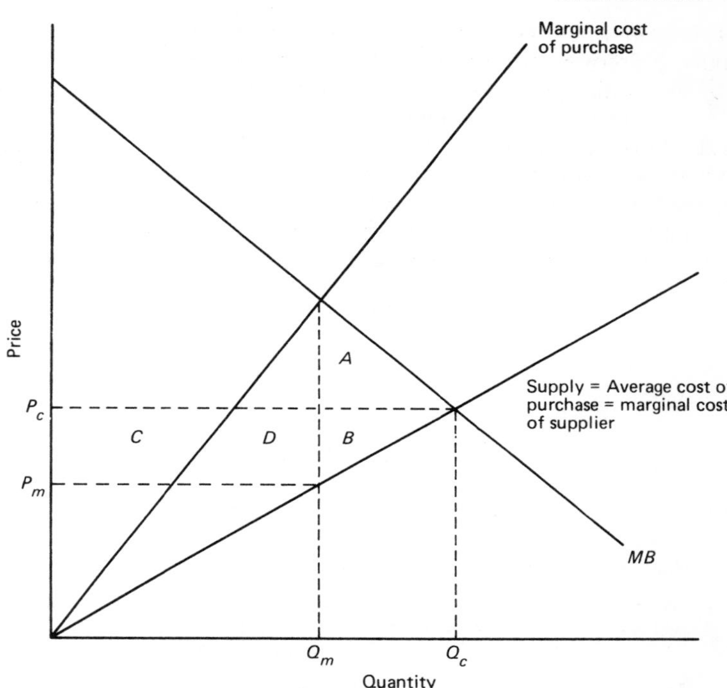

Figure 8.4 Social cost of monopsony

TABLE 8.4
THE SOCIAL COST OF MONOPSONY

Competitive equilibrium	$P_c Q_c$	
Monopsonistic equilibrium	$P_m Q_m$	
	Gain (+),	Loss (−)
Change in consumers' surplus	$+C+D$	$-A$
Loss of producers' surplus	$-C-D$	$-B$
Society		$-A-B$

Social cost of monopsony is $(A + B)$.

except perhaps in the labour market – for example, for doctors and nurses where incomes are disproportionately lower in comparison with foreign, market systems. In a few cases, some shops have monopsony power, e.g. Marks and Spencer in certain areas of retailing. In labour markets, one of the major results that is derived using monopsony analysis concerns minimum wage legislation.

If labour markets are competitive, then a minimum wage will reduce employment and increase unemployment[4]. If labour markets are monopsonistic, then a minimum wage can increase employment as well as wages even if it is above the competitive level. This case is illustrated in *Figure 8.5*. The monopsonist employs E_m workers at a wage of W_m. A minimum wage is then imposed at a level above the competitive wage W_c. This changes the marginal cost curve facing the employer. Whenever employment is less than E_s, all workers are paid the minimum wage.

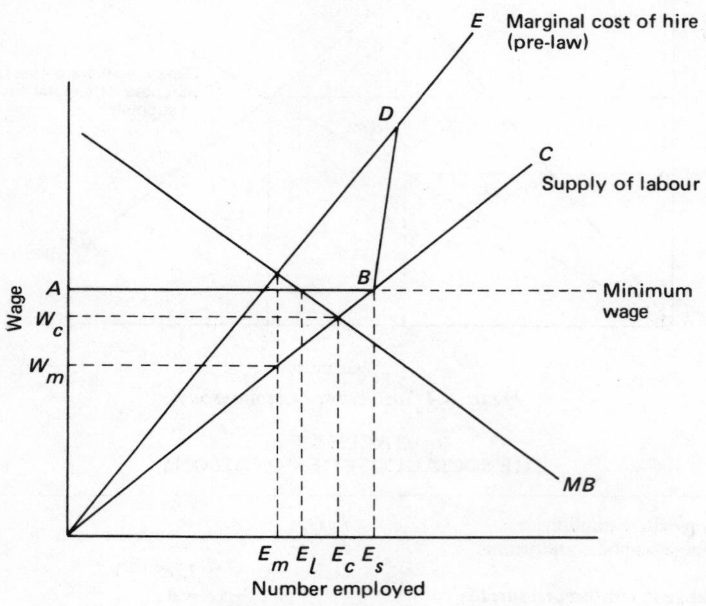

Figure 8.5 A minimum wage law increases employment

Thus, up to this point marginal cost of hire is equal to average cost of hire and both are equal to the minimum wage (marginal and average are equal as there is no need to pay extra to existing workers when an extra workers is hired). Beyond E_s, the old supply conditions prevail. Consequently the monopsonist now faces a supply curve *ABC* and a marginal cost curve *ABDE*. The intersection of marginal cost and marginal benefit is at E_l so employment is E_l and the wage the government-imposed minimum. Thus the imposition of a minimum wage has increased both employment and wages. To complete the paradox, output will

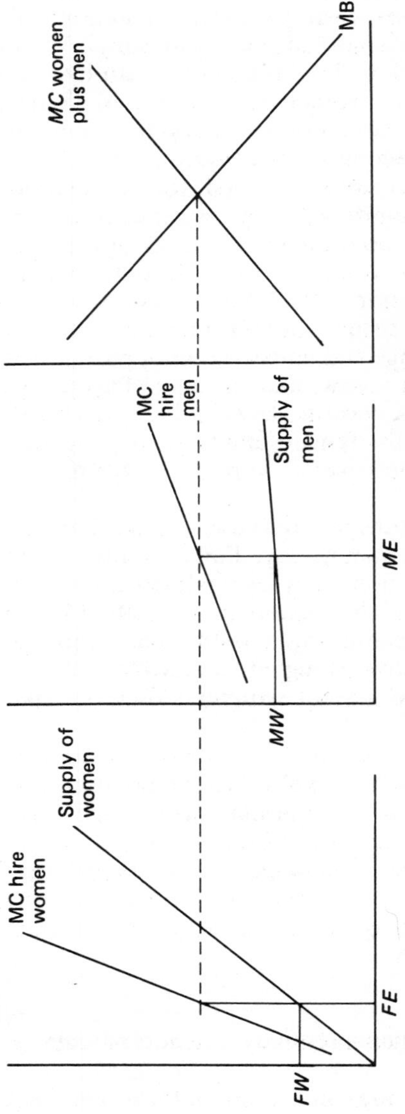

Figure 8.6 Profitable sex discrimination

probably be higher because of the extra workers, so prices will probably be lower! The paradox arises because the natural tendency of a minimum wage law to reduced employment is more than offset by the breaking of the monopsony. Any anti-monopoly or monopsony action should increase quantity. Thus there are two offsetting effects. Sometimes the one is greater, sometimes the other. Thus in monopsonistic markets a minimum wage can raise employment although it need not.

This analysis can be extended, for example, to a price discriminating monopsonist who can increase profit by paying workers different wages according to race, sex or religion (see *Figure 8.6*). Such analysis may be relevant to South Africa or the southern United States prior to the Civil Rights Revolution of the 1950s and 1960s. In this case anti-discrimination legislation may increase both the earnings and employment opportunities of the disadvantaged group. It seems that the Equal Pay Act may have had this effect in the UK because between 1971 and 1975 – the period of its implementation – female employment rose while male employment fell and the level of women's wages rose by 20% relative to male wages.

There are other extensions of market failure analysis to monopoly and monopsony. For example, a price discriminating monopolist's actions may be analysed by calculating the relevant areas. It is found that society may be either better off or worse off with a discriminating monopolist than a non-discriminating one but because output is higher society is normally better off. Other non-competitive market structures may be analysed in a similar fashion.

A particularly interesting market structure is bilateral monopoly. In this case a monopolist faces a monopsonist. This is the basis of most analyses of labour markets (see Chapter 6 above). In this case traditional economic analysis does not get very far. It merely established a minimum wage (the company level) and a maximum (the monopoly level) between which the actual wage will be. Hence, bargaining theory is necessary in order to analyse the problem further.

8.3.2 Natural monopoly and economies of scale

Economies of scale can produce a form of market failure which in its extreme form is called a natural monopoly (Scitovsky, 1952). The problem arises whenever there is a downward sloping marginal cost curve, as in *Figure 8.7*. This can occur either because of indivisibilities or for technological reasons. Examples include village shops, railways, the electricity national grid and parts of the gas supply industry.

If the marginal cost curve slopes downwards, and if price is equal to marginal cost, then the industry must make a loss. This is illustrated in *Figure 8.7*. Whatever price, P_1 chosen, so long as it is equal to marginal cost, there will be a loss represented by area A;

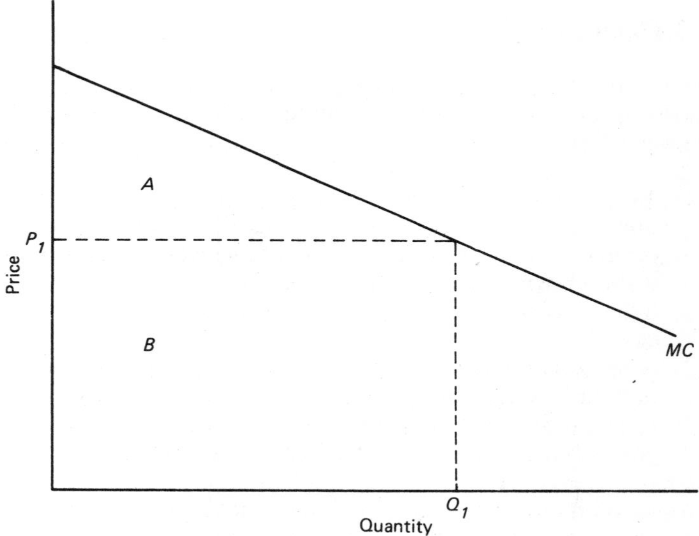

Figure 8.7 A natural monopoly

total revenue will be equal to B and total cost to area $A + B$. No firm will produce at a loss so there is no way in which the market system will produce the equilibrium output, i.e. where price = marginal cost = marginal benefit. State intervention might ensure this by means of a subsidy equal to A, but all subsidies raise problems of equity and efficiency (this is discussed below – see p. 196). Sometimes, two-part tariffs are used as devices to try to solve the problem. These aim to impose a flat-rate charge on customers unrelated to the use they make of the service and a second element where marginal cost is charged for the quantity concerned. British Gas and British Telecom both use such devices with the 'standing charge' and 'telephone rental'. The hope is that in this way the industry can cover costs and yet efficiency be achieved by marginal cost pricing. There are a number of practical problems with such devices but, in addition, there is a major theoretical problem. The standing charge may deter some consumers from purchasing the good at all. In this case, the effective price is not marginal cost. Thus efficiency has not been achieved. The theoretical condition is not merely that marginal cost is equal to marginal benefit but also that total benefit exceeds total cost. If there is a standing charge then the second condition may not be met even if the first is.

8.3.3 Public goods

One of the most analysed forms of market failure is that it is impossible to have a market in a 'public good' (Boadway, 1979). A public good has two characteristics, at least in its pure form:

(1) *Non-rivalry*. This means that consumption by one individual does not reduce the amount available for consumption by others. This is true of street lighting, where if one person walks down a lit street his behaviour does not reduce the light available to others, but is not true of, say, a cup of coffee.
(2) *Non-excludability*. This means that if a good is provided for one individual, there is no way in which others can be prevented from consuming it as well. this is not true of most goods but it is true of, for example, street lighting.

Besides street lighting, examples of public goods include, defence and lighthouses. Others may be public goods for a limited group. Thus the distribution of a tourist brochure describing York is a public good for all the hoteliers in York. The problem with a market for public goods is that everyone will rely on his neighbours to provide the good, the free-riding problem. No one has an incentive to build or pay for a lighthouse to guide his ships since otherwise his competitors may build or pay for one instead and he would receive the same benefit for nothing. Thus coercion may be necessary to ensure that all beneficiaries pay.

8.3.4 Merit goods

Musgrave argued that market forces would lead to underprovision of 'merit goods' just as they do of public goods (Musgrave and Musgrave, 1976). He defined merit goods as those which society feels benefit the individual by more than the individual's own valuation, in other words they are good for him. He cited education and health as examples. Some liberal economists have denied the existence of merit goods, either on individualist principle or by claiming that the extra benefit arises because the individual is badly informed, or because others benefit from his actions, i.e. there is an externality of the type discussed in section 8.3.7. Certainly the concept of a merit good is a paternalistic one and the validity of the concept is a controversial issue in political theory[5]. The major problem with the concept in practice is that anything could be a merit good. Its major virtue is that those relying on it as a defence for state action are forced to be very honest about why they support, say, a subsidy for the Royal Opera House. The concept thus is of value in making explicit an implicit argument often used to justify state intervention. Once the proposition has been made explicit it can be debated.

8.3.5 Transaction costs

One of the assumptions necessary to show the optimality of market allocation is zero transaction costs. This is, at best, an oversimplification. Market failure arises when the transaction costs in a market exceed the benefits, that is the increase in efficiency plus the costs of non-market allocation is less than transaction costs in a market. In this case some form of non-market allocation is to be preferred. The most common form of non-market allocation is queueing, the other principal form is rationing. The queue is certainly cheap for the sellers and may be beneficial to consumers as well. In some cases the idea of a market seems absurd even though it would be possible. For example, queueing at a supermarket cash desk is inefficient; those who value time most should be able to buy a quick exit from those who value time less. Alternatively the management could provide special tills where a quick throughput time is guaranteed in exchange for a surcharge. The reason that such schemes are not introduced is that the cost far exceeds the benefit.

8.3.6 Information

Another assumption implicit in the case for markets is that consumers and producers are the best judges of their own welfare. In fact, consumers equate *perceived* marginal benefit with price. If they lack information, perceived marginal benefit may not equal actual marginal benefit so misallocation would result. A full-blooded market liberal would argue that information should be made available and that the problem would then disappear. However, in many cases the cost of providing the extra information would exceed the benefit from it, and an administrative solution is simpler. For example, it is preferable to ban the sale of salmon containing mercury rather than have one tin labelled 10% risk of death, another 5% and so on. The liberal would also argue that information is another good and its provision should be left to the market, which will provide the optimal quantity. There is some evidence of a market in information, notably the existence of *Which*, the sale of railway timetables and *Radio Times* and arguably the growth of such magazines as *What Hi Fi?* However, virtually all observers would agree that there is some market failure in the information market.

A peculiar form of market failure, caused by lack of information, arises if price is treated as an indicator of quality. This habit seems to be widespread and is even rational in some circumstances (Deaton and Muellbauer, 1980). This may not merely mean that misallocation occurs but may even prevent any transactions taking place at all. This, it was claimed, means that there cannot be a market in good second-hand cars, sometimes called Akerlof's lemon after the economist who analysed it and the American term for a bad second-hand car (Akerlof, 1970). The essence of the argument is that if *X* asks £1500 for a car the potential buyer *Y* will think it's worth only £1200. If *X* reduces the price to £1200, this action will make *Y* think the car is worth only £1000 and so on. It might be argued that this is more relevant to explaining the non-existence of second-hand markets in good consumer durables and modern furniture than to cars, at least in the UK.

8.3.7 Uncertainty

Another assumption which is necessary to prove the optimality of market allocation is either perfect certainty or risk-neutrality. It is perhaps useful to distinguish between perfect information and perfect certainty, even though usage is not consistent. Information relates to all presently-available knowledge. Uncertainty is concerned with the future consequences of present decisions. A perfectly informed agent would have all the relevant knowledge presently available including the best estimate of the future consequences of his decisions. He need not be certain of them. For example, an individual selecting a holiday resort would be interested in the weather. He would be perfectly informed but uncertain if he knew that on each day there was a 70% chance of sun and a 30% chance of rain. There are arguments about the meaning of probability and about whether subjective probability can be used, i.e. whether an individual's beliefs about the future can be expressed in mathematical form. However, these fascinating arguments are irrelevant to the present problem. Perfect certainty clearly does not prevail so it is necessary to examine the consequences of uncertainty. In particular, the effect on investment needs to be considered. It is argued that the maximization of social gain requires investors to operate on the basis of expected return. Imagine a very risky project. There is a 50% chance of losing £1 m and a 50% chance of making £2 m. Thus the expected return is £1 m. This can be compared with one that offers a safe return of £100 000 on the same investment. Society should prefer the first since it is large enough to 'pool risks' and gain on the swings what it loses on the roundabouts. On the other hand an individual or firm might very well prefer the second because he might be risk-averse and prefer greater certainty to a higher expected return. If investors are risk-neutral, this problem does not arise. This argument was very popular in the 1950s and 1960s and was used to justify many state investments. However

(1) Some projects are so large that society might legitimately be risk-averse.
(2) Many companies are so large that any risk-pooling is done within the company's investment programme.
(3) Virtually all projects justified on these grounds have been disasters, of which Concorde and the Advanced Gas Reactor are the two best-known examples.

Finally uncertainty may mean that some markets do not exist. This is relevant to the work of Arrow and Debreu who argued that all markets have to exist if the market system is to be optimal[6]. This includes a complete set of future or contingent markets. For example, a farmer buying a farm should be able to sell his 1997 wheat crop in 1981 and insure against a drought in 1996. This rather abtruse and arcane literature highlights two relevant points:

(1) That forward markets are often crucial to the case for the free market system, as in the floating rate debate[7].
(2) That the absence of a futures market in labour may matter. In particular it is crucial to the 'reappraisal of Keynes' debate about why unemployment exists[8].

8.3.8 Measurement problems and moral hazard

One growth area in economic theory in the late 1970s was the implicit contract literature. This started by noting the large element of goodwill, unstated terms and general imprecision of contracts, especially wage contracts. It is rare to find a wage contract in which payment is directly related to output and employers seem anxious to move away from those that remain – for example, BL's desperate struggle to replace piece-work by the measured day-work system. Some reasons for this are related to transactions costs, uncertainty and lack of information. Some relate to the impossibility of measuring an individual's output as distinct from that of his colleagues jointly. However a crucial problem is that called 'moral hazard' – the way a contract is drawn up may affect behaviour. There is a possibly apocryphal Soviet story concerning a factory that made nails which illustrates this. Originally the target for output (and bonus payments) were in terms of the weight of nails, so only 6″ nails were made. Then it was changed to number of nails so the factory started to produce only panel pins. Finally the factory was given a target in terms of the value of nails – so it made gold nails. A similar problem arose in Chicago when teachers were paid according to their pupils' improvement in performance on standardized tests. In this case some teachers taught students only how to read (or even recite) the prescribed text.

Moral hazard may arise in other contexts, for example, having insurance may make individuals careless (the rationale for no-claims bonuses). The 'market failure' arises because all goods and services cannot be defined sufficiently specifically. Moreover contracts cannot be so tightly drawn up as to avoid problems. The solution may be provided by private action or by state intervention.

8.3.9 Disequilibrium

A frequently ignored assumption in the case for market forces is that all markets are in equilibrium, that is that they clear by the price mechanism. If this does not occur output will not be at the optimal level. Instead it will be, at best, at the higher of the quantity demanded and the quantity supplied at the prevailing price. Thus the range of possible price/quantity outcomes is traced by *ABC* on *Figure 8.8*. Not all possible transactions may occur because some buyers may not be aware of the existence of some

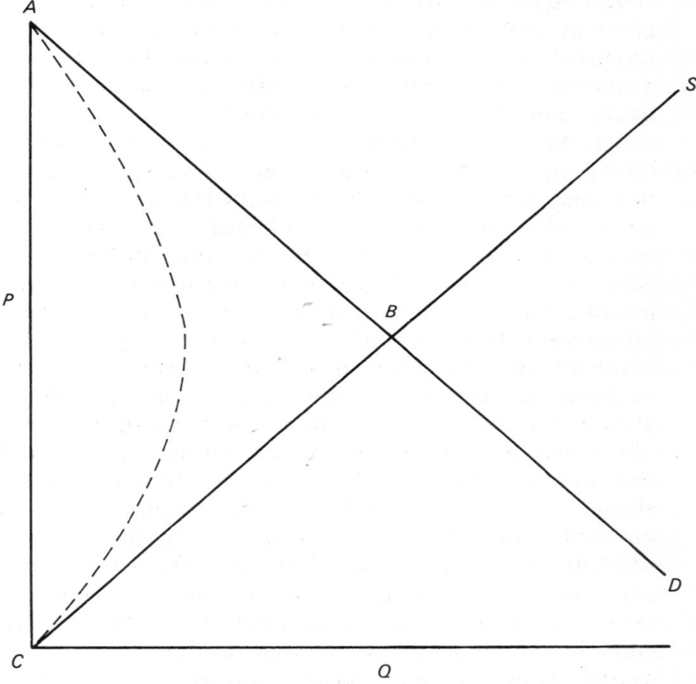

Figure 8.8 Disequilibrium

sellers and vice versa. In this case transactions will occur on the dotted line. In either case the welfare loss, the Marshallian triangle, can be calculated easily.

8.3.10 Distribution of income

The weakest element of the case for a totally free market economy concerns the distribution of income and externalities, which are discussed in this and the next sub-section. The market may secure efficiency but it is unlikely to ensure equity. It has been argued that inequality is itself a form of inefficiency or market failure because there is an economic case for redistribution, the diminishing marginal utility of income argument. This is not the place to discuss inequality save to say that the argument does not convince the author. There are moreover a number of other relevant considerations which do much to dilute the practical force of the criticism, that market allocation produces inequality.

(1) It may be possible to select the most equitable from amongst efficient market-determined outcomes, or from slightly modified market outcomes. In theory this should be achieved by either 'lump sum' taxation or a redistribution of factor endowments. Lump sum taxation is defined as taxes which have no substitution effects, for example, between labour and leisure or consumption and saving, even though they may have income effects. No practicable tax satisfies this criterion although some economists have toyed with the idea of an IQ tax or some other inherent attribute. Friedman at one time thought that inheritance taxes might increase equality without sacrificing efficiency through disincentives (Friedman, 1962). He later accepted the counter-argument that the desire to transmit wealth is a powerful incentive in Western society. Samuelson suggested the allocation of petrol ration coupons to old age pensioners (or other, preferably non-motoring poor) during the 1973 petrol shortage. If a market in the coupons could be developed cheaply, the price mechanism would operate to allocate petrol but redistribution would occur. The major problem with this argument is transaction costs. Transfers of factor endowments are equally as impracticable as lump sum taxes. However, at a less abstract level selection from amongst the efficient is sometimes possible.

(2) Market failure analysis makes it possible to calculate the costs of governmental redistributive policies. The cost of redistribution is then made explicit. Moreover, the costs of alternative methods can be assessed.

(3) It is rarely clear what is the precise objective of redistribution. Is it to reduce horizontal inequality, to reduce vertical inequality or to remedy some less precise but more powerful source of injustice? Inequality itself is a rather vague concept. Once the objective is defined, e.g. to eliminate poverty, it may be possible to achieve it at low cost in terms of efficiency and by little interference with market forces.

8.3.11 Externalities

The market system may ensure maximum benefit for producer and consumer but no account is taken of the impact on third parties. This impact is called an externality (Burrows, 1979). The analysis is sometimes called the analysis of social cost. Social cost is private cost plus external cost. Externalities include all forms of pollution and, in particular, lorry and aircraft noise. However, there are also external benefits conferred by some activities, for example by gardens and farms. The basic argument is that the market produces too much of goods with external costs (negative externalities) and too little of those with external benefits (positive externalities).

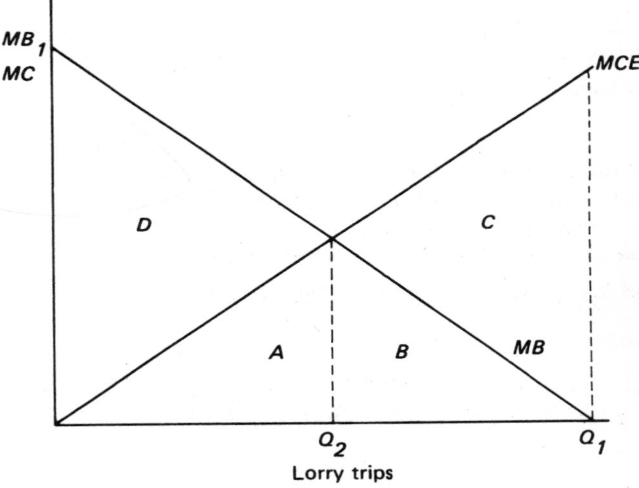

Figure 8.9 Externalities

The analysis is illustrated in *Figure 8.9*. The form of externality is the amount of noise produced by lorries. Thus the horizontal axis measures the number of lorry trips. Hauliers and their customers operating in a price takers' market will settle on an output of Q_1 trips. This is where the benefit to them is maximized, i.e. where their joint marginal benefit is zero. (In equilibrium the hauliers' net benefit, $MR - MC$, and the consumers', marginal benefit – marginal cost of purchase, are both equal to zero.) This marginal benefit curve is shown (MB), and is the sum of the consumers' and the producers' surpluses. The area under this curve gives net private benefit of the haulage industry, D + A + B. However no account is taken of the costs in terms of annoyance, disruption and so on inflicted on everyone else (possibly on only one person). This is converted to a monetary measure and shown as MCE, the marginal cost to everyone else. The total damage is $(A + B + C)$. Thus society is better off as a result of

TABLE 8.5
SOCIAL AND PRIVATE COST

At output Q_1	
Private Benefit (+) and Cost (−)	$A + B + D$
External Benefit (+) and Cost (−)	$-A \quad B \quad -C$
Social Gain	$(D - C)$
At output Q_2	
Private Benefit (+) and Cost (−)	$A + D$
External Benefit (+) and Cost (−)	$-A$
Social Gain	D

road haulage by $(D - C)$, which might be negative or positive: the calculation is set out in *Table 8.5*. Thus it is not clear whether society would be better off with Q_1 lorry trips or none. However there is an output preferable to both. This is where

Marginal Social Benefit = Marginal Social Cost;

i.e. where

Marginal Private Benefit + Marginal External Benefit = Marginal Private Cost + Marginal External Cost,

or

Marginal Private Benefit − Marginal Private Cost = Marginal External Cost − Marginal External Benefit.

In this case this is where $MB = MCE$, i.e. at Q_2 trips. At Q_2, private gain is $(A + D)$ and external cost (A) so social gain is D. It is easy to show that this is the maximum attainable. The crucial conclusions are

(1) That no pollution is rarely optimal – Q_2 is preferable to zero output and pollution.
(2) Market output is too high in the presence of pollution or other negative externalities.

The problem that has to be faced is how can an output of Q_2 be achieved? There are three possible solutions.

(1) Property rights

It is argued that the problem arises because of the non-existence of property rights, e.g. no one has a right to clean air in the way he has a property right against trespassers. It is argued, further, that if all property rights were allocated then no problem would arise. Thus if the airlines and/or the BAA had to compensate the residents of Middlesex for noise-pollution, flights at Heathrow would be at the optimal level. Three problems arise with this analysis:

(*a*) It would be impracticable – how can a property right to see the North Yorkshire Moors be established?

(*b*) When it would not be impracticable it would be very costly and there are enormous opportunities for exercising market power, for example, by mis-stating preferences.

(*c*) There are the ethical problems raised by Coase's theorem (Coase, 1960). Coase demonstrated that it did not matter how property rights were allocated; output would be the same, 'only' distribution would be altered. So in *Figure 8.9* whether the affected parties paid the hauliers not to make $(Q_2 - Q_1)$ trips or the hauliers paid the sufferers for the right to make Q_1 trips, the output would be the same Q_1. However, distribution does seem to most people to matter here. In fact, paying airlines not to fly over one's own house would strike most people as blackmail.

(2) 'Internalize externalities'

The argument is that taxes and subsidies should be imposed to equate marginal social with marginal private cost and benefit. Thus in *Figure 8.9*, a tax equal to *MCE* at Q_2 on each lorry trip would shift the *MB* curve downwards so that maximum private benefit was at the socially optimal output of Q_2.

(3) Regulation

The state could intervene to restrict the number of lorry trips (or compel the use of more – private – expensive routes with lower external costs).

The choice between (2) and (3) has been widely covered but should be looked at as a problem of minimizing private and public administrative costs rather than of high principle. The problem of how to resolve such problems is discussed further in the next section.

8.4 STATE INTERVENTION: OR THE ANATOMY OF COLLECTIVE FAILURE?[8]

The existence of market failure creates a *prima facie* case for state intervention. The potential social gain can then be calculated and compared with the direct and indirect costs of state intervention to determine whether or not it is desirable. State intervention can take different forms and each is appropriate in different circumstances. The three major forms are

(1) Subsidy and taxation
(2) Regulation
(3) State provision[9].

A brief discussion of the advantages and disadvantages of each follows. State provision is probably the most obvious form of intervention. This may be introduced where no private provision existed (street lighting), to supplement private provision (e.g. HMSO), to replace it (e.g. fire and police) or by taking-over, e.g. by nationalization of existing private agencies. Private provision can be forbidden, permitted or encouraged alongside state provision. Mail delivery, health and education and book publication provide examples of each of these cases. The problems of state provision are analysed in the economics of politics models of bureaucracy. The basic problems are that the agencies have an incentive to empire build and may have insufficient incentive to ensure efficient production. To achieve either or both of these they may conceal information or collude with outside bodies to pursue mutually advantageous policies against the public interest. That much-maligned body, the US Post Office, used to be a state agency and, it was alleged, colluded with its workers (the Postal Workers' Union) and its clients (the magazine publishers) to use political influence to ensure an overly large, inefficient postal service. Some observers have similar views about local authorities and public sector unions in the UK.

The dangers (or costs?) of a political market replacing an economic one are also present with subsidies. Subsidized industries have an incentive to overstate both costs and benefits to maximize subsidies, and to change behaviour to maximize political power. The other problem with subsidies is that they need to be financed. The tax necessary to finance a subsidy, or state provision if this is not self-financing, can impose more distortions than it removes. Externality taxes are every finance minister's dream and provide an extra justification for taxing alcohol and cigarettes.

Their precise, scientific use to equate social and private tax is probably impractical.

Regulation is superficially the most attractive method of intervention as its costs may be hidden from public view. However, many forms of regulation are very costly to consumers – e.g. the CAP's restrictions on food imports. It has been argued that regulation almost always works in the interest of the regulated[10]. The argument is that the regulated gain control of the regulatory machinery and use it for their own ends, for instance to create unnecessary barriers to entry.

Undoubtedly state intervention is necessary in some cases, but it is neither costless nor perfect. Its costs and benefits need to be assessed carefully.

8.5 CONCLUSION

The appropriate role for state intervention is probably the most contentious issue in politics in Western societies. Some of the arguments concern macroeconomic intervention, discussed elsewhere in this book. However the issue of the state vs. the market is a critical issue dividing left and right. It is thus vital to see how much light economic analysis can throw on the issue. The first section of this chapter stated the orthodox case for the market as the means to maximize social welfare. It is not clear how important this static-resource allocation argument is. Some authors have estimated it to be small, others large. There are other, possibly more important arguments in favour of market forces. One is a dynamic one, that the market is likely to produce a greater amount of innovation – this was Schumpeter's argument in his classic work (1943). The market system makes decentralization possible and avoids some of the problems inherent in planning. Perhaps the strongest case for the market is the appalling record that state intervention has. Such 'obviously right' actions as the one in 1973 increasing the capacity to produce oil rigs, have proved mistaken. If the state makes a mistake, then it is likely to be a large one – Concorde, for example. The market system probably produces fewer disasters, even if many small ones. Even the Ford Edsel pales by comparison with many official mistakes.

The analytical framework provided by the concept of market failure is useful in structuring the issue of when state intervention is desirable. It both forces a vigorous statement of the case for state intervention and makes it possible to calculate its potential benefits. However, it does not make it possible to say definitely when state intervention is desirable. Nevertheless, it does seem that the market in 'human capital' is far more prone to failure than others. Thus efficiency considerations overwhelmingly reinforce the powerful equity case for state provision of health and education (see Chapters 9 and 11).

Guide to further reading

Specific
Monopolies etc. The official publication, Hattersley (1978) is superb. The annexes summarize virtually all the worthwhile academic work on the subject.
Natural monopoly and economies of scale Hattersley (1978) and Webb (1979)
Public goods, merit goods Boadway (1979)
Information, uncertainty and moral hazard Hey (1980)
Externalities Burrows (1979)
General
Hartley and Tisdell (1981)

Notes

1 See Sugden (1981), Sugden (1980) and Rowley and Peacock (1975) for this argument.
2 See also Trade (1969)
3 For a summary of this literature see Hattersley (1978), Annex D.
4 See Maynard in Gowland (1979), Chapter 12.
5 See Wikler (1980) for a discussion of the problem.
6 See p. 64 above.
7 See Gowland (1979), Ch 2.
8 Title borrowed from Peacock's stimulating (1980).
9 Usually nationalization, see Webb in Gowland (1979), Chapter 10.
10 See the discussion in Hartley and Tisdell (1981).

Bibliography

AKERLOF, G. A. (1970), 'The Market for Lemons', *Quarterly Journal of Economics*, Vol. 84, No. 3 (August), pp. 488–500
BOADWAY, R. W. (1979), *Public Sector Economics*, Winthrop; Cambridge, Mass.

BURROWS, P. (1979), *The Economic Theory of Pollution Control*, Martin Robertson; London

COASE, R. H. (1960), 'The Problem of Social Cost', *Journal of Law and Economics*, Vol. 3 (October)

DEATON, A. S. and MUELLBAUER, J. (1980), *Economics and Consumer Behaviour*, Cambridge University Press; Cambridge

FRIEDMAN, M. (1962), *Capitalism and Freedom*, University of Chicago Press; Chicago

GOWLAND, D. H. (ed.) (1979), *Modern Economic Analysis*, Butterworths; London

HARTLEY, K. and TISDELL, C. (1981), *Microeconomic Policy*, John Wiley; London

HATTERSLEY, R. (1978), *A Review of Monopolies and Mergers Policy*, Cmnd 7198, HMSO; London

HEY, J. D. (1979). *Uncertainty in Microeconomics,* Martin Robertson; London

LEFRERE, P. (eds.), *Risk and Chance*, Open University; Milton Keynes

MUSGRAVE, R. A. and MUSGRAVE, P. B. (1976), *Public Finance in Theory and Practice,* McGraw-Hill; New York

PEACOCK, A. T. (1980), 'On the Anatomy of Collective Failure', *Public Finance* (Festschrift Paul Senf) pp. 34–43

PETERS, W. (eds.), *Contemporary Economic Analysis* (Vol. 1), Croom Helm; London

ROBBINS, L. (1931), *The Nature and Significance of Economic Science*, Macmillan; London

ROWLEY, C. K. and PEACOCK, A. T. (1975), *Welfare Economics: A Liberal Restatement*, Martin Robertson; London

SCITOVSKY, T. (1952), *Welfare and Competition*, Unwin University Books; London

SCHUMPETER, J. A. (1943), *Capitalism, Socialism and Democracy*, Allen & Unwin; London

SUGDEN, R. (1980), 'Individualism and Liberalism', in CURRIE, D. A. and

SUGDEN, R. (1981), *Welfare Economics*, Martin Robertson; London

TRADE (BOARD OF) (1969), *Mergers*, HMSO; London

WIKLER, D. (1980), 'Persuasion and Coercion for Health', in DOWIE, J. and

9
The Economics of Health

Alan Williams

Health economics emerged in the 1970s as a distinct field of study. Its roots were in the 'new' welfare economics, human capital theory, and the economic behaviour of non profit-seeking organizations. It is concerned not only with the specific economics of medical care, but also with the economics of all activities that affect health (e.g. investment in safety at home, work and on the roads, smoking, alcohol abuse, poverty, housing, education, environmental pollution, and so on). In this short survey I shall attempt to convey something of this work, in a necessarily selective manner, to show how relatively simple economic concepts can offer some insight into resource allocation problems faced both by private individuals and by public organizations in the health field.

9.1 THE DEMAND FOR HEALTH

If we start with the individual, 'health' is a desirable 'good', the supply of which, at the margin, can be increased or decreased by the population's behaviour both as workers and as consumers. It is helpful to view health as a capital good, offering a flow of services (in the form of healthy time) which we can then 'use' in a variety of ways. We could use it for paid work, and thereby convert it into income. Alternatively, we may use it for unremunerated work, such as housewife's services, 'household production'. Then again we could use it for leisure activities, which may be quite active and demanding of our health, like skiing, or fairly passive, like reading. We can also simply enjoy 'feeling good' at whatever we are doing. Thus 'healthiness' is a potentially very versatile 'good' which is associated with most of our activities, and which we can take for granted until we are unhealthy. This is perhaps the reason why much of the explicit thinking about the value of health has been concerned with the (dis)value of *ill*-health (or of premature death).

Some ill-health is, of course, truly 'exogenous' in the sense that it hits us 'out of the blue', but some is undoubtedly attributable to the fact that we choose to draw on our health stock quite deliberately in order to do things which we value more than the associated risk to our health. Eating, drinking or smoking too much are clear cases in point, but we may also risk our health deliberately in order to earn more money, or in order to 'get there' more quickly (i.e. to 'save time'). Thus if one adapts standard indifference curve techniques as conventionally applied to the individual's choices of consumption pattern (or of income/leisure choices), then we can add another dimension, such as the expectation of healthy life, treating it as a consumption good in itself, and allow individuals to 'trade-off' a short life, albeit a gay one, against a long but dull one, and each of us will come to some personal optimum at the margin!

Clearly, not everyone starts off with the same assets in this optimizing process. Our genetic endowment is different, we may have different levels of education, different inherited or acquired wealth, and so on, and it is obviously possible, within limits, to convert wealth into education and health, and vice versa, so that individuals have quite complex decisions to make, especially through time. For instance, a person with little wealth, poor education, but good health may 'sacrifice' some of his health to earn money and get more education, so that even if his initial genetic endowment were the same as that of a person with inherited wealth, the (chosen) health level of the former will be lower than that of the latter. Conversely, affluence may lead to very unhealthy (i.e. health demanding) consumption patterns ('over indulgence') so that the influences of wealth are not all in the same direction. An important influence here will be people's rate of time preference, reflecting the extent to which they 'live for today . . .', or are anxious to avoid dying 'tomorrow'. So healthy behaviour *now* is regarded as an 'investment' intended to generate a return in the form of additional healthy life expectation *later*. It can even be appraised explicitly in that way to the extent that people are conscious of, or can be made aware of, these optimizing decisions.

This has been one source of studies on the value of life, as implicit in individual decisions about safety etc. and buttressed by experimental evidence designed to elicit how much of their other resources people are willing to sacrifice in order to reduce the risk of death or injury. There is a set of different, but related, issues concerning the *relative* valuations placed by individuals on *different aspects* of health, e.g. length of life versus quality of life or one quality variable versus another, (such as mobility versus freedom from pain), to each of which indifference curve analysis can usefully be applied to elicit preferences at the margin, which are relevant, for instance, when someone has to decide whether it is worth having an operation which relieves pain by restricting mobility or which lengthens life but lowers its quality (e.g. through adverse side-effects from drugs). Clearly the resource costs still have to be considered too, but even at the level of pure *preference*, people may rationally choose *not* to have some recommended medical treatment because they do not see it as generating any benefit *on balance* (the cure is worse than the disease).

9.2 THE DEMAND FOR MEDICAL CARE

The demand for medical care will clearly depend also upon its cost, but now the interesting question concerns costs *to whom* and *in what terms*? The demand for medical care is not the same as the demand for health, since, as we have seen, medical care is but one of the 'inputs' into a healthy life. It is not uncommon for people to run down their health stock by adopting an unhealthy life-style, then 'demand' medical care to make good (at least some of) these depredations. Whether medical care achieves this depends upon its technical efficiency (is there a pill for every ill?) and its accessibility. Its technical efficiency I shall here take for granted, though there is no shortage of literature suggesting that much medical practice is ineffective (or even harmful). Its accessibility is a dimension more susceptible to economic analysis, and can be regarded as the price of medical care in demand studies.

Accessibility to medical care is controlled in different ways in different countries (and sometimes in a variety of ways even within one country). There are systems which rely essentially on private markets, though they are never really competitive markets, because entry into the medical profession is regulated, as is advertising and the dissemination of information generally (see the discussion of these problems in the abstract in Chapter 8). Because the treatments involved in much hospital care can be very costly the financing of 'private' care for 'catastrophic' illness is usually organized through insurance, and the insurance companies then have to enter the regulatory business as well, to protect themselves from exploitation both by patients and by practitioners. Some risks are not very profitable commercially (e.g. chronic conditions, mental illness) so the state has to move in to 'carry' the bad risks, and those who cannot afford private insurance. In addition there is the large 'self-medication' market, which is also subject to a variety of controls, concerned with drug safety, misleading advertising, restrictive practices and monopolies. Clearly there is a hornet's nest of problems here on which the economics of insurance, consumer protection and industrial policy all bear.

Accessibility may instead be controlled through comprehensive state insurance or, as in Britain, by simple 'nationalization' of the main sources of provision, with the costs met from general taxation and access (virtually) free at the time of need. But removal of prices does not remove the need for some other rationing device. On the consumers' side, the cost of obtaining medical care will now consist of time and inconvenience rather than cash, but this can be just as effective a 'deterrent', as many studies have shown which relate utilization of medical services, to people's distance from the point of service. Clawson type demand curves (see the guide to further reading) can be used to estimate the time-price elasticity of demand for such services, and, with an explicit value assigned to time, it is even possible to calculate the gain in consumer surplus due to choosing a more convenient location for a facility. Studies of patients' costs, and of accessibility more generally, have been one factor reversing an earlier trend towards the concentration of facilities on a single site so as to exploit economies of scale within the hospital. A balance needs to be struck which economic calculations can elucidate.

9.3 NEED AND THE AGENCY RELATIONSHIP

But in all medical care systems there is a rationing, or priority setting, process at work on the supply side too. In this the doctors play a dual role which has led health economists to lay great stress on their peculiar 'agency relationship', which undermines the conventionally sharp distinction between the 'demand side' and the 'supply side' in economics. Because of the technical 'mysteries' surrounding medicine, consumers have to rely on the experts to assess their 'needs' (of which more anon). But these experts are not just detached advisers working solely in the patients' interests. They are also the potential suppliers of the needed services, and it is from providing these services that they make their living. In principle the doctor merely 'advises' on the technical possibilities and their likely consequences, his own potential role in any subsequent action being irrelevant. The then well-informed patient chooses whichever course of action is in his or her best interests as he or she sees it (i.e. the assessment of benefits and costs is entirely the patient's, using information supplied by the doctor). Despite the inculcation of strong professional ethical rules attempting to make this idealized position the reality, it will be obvious that doctors are bound to have private motives which influence their behaviour too. For instance, even in systems where they are not paid a fee for each item of service, they will have an incentive to minimize the costs falling on themselves. These costs may simply be time costs, so that not wishing to spend hours on every consultation, the doctor takes a 'short-cut' and 'advises' the patient to 'take this medicine' (without going into the whys or wherefores) or to go to the hospital to have a test or to see a specialist, with the bare minimum of explanation. In a system where doctors are paid on an item-of-service basis, the inducement to modify one's advice in the light of what is (or is not) profitable obviously gives added weight to supply-side influences in what started out as a 'demand side' advisory process.

The assessment of 'need', and its relationship to 'demand', is a matter which highlights these problems. When it is said that someone 'needs' an operation, what exactly is meant? Here are some possibilities:

(1) It will do the patient good and he wants it and is willing and able to pay for it.
(2) It will do the patient good and he wants it, but he is not able to pay for it.
(3) The patient does not want it but the doctor thinks he should have it.
(4) It would probably not do the patient any good, but he nevertheless wants it and is ready to pay for it.
(5) The patient and the doctor are willing to go ahead with the operation, but 'society' forbids it.

Clearly each of these statements has a significantly different content, which needs to be analysed. If 'demand' is taken to be willingness and ability to pay by the potential consumer, then (1) is clearly such an instance, as are (4) and (5), but (2) and (3) are not. So if all five statements are really within the category of 'need', then it is clearly different from demand, but what is its essence? There are two possibilities, firstly that it is to do with capacity to benefit, and secondly that it is to do with *someone else's* (i.e. not the consumer's) judgement about the desirability of the operation in question. Under the first interpretation, the statement 'A needs X' is to be translated 'A would be better off with X than without it'. In this interpretation, it would be valid to say that I 'need' a bigger house, a better car, more foreign holidays, etc. Looking at the above statements (1) and (2) clearly qualify, and (4) does not. We do not know enough about (3) and (5) to be able to assign them one way or the other. It therefore raises the second issue, namely, whose judgements are relevant. Usually it is the 'expert' or 'society' whose views are adduced here. Thus while patients 'demand', doctors assess 'need' (i.e. the size *and value* of likely benefits). On this interpretation (3) and (5) count and possibly also (1), but we cannot assign the others. Note that in these cases the doctors may well be substituting their own valuations for those of their patients, so are not acting as perfect (demand-side) agents. And they may or may not be acting on behalf of 'society' in this process (5). They may reflect, or flaunt, wider social judgements when deciding whether a pregnant woman should or should not have an abortion, for instance.

This rather lengthy discussion of the role of the doctor in 'mediating' the demand for medical treatment is important because there is a tendency to apply ordinary demand and supply concepts rather unthinkingly in this area of social policy. For instance, if it is doctors who determine the demand for most hospital services (through the referral process) it is a bit pointless to advocate charging *patients* in order to cut out 'wasteful' or 'frivolous' use of services . . . it might be better to charge doctors! Similarly, waiting lists are taken as a measure of 'excess demand' or 'unmet need'. But since it takes at least one doctor to get a patient onto a waiting list, and doctors are influenced (to differing degrees) by supply side considerations when deciding whether to deal with a case urgently, or by waiting list, or by masterly inactivity, then clearly the size of waiting lists is determined in a complex way by doctors themselves, and is not an 'objective' measure of anything other than the outcome of their judgements. In this connection it may be noted that it is advantageous to the system (when planning the workload) to have a waiting list, so that even setting aside the above reservations, the optimum waiting list as seen by doctors is not zero! This is not to deny that there may be people on waiting lists who would be better off if treated sooner, but whether anything should be done to make that possible is not sensibly decided by reference to the *size* of waiting lists, nor even to average waiting *times*, but rather by reference to some kind of cost-benefit calculus, a matter to which we shall return below.

9.4 EFFICIENCY

The pursuit of efficiency in the provision of health care is bedevilled both by conceptual confusion and by lack of relevant information. Let me start with some typical indicators of efficiency that are widely used in hospital care. It is held to be a good thing to reduce costs per bed-day and/or costs per case. In order to reduce these one can concentrate on length of stay and turnover interval (the length of time a bed is empty between patients), both of which should be reduced, and the bed occupancy rate, which needs to be increased. So data is collected and presented on these variables in order to judge whether the system is operating efficiently or not.

Let us consider their respective meanings and interrelationships. Suppose that the day to day costs when someone (patient A) is in hospital are characteristically as shown in *Figure 9.1a*, i.e. they rise to a peak on the second day, then decline steadily until virtually the only costs still being incurred are the 'hotel' type costs. Suppose the patients stay for 7 days, and that there is a 2-day 'gap' between the discharge of patient A and the admission of patient B, who then goes through the same routine. On this basis cost per case is the area of the histogram, and cost per bed day comes in two variants: cost per *occupied* bed day, which counts only the days the bed is in use, and cost per *available* bed day, which is always lower than the former if turnover interval is positive and if vacant days are less costly than occupied days. The bed occupancy rate is simply the ratio of occupied days to available days within a given time period, which in this highly simplified example is taken to be one complete cycle (from one admission to the next).

What happens to these various indicators if we shorten length of stay by 2 days, keeping the turnover interval constant? *Figure 9.1b* shows the new situation, from which the following conclusions can be drawn: cost per case is less; but both cost per available bed day *and* cost per occupied bed day are higher; and the bed occupancy rate has declined (even though turnover interval is unchanged). *Figure 9.1c* shows what would happen if, in addition to shortening length of stay, turnover interval were also reduced. Although this leaves costs per case and cost per occupied bed day unchanged, it *increases* costs per available bed day. Further behaviour changes may be analysed at will, but the general point should already be clear, namely that these measures cannot all be good indicators of efficiency since they often move in contradictory ways. Indeed, this is hardly surprising when we have not defined what we mean by 'efficiency', but rather taken it for granted that high costs are bad, empty beds are bad, and so on.

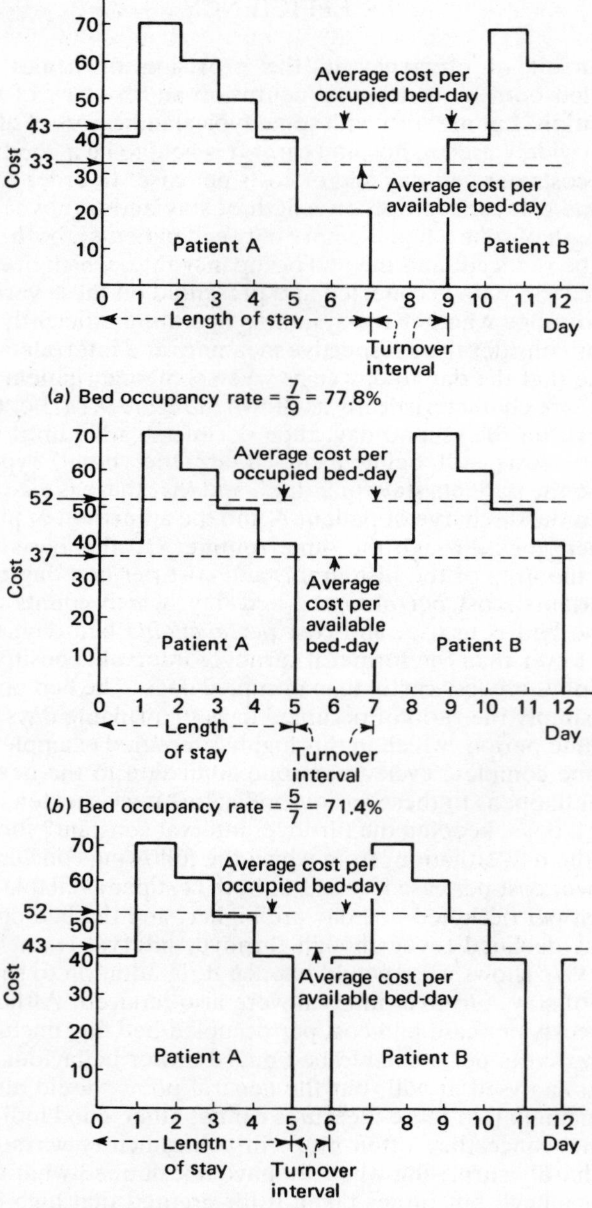

Figure 9.1 Three patterns of bed occupancy

The fundamental problem in defining efficiency is deciding what the 'product' is that a hospital provides. Is it 'available beds', 'used beds', or 'cases'? 'Cases' seems in many ways the more sensible unit, but even this is suspect in actual hospital statistics, for it is actually just an episode of inpatient treatment, not the whole 'case' (i.e. all the treatments given to a particular patient with a particular condition) so that if a case is treated with a succession of episodes of hospital treatment, each episode will be counted in the data as a separate 'case'. Moreover, an 'episode' may be terminated either by discharge or by death, and although the latter instances can be separated out, they are frequently not separately noted in the routine statistics. This highlights what is, perhaps, the most fundamental weakness of all, namely that none of the above 'units' is a measure of the gain in health resulting from expenditure on medical care, and this is presumably what we want to have if we are to discuss efficiency sensibly. To know whether the system is or is not efficient, we need to know what gain in health has been achieved at what cost, and whether there is *either* a less costly way of getting the same gain, *or* a bigger gain that one could get for the same cost.

The difficulties involved in answering these more fundamental questions should not be underestimated. They entail the definition and measurement of health (or, at any rate, those dimensions of health that are immediately relevant to the comparison in question), a clear statement and systematic analysis of the alternative courses of action and their effectiveness in influencing health, and a careful examination and estimation of the relevant costs. Even in relatively simple cases there are many pitfalls for the unwary in trying to carry out such studies.

Let us take the example of chronic renal failure, and the choice between kidney transplants and dialysis. This choice is not straightforward, because there are (at least) two different dialysis strategies, at home or in hospital. Moreover people on home dialysis will normally need episodes of hospital dialysis. Dialysis is also provided for people who are awaiting a transplant, or when a transplant fails. So we are not considering either/or alternatives, but a number of different (and complicated) *mixes* of treatment modes. In a classic American study of this problem by Klarman *et al*. (1973), it was found that the best value for money (in terms of costs per year of life gained) was from transplantation. But the authors recognized that a 'year of life' is not a homogeneous measure of health gain, so they counted 1 year gained by transplant as equivalent to 1.25 years under dialysis, to allow for the higher 'quality' of life which a successful transplant provides (average survival with a transplant is also about twice as long as average survival on dialysis). No more sophisticated measure of health gain was undertaken, and the notion of cost was restricted to service costs (though the costs of obtaining transplantable kidneys was ignored). Costs falling on households and other public services, and loss of production, were also not taken into account. A subsequent British study (by Buxton and West, 1975) filled some of the gaps on the cost side, but treated as the 'benefit' the increased production attributable to patients being more able to work. Thus the improvement in health *per se* is not valued independently of its 'market' value. But if the excess of the costs of those programmes over these (narrowly productive) benefits is taken as an estimate of what the 'humanitarian benefits' are explicitly thought to be worth, then these were running at about £2500 to £5000 per additional year of life expectancy (at 1975 prices).

Before high-level efficiency issues can satisfactorily be resolved, judgements have to be made about the value of *resource* gains compared with health gains *per se*. Productivity gains are undoubtedly relevant and in some cases they alone may justify investment in health care. But in general I think that productivity gains are best seen as offsets to the resource costs of providing the medical care, and 'netted out' accordingly, so that we can see, separately and clearly identified, the actual health gains that have been achieved, be they in years of additional life expectation, reduction of physical disability, relief of pain, or whatever. Thus we might find that a particular kind of treatment extended life by three years on average, and cost the health service £1000 to provide, against which might be set £800 of additional output through the enhanced productivity of the patient, so that the net cost to society is only £200. If the productivity gains outweigh the service costs, the treatment is a good investment anyway, and the 'health gains' come as a bonus! If health service policy is to be 'hard-headed' (as may be necessary in very poor countries where large numbers of people are suffering from malnutrition and low living standards) it may be necessary to give dominant weight to productivity gains and virtually ignore life expectancy etc. *per se* (i.e. it will count only if the person concerned is a 'worker' and then only to the extent that it generates extra output). In richer countries the reverse may hold, and a high value may be placed on the humanitarian aspects and relatively little on additional production. In these latter societies more generous provision will be made for the elderly, the handicapped, and other 'unproductive' members of the group, than in the former societies. It is a choice facing every society, which health economics can illuminate, but which the population at large has to make.

9.5 EQUITY

Economics has been criticized for being obsessively concerned with efficiency at the expense of equity, and there is undoubtedly some substance in that charge. But in the health service field economists have in fact been in the vanguard of those analysing the distribution of resources and in putting forward schemes which would generate a more 'equitable' distribution.

But before plunging into that territory we must ask ourselves what we mean by equity. It could be 'getting what you deserve', and, in the case of health care, notions of this kind undoubtedly manifest themselves from time to time in discussions about drunkenness, smoking, and the non-wearing of seat-belts. The principle seems to be that contributory (or wilful) negligence undermines one's 'entitlement' to free health care. There is little an economist (as such) can say about that principle, but we do have an analytical tool which helps to clarify thought on the subject, namely the notion of 'externalities'. If it is held that people should, wherever possible, seek to reduce the costs they impose on others (i.e. the external costs of their actions) then estimating these costs might be helpful in focusing the above discussion. For instance, do drinkers, smokers and motorists impose costs on the health system in excess of their contributions to it? This is not an easy question to answer, because the NHS is largely financed out of general taxation, and if NHS expenditure were cut, we do not know which taxes would be reduced (i.e. at the margin we do not know who is making the additional contributions generated by the need to care for drunks, smokers and motorists).

But there are other notions of equity to which economics can relate more readily. The crucial role of the valuation of people's health has already been mentioned several times, as is only right and proper, since it is the central issue. In principle, doctors are supposed to provide care for people irrespective of such personal qualities as whether they are beautiful or ugly, pleasant or unpleasant, black or white, rich or poor, well-known or anonymous. Does this imply that, say, a year of healthy life expectation should be equally valued for everybody? Does it imply that a person's 'productivity' should be ignored? Or age? Or sex? Is one year of healthy life equally valuable to a beautiful 15-year-old and a friendless 95-year-old? If not, what is the principle by which such relative valuations should be made? How are they made? (For they must be made as part of the inescapable priority setting that goes on, consciously or unconsciously, in any health service.) In most studies (such as that by Klarman, 1973) the identity of the individual receiving the extra life expectancy is ignored, and this is the common practice in most epidemiological as well as most economic studies. So we are all implicitly taking the strong egalitarian stance that a year of healthy life expectancy is of equal value to everybody . . . in other words, every 'efficiency' study contains within it a strong 'equity' principle of some kind or other, which one can readily detect by noting what is being 'added together' as the benefit measure (in this case, years of life expectancy no matter who gets them, except that post-transplant years count for more than dialysis years).

Curiously, there is a lot more discussion of 'geographical equity' in the literature, than there is of either of the above mentioned equity notions. Whole communities of people are regarded as the subjects of equity judgements as if they were individuals, so that we have rich communities and poor communities, despite the fact that the former may contain many poor people and the latter many rich people, raising the question: what is it about 'communities' that justifies making equity judgements about them over and above those that are made about the individuals within them? The answer seems to lie in the collective nature of health service provision in the NHS. Because a rich community can afford better health services than a poor community, and because the basic ethic of the NHS is an egalitarian one (e.g. that people should have equal access to health care no matter where they live), this logically leads to the replacement of local finance with national finance, and the consequent need for a system to distribute funds among areas irrespective of where the funds were raised. This can be done by following existing historical patterns of provision, by political bargaining, by objective criteria, or by some mixture of all three. In the UK since the mid 1970s there has been increasing pressure to use a distribution formula which breaks out of the historical pattern (since large inequalities in the level of provision exist among different parts of the country), and this has, predictably, led to the 'political bargaining' concentrating on the precise nature of the formula. The formula propounded by the DHSS's Resource Allocation Working Party (RAWP) was essentially based on population, weighted by age (to reflect the markedly differing demands on health services by the young, the middle age groups, and the elderly) and by differential morbidity (as measured by age-specific mortality) reflecting general conditions of living in the different regions. This has raised interesting questions about the extent to which mortality is a good measure of morbidity, whether it is really the NHS's job to make up for deficiences in housing, or for an unhealthy pattern of industrial activity, in an area, if these are the fundamental causes of their poor health record. It has also raised an associated efficiency point, in that the system appears to give perverse incentives to the NHS, in that the healthier they make people the less money they will get! It also clashes with another strongly held view that if people wish to add to local provision by voluntary effort they should be encouraged to do so. But then we are back with the 'inequity' that people in rich areas will have better health services than people in poor areas!

A further sense of inequity in all this debate has stemmed from capital provisions (mainly hospitals). For decades major hospital complexes were concentrated in the major cities, with London having a disproportionately large share. Capital allocations were distributed independently of 'current' allocations, but when a new hospital was ready to be opened, a supplementary current allocation was given under a special head called 'revenue consequence of capital schemes' (RCCS). This meant that every authority had a strong incentive to get all the capital allocation it possibly could, knowing that it would later automatically get more 'revenue' money too. Economists have argued for years that this is illogical, since authorities should be put in the position of 'servicing' capital (i.e. paying an interest charge on the debt) so that they have to think hard whether a particular investment is or is not worthwhile in terms of the *sacrifice* of subsequent revenue that may be involved. This is the normal context in which most organizations (and individuals) have to conduct investment appraisal, and its absence has been adduced as one reason why the NHS has taken relatively little interest in such techniques as discounted cash flow financial appraisal, let alone cost-benefit or cost-effectiveness analysis, in connection with major capital schemes. When the RAWP formula was introduced, RCCS was eliminated from the allocations made by the DHSS to the Regional Health Authority (though some regions still tried to sustain it between them and their constituent authorities). This led to the phenomenon of hospitals being completed (which had been planned on the assumption that RCCS funds would be available) which authorities could no longer afford to run at their full design capacity, because the sacrifices which *now* had to be made were judged too great (i.e. they would not have planned the hospital in that way had they been faced with the prospect of finding most of the running costs from their existing budgets). The NHS still does not face interest charges on its capital, but there is now a clearer 'trade-off' between capital and current expenditure, which is one step towards greater 'efficiency'. But during the transition period, it generates an understandable sense of inequity, in that while hospitals are still being completed from the earlier era, 'legitimate expectations' are not being fulfilled.

Equity is a tricky matter! It gets even trickier when we enter the delicate area of the respective roles of the NHS and private medicine. This issue can be joined at a variety of levels. There is a factual question as to whether the private sector competes away resources from the public sector, and, even if it does, whether it does not also reduce the public sector workload, so we would need to estimate the balance of advantage as regards the net effect on the NHS. There is also a delicate ethical issue on the supply side, as to whether NHS-employed doctors with large waiting lists should be offering private treatment to those same patients, thereby enabling them to avoid waiting. The various pressures at work here need to be considered in the light of the 'agency relationship' discussed earlier. Then there is the issue of the terms on which the private sector uses NHS facilities, and vice versa. For instance, should each sector base its charges to the other on 'marginal cost' or 'average cost' terms, and how do we do these calculations? The size of 'marginal cost' is very sensitive to the level of utilization of capacity, and in those parts of the system that are at full stretch the marginal cost is really the cost of new capacity (which is much higher than current operating costs, even if the latter included an imputed rental element based on historical costs). But deep down the argument is less about these issues, and more about two conflicting ethical notions about the provision of medical care. The NHS is based on the notion that access should depend on need (however interpreted!) while the private sector controls access by demand (i.e. willingness and ability to pay). The NHS principle follows from a more general view that society should treat access to medical care like access to the courts, namely that all citizens have equal rights which should not be affected by wealth etc. In practice we do not achieve this, of course, but that is the principle we seek to uphold. The latter position follows from a more general view that society should treat access to medical care like access to all the other good things in life, namely it is part of society's reward system. There is no point in offering people the inducement of higher income to do particularly highly valued jobs if they are then denied the opportunity to spend those incomes on the things they value, and medical care is, on occasions, one of the most highly valued goods and services that one can have. Here is a clash of equity notions of a truly fundamental kind which has a profound influence upon the role of economics in health and medical care.

9.6 CONCLUSIONS

The role of economics in the study of health and medical care is to identify and clarify the nature of the choices that have to be made, to explain their consequences, and to distinguish those matters which can only be resolved by recourse to ethical judgements, and those that are susceptible to empirical evidence. Whether a particular charge will reduce demand, and by what kinds of people, is a factual matter, as is the effect of different systems and levels of remuneration upon the behaviour of doctors, or the effect of different distribution formulae upon the behaviour of health authorities. On the other hand, the respective roles of the private and the public sectors is essentially an ethical matter, though the actual consequences of different 'demarcation' rules are clearly an empirical matter. In between are important issues, such as the comparative evaluation of different health-affecting policies or practices, where what is required is a mixture of empirical evidence about their effects and costs, and explicit valuations of health gains which cannot necessarily just be culled from readily available data and adapted without further consideration. Thus the economics of health and medical care is bound to be a subtle blend of ethics and economics, often working on raw material generated by epidemiologists. As such it seems an excellent focus for inculcating the skills of synthesis which are essential to mature intellectual development and a prerequisite for the exercise of one's role as a responsible citizen.

Guide to further reading

General background

A great deal of the literature on health economics is American. Here a deliberate bias has been exercised in favour of British material wherever possible, because the institutional background of the NHS provides a distinctly different context from the US system. However, those interested in the comparisons of different *systems* may care to refer to

MAXWELL, R. (1978), *Health Care: The Growing Dilemma: International Comparisons of Health Needs and Health Services*, McKinsey and Co., Ltd; New York

MAYNARD, A. K. (1975), *Health Care in the European Community*, Croom Helm; London

KASER, M. (1976), *Health Care in the Soviet Union and Eastern Europe*, Croom Helm; London

OECD (1977), *Public Expenditure on Health*, Studies in Resource Allocation No. 4, OECD; Paris

For general background on the problems facing the NHS the best summary source is the Report of the Royal Commission on the NHS (Cmnd 7615, HMSO, July 1979). Their five research reports are also a mine of more detailed information and analysis. These include

(1) A study of the working of the reorganized NHS, primarily aimed at establishing the truth of the frequent allegations of delays resulting from NHS reorganization, undertaken by Professor Maurice Kogan and a team of researchers at Brunel University (published as *The Working of the NHS*, Research Paper Number 1, London, HMSO in June 1978).

(2) A study of the local administration of NHS finance, intended to help tackle that part of the terms of reference which refers to the 'best use and management of the financial . . . resources' of the NHS, undertaken under the supervision of Professor John Perrin of Warwick University (published as *The Management of Finance in the NHS*, Research Paper Number 2, London, HMSO July 1978).

(3) A commentary on the health department's resource allocation arrangements prepared by Professor Rudolf Klein of Bath University and Mr Martin Buxton of the Policy Studies Institute (published as *Allocating Health Resources, A commentary on the Report of the Resource Allocation Working Party*, Research Paper Number 3, London, HMSO, August 1978).

(4) A report on medical manpower forecasting prepared by Mr Alan Maynard and Mr Arthur Walker of York University (published as *Doctor Manpower 1975–2000: alternative forecasts and their resource implications*, Research Paper Number 4, London, HMSO, September 1978).

(5) A study by the Social Survey Division of the Office of Population Censuses and Surveys of patient attitudes towards hospital services which complemented one already

commissioned by the Department of Health and Social Security on access to primary health care services (published as *Patients' attitudes to the Hospital Service* Research Paper Number 5, London, HMSO, Janaury 1979).

(6) Jointly with the National Consumer Council a survey of problems of certain groups in gaining access to primary care services (published as *Access to Primary Care*, Research Paper Number 6, London, HMSO, February 1979).

Still more background material is contained in a series of booklets, published by the King's Fund Centre as a set of project papers, reproducing position papers prepared for the Royal Commission in the course of their deliberations. They cover (*inter alia*) topics such as Health Service objectives, the nation's health and the NHS, international comparisons, NHS finance and resource management, health education and self-help, ideology and class and Consumer and Community Councils as well as many aspects of manpower use and planning, especially relating to nursing and the roles of doctors and dentists, and a full list and details of prices etc. can be obtained by writing to: The King's Fund Centre, 126 Albert Street, London NW1 7NF. Finally, the *Office of Health Economics*, a body sponsored by the British Pharmaceutical Industry, publishes periodic 'Briefings', giving up-to-date factual data and analysis of current trends in, for instance, sickness absence, disability, European health spending, and so on. It also produces more substantial booklets on particular health problems such as mental handicap and hypertension. Their address is 12 Whitehall, London SW1A 2DY.

The economics of health and medical care in general

The closest thing to a British textbook in this field is CULLIS, J. G. and WEST, P. A. (1979), *The Economics of Health: An Introduction*, Martin Robertson; London, which covers most of the territory in this essay, 'geared to students of economics and social sciences in general, and of health care services in particular, who have successfully completed a first-year degree-level course in economics or its equivalent'. At a more elementary level there is WILLIAMS, A. and ANDERSON, R. (1977), *Efficiency in the Social Services*, Basil Blackwell; Oxford, a textbook of microeconomics using *only* non-market examples. Its coverage is broader than the health services, and includes an explanation of Clawson-type demand curves. An even less technical exposition (using epidemiological evidence in an economic framework) is to be found in CULYER, A. J. (1976), *Need and the National Health Service*, Martin Robertson; London. On the appraisal of alternative forms of treatment etc. the best explanation is by DRUMMOND, M. W. (1980), *Principles of Economic Appraisal in Health Care*, Oxford University Press; Oxford. (There is a companion volume, *Studies in Economic Appraisal in Health Care*, OUP, 1981, which offers a critique of 101 published studies in this field.) A fuller treatment of financial and economic appraisal generally, but not specifically focused on health, is to be found in SUGDEN, R. and WILLIAMS, A. (1978), *Principles of Practical Cost-Benefit Analysis*, Oxford University Press; Oxford. This too is at the level of the second or third-year undergraduate, whereas the previous two works are less technical.

There is a useful book of readings, COOPER, M. H. and CULYER, A. J. (eds.) (1973), *Health Economics*, Penguin; Harmondsworth (in the Modern Economics Readings series), which includes the work by Klarman and others referred to in the body of this chapter, (it is reviewed in the books by Drummond cited above). For anyone wishing to plunge still deeper into the literature, there is CULYER, A. J., WISEMAN, J. and WALKER, A. (1977), *Annotated Bibliography of Health Economics*, Martin Robertson; London, and covering English language sources up to 1974. A subsequent companion volume covering other Western European sources, edited by A. Griffiths and others was published by Martin Robertson in 1980. Though the original articles were in many languages, the summaries are all in English, and it includes material up to 1978.

Some specific issues

THE VALUATION OF LIFE AND ILLNESS

The best general summary of the literature on the value of life is contained in MOONEY, G. (1977), *The Valuation of Human Life*, Macmillan; London. On the measurement and valuation of various states of health see WRIGHT, K. G. (1978), 'Output Measurement in Practice', in CULYER, A. J. and WRIGHT, K. G. (eds.), *Economic Aspects of Health Services*, Martin Robertson; London. A more psychometric approach is to be found in ROSSER, R. and WATTS, V. (1974) 'The Development of a Classification of Symptoms and Sickness and its use to measure the output of a hospital', in LEES, D. and SHAW, S. (eds.) (1974),

Impairment, Disability and Handicap, Heinemann (for the Social Science Research Council); London. This work was developed further and the most recent results are reported in ROSSER, R. and KIND, P. (1978), 'A Scale of Valuations of States of Illness: Is there a Social Consensus?', *International Journal of Epidemiology*, Vol. 7, No. 4, pp. 347–358.

NEEDS AND DEMAND

For contrasting approaches to this problem see BRADSHAW, J. (1972), 'A Taxonomy of Social Need', in McLACHLAN, G. (ed.) (1972), *Problems and Progress in Medical Care*, 7th Series, Nuffield Provincial Hospitals Trust, (1978), CULYER, A. J. (1978), 'Need, Values and Health Status' and WILLIAMS, A. (1978), 'Need – An Economic Exegesis', in CULYER, A. J. and WRIGHT, K. G. (eds.), *Economic Aspects of Health Services,* Martin Robertson; London.

CHRONIC RENAL FAILURE

The Klarman study is in the Penguin Readings cited earlier. The Buxton and West study was called 'Cost-benefit Analysis of Long-term Haemodialysis for Chronic Renal Failure' and published in the *British Medical Journal* (1975), Vol. II, pp. 376–379. Drummond's *Principles* cited above has an extended commentary on these studies.

INEQUALITY

The two classic sources for the UK are the Report of the Resource Allocation Working Party (RAWP), DHSS, 1976; Research Paper Number 3 of the Royal Commission on the NHS referred to earlier, and the 'Black Report' *Inequality in Health*, DHSS, London 1980 (now available as TOWNSEND, P. and DAVIDSON, N. (eds.)' *Inequalities in Health*, Penguin; Harmondsworth).

The epidemiological and sociological background

There has been a spate of books recently on the issue of whether medical care has really been responsible for the improvements in health that have been witnessed in the richer countries of the world over the past century. Classic texts are COCHRANE, A. L.

(1972), *Effectiveness and Efficiency*, Nuffield Provincial Hospitals Trust; McKEOWN, T. (1976), *The Role of Medicine*, Nuffield Provincial Hospitals Trust; DOLLERY, C. (1978), *The End of an Age of Optimism*, Nuffield Provincial Hospitals Trust; and (for an extreme political view) ILLICH, I. (1975), *Medical Nemesis*, Calder and Boyers; London. The Nuffield Provincial Hospitals Trust produces a steady stream of informed commentary by eminent people (mostly medical) on health problems, and for an up-to-date list of their publications write to 3 Prince Albert Road, London NW1 7SP.

For a good example of the kind of statistical work which puts the cat amongst the pigeons in this field, see COCHRANE, A. L.; ST. LEGER, A. S.; and MOORE, F. (1978), 'Health Service "input" and mortality "output" in developed countries', *Journal of Epidemiology and Community Health*, Vol. 32, No. 3, pp. 200–205, which appears to demonstrate (*inter alia*) 'a marked positive association between the prevalence of doctors and mortality in the younger age groups', and no noticeably favourable effects of health care on mortality for any other age group. It is a challenge!

For a selection of sociological writings on the problems of the NHS, see STACEY, M. (ed.) (1976), *The Sociology of the NHS*, Sociological Review Monograph No. 22, University of Keele. A textbook reviewing and explaining the current state of the art is TUCKETT, D. (ed.) (1976), *An Introduction to Medical Sociology*, Tavistock Publications, and its companion volume *Basic Readings in Medical Sociology*, Tavistock Publications, 1978.

Ethics and economics

The best statement of the rival ethical positions underlying different approaches to the provision of health care is contained in DONABEDIAN, A. (1971), 'Social Responsibility for Personal Health Services: An Examination of Basic Values', *Inquiry*, Vol. 8, No. 2, pp. 3–19.

There is also a useful collection of essays, BOYD, K. M. (ed.) (1979), *The Ethics of Resource Allocation in Health Care*, Edinburgh University Press; Edinburgh of which the first two chapters set out the problems and report on a group experiment in which a varied group of people were asked to grapple with the issues in a practical setting. There is also a *Journal of Medical Ethics*, published by the Society for the Study of Medical Ethics, Tavistock House North, Tavistock Square, London WC1H 9G, which occasionally has articles relevant to resource allocation dilemmas.

My own views are set out at greater length in LUMLEY, J. and CRAVEN, J. (eds.) (1979), *Surgical Review I*, Pitman Medical, Tunbridge Wells, Kent, in an essay called 'The Costs and Benefits of Surgery'.

A sensitive treatment of much of the material in this chapter, set in an American context, is to be found in FUCHS, V. R. (1974), *Who Shall Live?*, Basic Books; New York.

The best 200 pages?

When the UK Health Economists Study Group had a joint meeting with the Society of Social Medicine in 1978, its members were canvassed for their views as to which would comprise the 200 pages of health economics they would recommend to an 'outsider' to give the best representation of what the field is about. This was the resulting list:

ARROW, K. J. (1979), 'Uncertainty and the welfare economics of medical care', in COOPER, M. H. and CULYER, A. J. (eds.), *Health Economics*, Penguin; Harmondsworth

CULYER, A. J. (1971), 'The Nature of the Commodity "Health Care" and its Efficient Allocation', *Oxford Economic Papers*, Vol. 23, pp. 189–211 (also in COOPER, M. H. and CULYER, A. J. (eds.), *Health Economics*, Penguin; Harmondsworth.

CULYER, A. J., LAVERS, R. J., and WILLIAMS, A. H., 'Social Indicators: Health', *Social Trends*, No. 2, 1971. Also reprinted with minor changes in Social Indicators, SHONFIELD and SHAW, 1972.

FELDSTEIN, M. S. (1974), 'Econometric Studies of Health Economics', in INTRILIGATOR, M. D. and KENDRICK, D. A. (eds.), *Frontiers of Quantitative Economics*, Vol. 2, pp. 377–447, North Holland; Amsterdam.

GROSSMAN, M. (1972), 'On the Concept of Health Capital and the Demand for Health', *Journal of Political Economy*, Vol. 80, No. 2, March/April, pp. 223–255.

JACOBS, P. (1974), 'A Survey of Economic Models of Hospitals', *Inquiry*, Vol. 11, June, pp. 83–97.

KLARMAN, H. E., FRANCIS, J. O'S., and ROSENTHAL, G. D. (1973), 'Efficient Treatment of Patients with Kidney Failure', in COOPER, M. H. and CULYER, A. J. (eds.), *Health Economics*, Penguin, Harmondsworth.

WILLIAMS, A. H. (1974), 'The Cost Benefit Approach', *British Medical Bulletin*, Part 3, Vol. 30, pp. 252–256.

WILLIAMS, A. H. (1977), 'What can economists do to help health service planning?', in ARTIS, J., and NOBAY, A. R. (eds.), *Studies in Modern Economic Analysis*, Basil Blackwell; Oxford.

Bibliography

BUXTON, M. J. and WEST, R. R. (1975), 'Cost Benefit Analysis of Long-term Home Dialysis for Chronic Renal Failure, *British Medical Journal*, 4, pp. 376–379.

KLARMAN, H. E., FRANCIS, J. O'S. and ROSENTHAL, G. D. (1973), 'Efficient Treatment of Patients with Kidney Failure', in COOPER, M. H. and CULYER, A. J. (eds.), *Health Economics*, Penguin, Harmondsworth

10
The Economics of Housing

Alan Maynard

10.1 INTRODUCTION

During the last 100 years, particularly since 1919, the role of the government in the housing market has increased very rapidly. Housing is a major item in all family budgets and its cost is greatly influenced by government intervention by rent controls and rebates, tax relief, and subsidies. The poor receive housing finance from government both in the form of cash benefits (e.g. supplementary benefits) and of indirect subsidies (e.g. rent rebates). Many non-poor families are subsidized by tax reliefs on mortgage interest repayments which makes owner-occupation a very attractive form of investment. The state manipulated the opportunity cost of housing by policies which appear uncoordinated and ineffective. It is clear that a major reform of the housing market could lead to the more efficient use of resources.

This chapter will describe the main characteristics of the housing market and analyse the effects of government intervention. An alternative policy will be presented and the reasons for its likely rejection by policy-makers will be presented.

10.2 THE ECONOMICS OF HOUSING

A house is a durable asset which yields a flow of income, the monetary value of the housing services it provides. The asset may depreciate through time and its opportunity cost can be affected directly and indirectly by government intervention in housing and financial markets. This intervention has, together with increased incomes, changed radically the pattern of housing tenure. For instance only 10.6% of dwellings in Great Britain in 1914 were owner-occupied: most houses were rented. The changes in the post-war period have been rapid as can be seen from *Table 10.1*.

TABLE 10.1 HOUSING TENURE IN 1951 AND 1976[a]

	1951		*1976*	
	Nos. (m)	*%*	*Nos. (m)*	*%*
Private rented	6.4	52	2.6	15
Owner-occupied	3.9	31	10	55
Public sector[b]	2.2	17	5.5	30
Total	12.5	100	18.1	100

a The data are for England and Wales.
b Local authority, new town and housing association.

Source: Secretary of State for the Environment (1977), p. 14.

In 1951 the majority of the housing stock was still rented from private owners. The public sector had grown rapidly since the beginning of large-scale intervention in this sector after 1919 to own 2.2 million houses or 17% of the stock. Owner-occupation had also grown rapidly since 1914 so that by 1951 over 30% of the stock was in this sector. By 1976 it can be seen that this growth path had continued and 55% of housing in England and Wales was owner-occupied. The private-rented sector had shrunk to only 15% of the total stock, some 2.6 million dwellings. The public sector had continued its expansion to 30% of the stock. Thus since 1914 and particularly in the post-1945 period, there has been a rapid and substantial growth in the owner-occupied sector and the public sector, and a rapid and substantial decline in the size of the private-rented sector. How can these trends be explained? Each sector will be analysed separately in an effort to explain these outcomes.

10.2.1 The private-rented sector

The private-rented sector has declined in size both relatively and absolutely. To explain this trend it is necessary to analyse both the supply and the demand for private-rented accommodation. This section will emphasize supply side factors: the changing incentives for landlords to invest in housing for renting.

When investing in housing the landlord will appraise the benefits (rent) at the margin and the costs (depreciation and maintenance) at the margin. His investment in housing will be determined by these costs and benefits, and how they move, as a result of market and government forces through time; and how the resultant rate of return compares with that on other assets. One factor that affects the landlord's costs and benefits is rent control.

In1916 munition workers in Glasgow rioted about the high cost of housing. In order to maximize the production of shells for the Western Front, the government introduced, as a temporary measure, rent control. Like that temporary measure first introduced by Pitt, the income tax, rent control has tended to have a long life and although altered from one piece of legislation to another, it is still with us!

The effects of rent control can be analysed using *Figure 10.1*. If we assume that the supply of rented accommodation is relatively

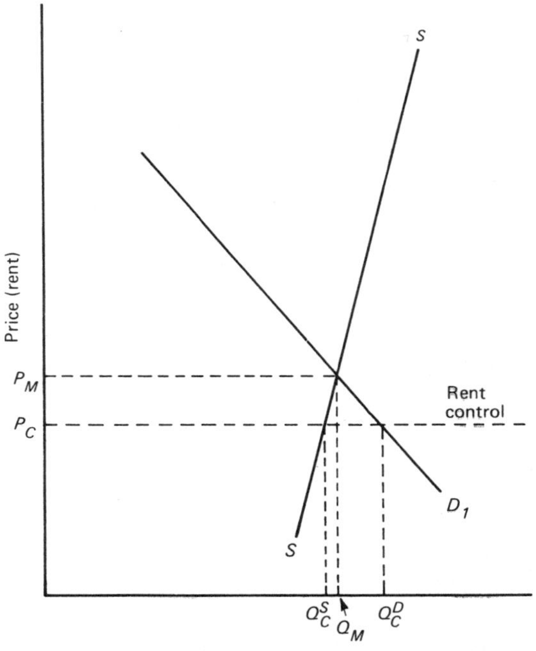

Figure 10.1 The effects of rent control

inelastic in the short run, we have the supply schedule S and a competitive market outcome with price P_M and quantity Q_M. If the government responds to the munition workers' riots by reducing the price by law to P_C, the quantity demand will exceed the quantity supplied ($Q_C^D > Q_C^S$).

How will demanders and suppliers respond to these changes? The suppliers – landlords – have been made poorer by rent control because the price (rent paid) has declined. Thus the rate of return to housing, in comparison with other assets, is depressed and, *ceteris paribus*, landlords will seek to readjust their investment portfolios, shifting out of housing and into other assets. Thus the first prediction is that the supply of rented accommodation will decline, the supply curve will shift to the left and the gap between supply and demand at price P_C will widen.

To appease the munition workers, voters, and users of private-rented accommodation, the government may (and did!) respond to these wicked (i.e. rational) capitalist inclinations of the landlords by restricting their ability to sell their assets. However, such regulation is not going to be without its effects on the landlords' behaviour. A restriction on sale means that the landlord is forced to hold an asset whose rate of return is low. To raise the net benefits of this asset the landlord can cut his costs by failing to maintain the quality of the asset. Thus we would predict that the quality of private-rented accommodation will be low and this prediction is consistent with the findings of government surveys that the highest proportion of slums (defined by explicit government criteria) is located in the private-rented sector.

The landlord who retains assets in the housing market is faced by excess demand. How is demand rationed? The landlord, because of rent control, has the power to discriminate. He can discriminate in a variety of ways. For instance he can rent his property to people with no children and no pets as this may reduce his maintenance costs. He can charge 'key money' or other side payments which ration demand by price. He can discriminate in favour of people he likes or against people he dislikes, e.g. blacks, Jews, homosexuals, communists or whatever his preferences dictate. Those unable to get private-rented accommodation of the required quality have to look elsewhere for housing: thus rent control 'creates' a demand for public sector and owner-occupied houses.

Rent control reduces the price below the market level and redistributes income from landlords to tenants. However, because the supply of property may fall, because of its depressed rate of return, tenants will have to compete for houses and will be discriminated against (rationed) in a variety of ways. The majority of landlords are not rich and the state is thus 'robbing' them to pay people who may or may not be rich: the redistribution of income is random almost and unlikely to be related to income or ability to pay. Government intervention, motivated by short-term policy objectives in World War I, has created a set of incentives which affect the behaviour of suppliers and demanders both within the private-rented sector and without.

10.2.2 The owner-occupied sector

Rent control affected, and still affects, the availability and the quality of private-rented accommodation. If such accommodation is not available the consumer can look elsewhere for housing, in either the owner-occupied or public sector.

In the owner-occupied sector the investor is the individual. His benefits from the purchase of a house are a flow of housing services over time. The costs of such an investment are, for the average individual, the cost of a mortgage and the cost of maintenance.

The basis of government taxation of the owner-occupied sector goes back to the budget of Lloyd George in 1909. A house is an asset which generates an income, the monetary value of its housing services, and which depreciates over time. A firm with a machine would be taxed on the income yielded from the sales of the machine's output, net of the costs of depreciation and maintenance. Thus Lloyd George provided for, under Schedule A taxation, the taxation of the income of housing net of its cost of maintenance. Thus until 1963, a calculation of the notional income of a house was made, maintenance costs were offset against this, and then the householder was taxed on this income. In 1963 this tax was abolished. The mortgage tax offset was introduced by Lloyd George also and its objective was 'to encourage owner-occupation': an effect it seems most successful in achieving!

The opportunity cost to the Exchequer of the mortgage tax offset is not inconsiderable as can be seen from *Table 10.2*. In 1970/71 the income tax yield in the absence of such offsets would have been £262 million greater. In the same year the option mortgage scheme, a scheme whereby the state subsidizes the mortgage interest payments of some low-income households, cost £15 million and the average owner-occupier received a subsidy of £32. This average subsidy had grown to £185 by 1980/81. The maximum mortgage level for such tax offsets is £25 000 but up to this level the higher the marginal tax rate of the mortgage holder, the larger the mortgage and the higher the interest rate charged by

TABLE 10.2 MORTGAGE TAX RELIEF IN GREAT BRITAIN

Year	Mortgage tax relief (1) (£m)	Option mortgage subsidy (2) (£m)	1 + 2 per owner occupied dwelling (£)
1970/71	282	15	32
1973/74	504	51	55
1976/77	1078	140	114
1978/79	1110	150	112
1979/80	1450	n.a.	145
1980/81	1960	n.a.	185

Sources: *Hansard*, 13 July 1979 and 15 May 1981; Building Societies Association (1981), table 6, p. 22.

the building societies, the larger the subsidy he receives from the tax system.

As a person has to be in receipt of an assured and not insubstantial income in order to acquire a building society loan, the effect of the mortgage tax offset is to subsidize families that are not poor. Furthermore this subsidy is augmented by another fiscal device: exemption from capital gains taxation. Most assets, for instance stocks and shares, are liable to capital gains taxation. The exemption of housing gives further subsidies to the non-poor and makes housing an even more remunerative asset in which to invest.

The market for housing finance is highly imperfect: effectively the building societies work as a cartel. However, borrowing from these bodies is highly rewarding because of the fiscal devices outlined above. Consequently it is not surprising perhaps that the housing stock has increased in size (see *Table 10.1*), that house prices have generally risen at a rate in excess of inflation, and that resources have been 'diverted' out of less remunerative activities and into housing. The effects of government fiscal subsidies to owner-occupiers has been to make the real cost of a mortgage very low or negative during most of the last 20 years. The government policies that have reduced the supply of private rented accommodation have created an incentive to invest in owner-occupation. This incentive has been increased by the substantial fiscal incentives via tax offsets and capital gains taxation exemption. Such policies can be questioned on equity grounds: why is it necessary to subsidize people who are not poor? Also such policies can be questioned on efficiency grounds: by reducing costs subsidies encourage over-investment in housing and a diversion of resources from more productive activities.

10.2.3 The public sector

Large-scale intervention by central government in the provision of housing by local government began in 1919. Since then a multitude of Acts of Parliament have offered a variety of subsidies to local authorities. These subsidies have the effect of shifting part of the cost of constructing housing off local government and onto central government. In exchange for financial support, central government has demanded and acquired construction policies in line with centrally-determined policy objectives. Two examples of this are the Parker Morris standards and high rise subsidies.

The Parker Morris standards were established to ensure that local authorities built houses to 'adequate' standards. The word adequate is ambiguous: like beauty, adequacy is in the mind of the beholder! Consequently the Department of the Environment has set out detailed specifications about heating, lighting, ceiling height, storage facilities, sanitary and washing facilities, and a variety of other attributes of a house. The implementation of these minimum standards is enforced by making subsidies and access to the capital markets dependent on their being met. The standards are, in some respects, generous and have led to disputes. Central government claims it is 'building for the future' and assumes that the future population with higher incomes will demand better housing: it is claimed it is 'best' to build this now rather than renovate at great expense in the future. Some local authorities would like to build at standards below the Parker Morris scale. They point out that high quality construction uses resources which could be used to construct more, less good houses. Further they point out that private building firms build to standards which are in some cases below Parker Morris standards. This debate about 'better or more' has gone on for 20 years and was summarized by Anthony Crosland when he was Secretary of State for the Environment as a choice between a Rolls-Royce and a Mini. Any such choice, like any in economics, depends on the policy objectives you are seeking to achieve and the policy debate is about these objectives and the alternative means of achieving them.

The high rise subsidies were a policy pursued by governments in the 1950s that were concerned with economizing on the use of land. The conventional wisdom was that land was expensive relative to other inputs used to produced housing facilities so it was economical to build high even if the construction costs were high. This subsidy system was a nice example of a policy which had not been analysed rigorously. The costs of building multi-storey flats increase very rapidly with the number of storeys. Further such buildings have economic costs (the costs of maintenance may be higher) and serious sociological implications: a high rise set of flats is rather like a set of terrace houses set on their end and such a pattern of housing provision breaks up social relationships (door-step chats with the neighbours are no longer possible). To service such flats it is necessary to have play areas, social facilities and effective (vandal proof) lifts if people are to be integrated into their local societies. However, the opportunity cost of some of these facilities, in terms of land, is substantial and, as a consequence, the land-economizing attributes of high rise flats are less significant at best, and non-existent at worst.

Subsidies and standard-setting have opportunity costs. The high rise flat subsidies encouraged local authorities to build accommodation whose full opportunity cost was sometimes greater than that of comparable private 'estate' housing. The Parker Morris standards encourage quality at the expense of quantity. However, all policies have opportunity costs: there is no such thing as a free lunch!

The policies by which central government has subsidized housing have varied from year to year since 1919 but the trend has been always, until quite recently at least, upwards. *Table 10.3* sets out the cost of housing subsidies in England and Wales which were financed from central government and out of local authority rates.

TABLE 10.3 GENERAL PUBLIC SECTOR HOUSING SUBSIDIES FROM CENTRAL GOVERNMENT AND THE RATE FUND (ENGLAND AND WALES)

Year	*Total (£m)*	*Subsidy per local authority/ new town dwelling (£)*
1975/76	864	166
1976/77	1062	199
1977/78	1136	208
1978/79	1266	229
1979/80	1673	301
1980/81	1904	364

Sources: Building Societies Association (1981), Table 7, p. 22; *Hansard*, 19 June 1981.

By 1980/81 the expenditure was £1904 million, equivalent to a subsidy per local authority/new town dwelling of £364. *Table 10.4* sets out the growth in rent rebates in England and Wales. By 1979/80 the cost of these policies was £408 million, equivalent to £73 for each local authority/new town dwelling. (Their cost would be much greater if all those eligible for such rebates claimed them.

TABLE 10.4 RENT REBATES (ENGLAND AND WALES)

Year	*Total (£m)*	*Rebate per local authority/ new town dwelling (£)*
1972/73	77	16
1974/75	199	39
1976/77	290	54
1978/79	363	66
1979/80	408	73

Source: Building Societies Association (1981), Table 8, p. 22.

The low 'take-up' rate reduces public expenditure on this item quite considerably.) These subsidies are substantial and the Thatcher administration plans to cut them savagely in the near future, e.g. they plan to cut general subsidies to £1011 million (in 1980 prices) in the year 1981/82.

The rationale of such subsidies can be debated on equity and efficiency grounds. The general public housing subsidies, unlike the rent rebates, are not, even remotely, related to ability to pay: subsidies go to tenants on the basis of the housing they occupy rather than in relation to their financial means. The efficiency effects of the subsidies depend on the nature of the legislation under which it is paid and this has shifted regularly. High rise flats are no longer encouraged with such misplaced financial vigour but the sins of the past are still being met out of the taxes of the present as most subsidies are paid for substantial (40 to 50-year) periods.

10.3 THE REFORM OF THE HOUSING MARKET

The preceding section has analysed briefly and somewhat selectively some of the economics of the housing market. This section appraises some suggested reforms to alter the existing chaotic pattern of government intervention. The owner-occupied section of the housing market will be discussed first and then the reform of rents will be analysed.

10.3.1 Reform of the owner-occupiers' market

Part of the theoretical basis of Lloyd George's tax treatment of housing was sound but this basis was consistently undermined until, in 1963, Selwyn Lloyd rendered it illogical by abolishing Schedule A taxation. The first elements of the reform of the market for housing must be a restoration of sound economic principles by restoring Schedule A taxation, the abolition or reduction of the mortgage interest tax offset, and the application of capital gains taxation to housing.

The tax offset policy can be handled in at least one of two ways. Firstly the present £25 000 ceiling could be maintained in money terms, i.e. eroded by inflation and reduced in real terms over time. An alternative would be to restrict the tax relief to a common rate of tax (e.g. the basic rate). This measure would enable policy-makers to replicate life insurance premia arrangements and permit the payment of interest net of tax in a much simpler way than the cumbersome scheme introduced in 1982. Both measures, given continued inflation and a gradual reduction in the allowable base rate, could enable policy-makers to phase out this subsidy over time.

Such a policy would increase the opportunity cost of housing to owner-occupiers but may be acceptable given social redistribution goals. It seems inconsistent with most equity goals to maintain the high level of subsidy to owner-occupiers who are not poor.

The second strand of the reform policy would also increase the opportunity cost of owner-occupation: the restoration of Schedule A. All capital assets yield services which have a monetary value e.g. dishwashers, cars, houses, etc. The usual consumer durables are taxed at purchase (value added taxation) and this tax could be viewed as a levy on the capitalized value of the services yielded by the asset. Housing services are not taxed and this omission could be rectified by the restoration of Schedule A taxation. Such a tax was supported by the 1955 Royal Commission on the Taxation of Profits and Income and similar taxes are levied in other European countries.

The form of the tax needs careful consideration. The estimation of the value of the notional rent of a dwelling is difficult because the size of the private rented sector is small and its rents are distorted by rent controls. King and Atkinson (1980) suggest that the Schedule A taxation should be levied on the capital value of the dwelling. If the rating structure is reformed and rates are based on capital values, the Schedule A tax will be made much easier to levy.

The gradual removal of mortgage tax offsets and the restoration of Schedule A taxation might affect the price of owner-occupied housing. Because these reforms would affect the cost of house ownership, the demand for houses might fall and depress prices.

This might make the yield on capital gains taxation applied to housing, limited. The weak case for the exemption of owner-occupied housing from this tax does not appear to be other than the result of clamour of self-interested groups and its exemption, on equity and efficiency grounds, should be abolished.

The effect of these three reforms on owner-occupiers would be substantial. Depending on the speed with which the reforms were introduced, the opportunity cost of owner-occupation would rise in a manner that would be felt by all house-owners.

10.3.2 Reform of rents

The rents of both the private-rented sector and the public sector have to be related to depreciation costs (on a replacement cost, and not an historic cost basis) and the desired rate of return on housing. King and Atkinson (1980) argue that the target rate of return for public sector housing is a social decision reflecting the priority society assigns to housing. Once this social decision is reached the rents of the public sector houses can be fixed, and these rents will incorporate this social decision (and the resultant subsidy if the rate of return is fixed at a level below that elsewhere in the market). This type of argument seems to perpetuate subsidies through product or service prices rather than through subsidies to 'needy' individuals. It is argued below that redistribution to individuals is to be preferred and that public sector rents should reflect the full social costs of the housing provided.

The rents of private accommodation would be determined by individual landlords. Thus rent control, in this reformed housing market, would be abolished, and prices would be used as the main mechanism to clear markets. If the rate of return to such activities rose – this would depend on private sector rents relative to housing costs elsewhere and resultant consumer movements in the market – this might attract some landlords into the market and reverse the decline of the private-rented sector in Britain.

10.3.3 Reform: an overview and a proposal for subsidization

The housing market should be analysed as a whole and a consistent set of economic principles should be applied to each sector of the market. Decision-makers should be obliged to face the full opportunity costs of their housing decisions whether they use owner-occupied, private-rented or public sector housing. If prices reflected opportunity costs, the problems associated with the provision of housing for the poor would remain.

King and Atkinson (1980) advocate the provision of a housing allowance to meet the problems of the poor. The allowance would be based on family composition and is really part of the reform of the income maintenance system. It could be viewed as a housing voucher or integrated into a reform of income maintenance which included the introduction of a comprehensive system of negative income taxation. (Such matters were discussed in Maynard, 1979a.) Subsidies of individual demanders rather than groups of suppliers may be more efficient means of achieving social objectives.

The proposals are radical and offer the possibility of acquiring housing policies which are integrated and consistent with economic principles of managing scarce resources.

10.4 THE IMPOSSIBILITY OF REFORM?

The economic principles behind the reforms suggested in the preceding section might permit policy-makers to use resources more efficiently and to achieve their redistributional policies more effectively. Why are not such policies implemented? The crude answer must be that when government regulates or intervenes in a market, some people gain and some people lose. To alter any regulation or intervention brings with it a new harvest of gains and losses and it is the latter in particular which make the reform of the housing market so difficult: interest groups oppose reform because they will lose.

Let us develop this argument briefly in relation to the owner-occupied housing market. At present owner-occupiers are subsidized generously but the proposed reforms would remove these subsidies. In 1980 the building societies had 5.383 million mortgage accounts. If we assume conservatively that each household has two voters, it can be seen that 10.766 million voters might be affected by our policy proposals and perhaps vote against any party proposing them. The building societies themselves employ voters and their funds finance house building and expansion which employ construction firms and their workers. Thus the political constituency affected by the reformation of the finance of the owner-occupied sector of the housing market is not inconsiderable. When these voters are added to other voters who could be affected by increases in public and private sector rents, it is not surprising that politicians and bureaucrats are wary of adopting the reforms so generously offered by economists!

If we assume that politicians are vote maximizers and bureaucrats are budget maximizers, we can predict the likely behavioural responses of these decision-makers (see Maynard, 1979b) for an elaboration of this analysis). Politicians will 'market' those policies that appeal to the median voter for only if they 'buy' the support of such people will they achieve or maintain political power in a world where voter preferences are normally distributed. Bureaucrats are viewed as 'successful' if their bureaux or departments grow. Thus they will oppose policies that reduce their empires. Such theories of public choice or decision-making imply that any reforms of the housing market must be put forward with care. Certain policies appeal to certain parties, e.g. the Tories might favour public expenditure cuts that affect Labour voters (e.g. general housing subsidies to council houses?), and Labour may favour policies that effect Tory voters (e.g. subsidies to owner-occupiers?). However, political constituencies overlap (many Labour voters are owner-occupiers) and hence the implementation of even part of the reform package may be difficult. The housing market may be efficient in that it is consistent with the self-interest of politicians and bureaucrats even though in Paretian terms its efficiency can be questioned.

Guide to further reading

There are many useful texts on the economics of housing policy e.g. Grey, Hepworth and Odling-Smee (1978) and Stafford (1978). However, perhaps the two most useful pieces of work are Robinson (1979) which is a textbook on housing economics, and King and Atkinson (1980) which is an excellent bank review article on the reform of the housing market.

Bibliography

BUILDING SOCIETIES ASSOCIATION (1981), *BSA Bulletin*, 27 November, July

GREY, A., HEPWORTH, N. and ODLING-SMEE, J. (1978), *Housing Rents, Costs and Subsidies*, Chartered Institute of Public Finance and Accountancy, London

KING, M. A. and ATKINSON, A. B. (1980), 'Housing Policy, Taxation and Reform', *Midland Bank Review*, Spring, pp. 7–15

MAYNARD, A. (1979a), 'The Economics of Social Policy', in GOWLAND, D.H. (ed.), *Modern Economic Analysis*, Butterworths; London

MAYNARD, A. (1979b), 'The Economics of Public choice', in GOWLAND, D. H. (ed.), *Modern Economic Analysis*, Butterworths, London

ROBINSON, R. (1979), *Housing Economics and Public Policy*, Macmillan; London

SECRETARY OF STATE FOR THE ENVIRONMENT (1977), *Housing Policy: a consultative document*, Cmnd 6851, HMSO; London

STAFFORD, D. C. (1978), *The Economics of Housing Policy*, Croom Helm; London

11
The Economics of Education

Alan Maynard

11.1 INTRODUCTION

Before 1960 the title of this chapter would have appeared a contradiction in terms. Education was the domain of the psychologist, the sociologist, the statistician, in fact of everybody but the economist. One of major advances in microeconomics since 1960 has been the realization that it can offer valuable insights into a wide range of social policy problems and, in particular, into education and health. Schools, colleges and universities use large quantities of capital and labour inputs, not least their students' time. They aim to produce various outputs, especially better-educated and more skilled students. This production process can be analysed using the normal tools of economics, efficiency, opportunity cost and marginality, to determine whether the objectives of education policy are being achieved in an optimal fashion. Moreover education in the UK involves many allocation decisions such as who goes to which school and who goes to university. This allocation is normally determined in a non-market system by the producers, educational bureaucrats, academics, principals and headmasters. As 'the science of choice' economics has much to offer in analysing this process. A fundamental insight into the education process is given by emphasizing that the inputs are consumed usually many years before the benefits of the outputs are achieved. In this respect education expenditure is an investment so again economic analysis has much to offer. This usually involves the concept of 'human capital' (Becker 1964, 1976). Becker argues that investment is made in people by expenditure on health and education in an exactly analogous manner to expenditure on machinery or buildings. The benefits of the investment may be greater output (the productivity of a skilled worker is greater than that of an unskilled worker) or a more enjoyable life.

11.2 THE SUPPLY OF AND DEMAND FOR EDUCATION

In this section the supply of and demand for education will be analysed in the human capital framework. Following Becker (1964, 1976), we will examine the benefits and costs of investing in human capital, seek to identify the nature of the supply and demand curves, and analyse how these curves can be shifted by alternative policy measures.

What are the determinants of earnings? The basic human capital equation for earnings is

$$E_t = x_t + k_t - c_t, \tag{11.1}$$

where

E_t = earnings in time period t;
x_t = raw returns to basic ability (i.e. net of all human capital investment);
k_t = returns to human capital investment made in previous periods;
c_t = human capital investments made in period t.

If we assume that x_t is small, earnings in any particular time period are determined by the returns to human capital investments made in previous periods (k_t), minus the cost of additional human capital investments in this period (c_t). Let us assume for simplicity that human capital is homogeneous. What determines an individual's investment in human capital and the yield from his investment? The answer is supply and demand.

In *Figure 11.1* the demand for human capital is determined by the marginal net benefit of human capital investment. The marginal net benefits accrue over time, or over the life-cycle of the owner of the human capital. Thus the marginal net benefit is a time series, suitably discounted to take account of time preference, of marginal returns minus marginal production costs. The marginal net benefit will fall as people age because the pay-off period

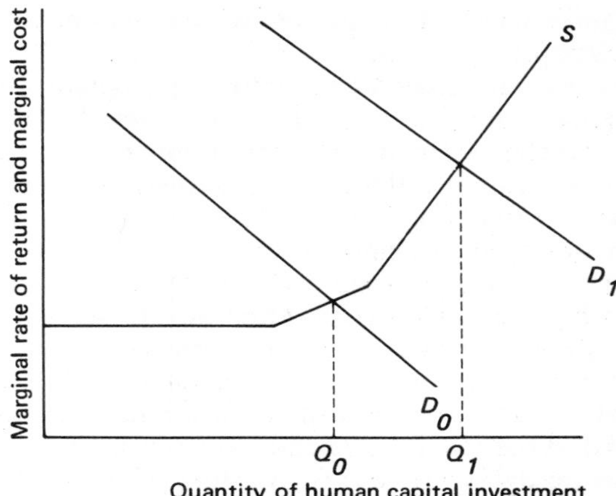

Figure 11.1 The supply and demand for human capital investment

(remaining length of working life) is shorter and it is likely that the costs of accumulation rise with age as the opportunity cost of learning rises.

Why do the demand curves in *Figure 11.1* slope downwards to the right? There are a variety of factors which may cause this outcome. Firstly we could argue that the individual's memory capacity is limited and that this will cause diminishing returns to set in. Secondly one of the main costs of investment is time costs and the substitution possibilities between own time and other inputs is limited. The consequence of this limitation is that marginal returns will decline. A third determinant of the slope of the demand curve is that human capital is part of the individual. The individual has to take himself along to be educated and in so doing takes his human capital stock with him and out of remunerative activity. As the stock increases in size, the opportunity cost of investment rises, i.e. the marginal production costs rise and give us the demand curve shown in *Figure 11.1*.

Whilst the demand curve slopes downwards to the right, the supply curve is in segments and slopes generally upwards to the right. The supply curve is the marginal cost of financing human capital investment, i.e. it is the opportunity cost (reflected by the rate of interest on the resources used) of investing an extra pound in human capital. The capital market for human capital is imperfect: there is the problem of a lack of collateral in the absence of slavery! The market for resources is segmented and the price of resources is likely to vary geographically and among different age and social groups.

A variety of sources of finance may exist. Gifts from parents, relatives or the state are represented in *Figure 11.1* by the first horizontal 'tranche' of funds. The opportunity cost of such funds is the investment returns you forego from investing in yourself rather than investing in the stock market. The size of this tranche will depend on the affluence and generosity of the state and your relatives: the Grosvenor family with £600 million wealth may be able to afford more gifts than our families! The second tranche of loans are subsidized loans from institutions such as human capital banks. The final section of the curve is open market loans, offered at rates that recognize the lack of collateral and the fact that you may abscond to the USA at the end of the training period, taking your human capital with you and avoiding repayment!

If we assume that individuals maximize the present value of profits, i.e. the difference between the costs and benefits at the margin in present value terms, the initial equilibrium is at Q_0 with D_0 and Q_1 with D_1.

What are the implications of this model? The first implication is that earnings vary among individuals because equilibria vary. Supply and demand conditions determine the level of human capital investment that determines earnings. Supply and demand conditions differ among individuals and hence investments in human capital differ and earnings differ.

If we assume that human ability is identical, the egalitarian point of view, then inequalities in earnings are attributable to supply-side problems or inequality in access to funds. Thus in *Figure 11.2*,

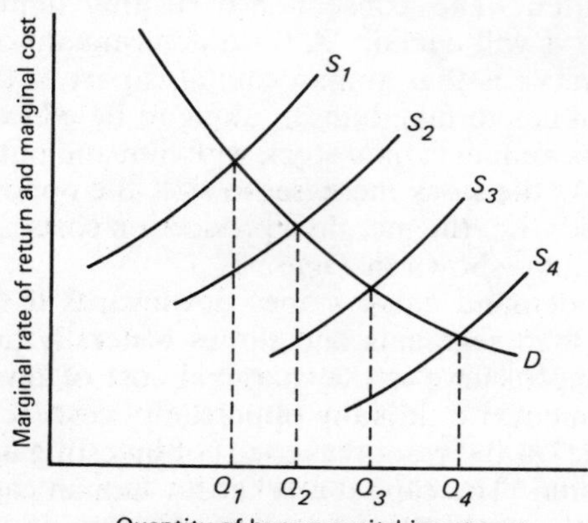

Figure 11.2 The egalitarian point of view

demand (D) is identical for all as the marginal benefits and the marginal production costs are equal. However individuals have differing access to financing, represented by S_1, S_2, S_3 and S_4 in *Figure 11.2*. Because of this inequality, the quantity of human capital investment varies (Q_1, Q_2, Q_3 and Q_4) and because of differing investments, earnings will differ (equation 11.1). Thus the cause of earnings inequality is a supply-side problem and a relative lack of access to investment funds for some individuals in society.

An alternative view is given in *Figure 11.3*, the elitist view. Here it is assumed that human ability is unequally distributed but the supply of funds is the same for everybody. Thus individuals differ in their capacity to benefit from human capital investment and the alternative demand curves represent this ranging from D_1 (the dim) to D_4 (the intelligent). Because of differing demands, the quantity of investment differs (Q_1, Q_2, Q_3 and Q_4 in *Figure 11.3*) and this causes the inequality in earnings.

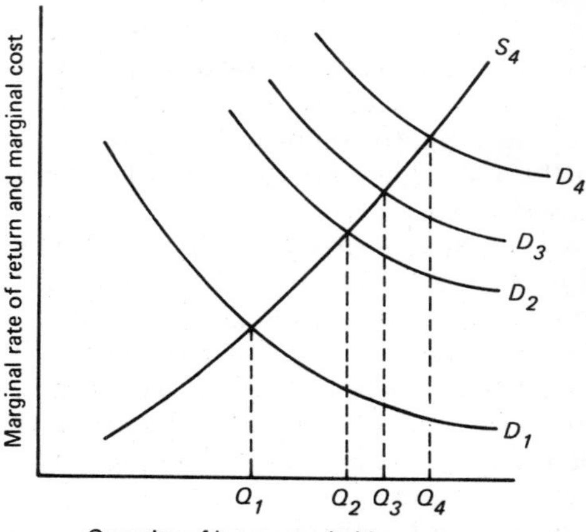

Figure 11.3 The elite point of view

The polar cases depicted in *Figure 11.2* and *11.3* illustrate how the model explains earnings outcomes. In the real world people do not have equal access to investment resources. Thus earnings outcomes are likely to be the result of supply and demand-side differences, and any public policy which seeks to reduce earnings differences can work on either or both sides of the market for human capital investment.

11.3 ALTERNATIVE EDUCATION POLICIES I: VOUCHERS

Education vouchers could be used to change the way in which education is financed and such a change in finance might have effects on the supply side as well. In this section a brief description of how a voucher system might work will be presented. This will be followed by an analysis of the effects of vouchers on equity and efficiency. The former section, on equity, will consist of an investigation of how vouchers might be used to reduce earnings inequality. The discussion of efficiency will appraise whether vouchers will have effect on the supply of education.

11.3.1 What is a voucher?

An education voucher is a piece of paper worth some monetary value which can be spent only on education. In the UK education vouchers tend to be associated with the radical right (e.g. Seldon, 1978) whilst in the USA they are associated with the socialist left (e.g. Jencks, 1970). In fact voucher systems can be designed to achieve virtually any right-wing or left-wing policy goal which you might like to think of: like the products of Mr Heinz, vouchers come in at least 57 different varieties!

The voucher is a mechanism by which cash to finance education is distributed to providers (teachers) by parents choosing to send their children to a school and paying for their education with the voucher. Thus some state agency may pay the voucher to parents. The parents will select a school and pay over the voucher to that school. The schools' ability to attract pupils (and their vouchers) will determine their income and their ability to stay in business: no vouchers equals no income and closure.

This crude outline of the mechanism disguises many problems. Who will determine the price of schooling? If the price exceeds the value of the voucher, parents will have to 'top-up' the voucher out of their income. Will vouchers be taxable? What will be the value of vouchers? Can vouchers be spent in all schools regardless of whether they are in the public or private sector?

The answers to these questions depends on the policy objectives that we are seeking to achieve. For instance if we wish to redistribute education resources radically we could give vouchers equal to twice the cost of education to all children whose parents earned incomes that placed them in the bottom 50% of the income distribution, and vouchers equal to £1 for all other children. We would maintain present tax levels and oblige all to stay at school until 16 years of age as now. Thus the school with children from poor families on their rolls would find their income increased significantly. More affluent parents would have to pay the full cost of education minus the £1 voucher. Clearly such a voucher scheme could have radical redistributive effects, and this variant of the voucher demonstrates clearly that its design is flexible and dependent on the policy of objectives you are seeking to achieve.

What problems might arise with such a mechanism? The first problem is inherent in its flexibility. Changing political masters may lead to changes in the design of voucher schemes as one ideology replaces another and one set of policy objectives yields its primacy to another. The effects of such fluctuations are difficult to forecast but could make the planing of education facilities difficult.

A second problem with any voucher scheme is that the demand for places in 'popular' schools might exceed supply. This outcome may generate a variety of problems. If the capacity of the school is fixed and demand exceeds supply, how will supply be rationed amongst competing demanders? One obvious way is price, i.e. adjust price upwards until supply and demand are equilibrated. The alternative is non-price rationing, e.g. an '11-plus' test, religion, sex, etc. If capacity is flexible, the crucial question is whether as size increases the quality of the school's product remains the same. Temporary classrooms (e.g. Portakabins) and the hiring of new teachers may make it possible to equate demand and supply by increasing the latter.

However this expansion raises another problem: teacher tenure. If demand fluctuates or if demand for places in a particular school declines, will teachers be made redundant or will they be offered retraining opportunities and given tenure in the system but not in the individual school? Such problems cannot be ignored and may lead to strong professional views on vouchers.

Another criticism of the voucher system is that parents and/or children cannot make efficient choices in education. Education is characterized by a lack of evaluation of practice and by little peer review and audit. Whether teachers are well-informed enough to make choices for their pupils is a moot point. Certainly if parents are to choose they will need more and better information about the relative merits of alternative schools. Such information will be expensive to provide and may lead to 'competitive' advertising of a trivial kind.

It is difficult to reach conclusions about these problems. Their existence and magnitude depends on the nature of the voucher scheme that is adopted. The exact nature of the problems of such innovations can only be detected in careful monitored social experiments (Maynard, 1975). Such experiments would select control and experimental groups of similar economic and social characteristics, and expose the latter group to some form of voucher innovation. The effects on teachers, parents and children of this experiment could then be compared with the outcomes of the control group. In this way a body of data could be acquired which might enable us to determine the answers to some of the problems that may arise in voucher schemes.

11.3.2 Vouchers and equity

The effects of education vouchers on the distribution of earnings depends on the type of education voucher scheme that is adopted. A variety of distributional goals can be achieved by careful design of the voucher system.

If we take the egalitarian view of the world outline in *Figure 11.2*, we might design the voucher scheme so that it advantaged those with limited access to the financial market (e.g. S_1 and S_2) and reduced the dispersion among the supply curves. This, if successful, would mean that the differences in human capital formation and as a consequence earnings, might be reduced.

However if we take an elitist view of the world the effects of vouchers on the distribution of earnings may be quite limited. The voucher affects the supply side of the education market principally and to reduce earnings dispersion in an élitist world it is necessary to use policy to affect the demand side of the market. If vouchers have efficiency effects (see below), the production costs of human capital form may be reduced and thus may increase marginal net benefit, i.e. demand curves will shift to the right. However there is no reason to believe that these shifts will be other than equal across all individuals and consequently the dispersion among the demand curves may not be affected.

Consequently vouchers are only likely to be effective if the cause of earnings differences are essentially generated by the supply side (the egalitarian view). If inequality is caused by supply-side problems, vouchers may be an effective policy. However the effectiveness of the alternative voucher schemes and current programmes of education must be carefully assessed in experiments if policy shifts are to be better informed and not biased merely on guesses, hunches and prayers!

11.3.3 Vouchers and efficiency

The question to be addressed here is whether education vouchers alter incentives and whether these different incentives induce producers to use resources more efficiently.

Who are the producers? Most of the literature on education vouchers assumes that the main resource allocation is the teacher and that vouchers would induce schools to organize more like firms with the headteacher being the managing director primarily involved in resource allocation. The headteacher would be a budget holder and the success of his/her school in attracting resources would determine the size of the budget available for use.

This dependence might induce headteachers to introduce greater variety in remuneration practices in order to induce labour supply responses of the required type. Thus salary scales might be incremental and 'decrimental' i.e. teachers might go up and down the scale depending on their performance. Presumably their performance would have to be judged in relation to output criteria that were relevant to attracting 'customers'. In addition to the salary scales teachers in the teaching workers' co-operative might share in budget surpluses by being eligible for bonuses.

Those familiar with Soviet and Yugoslavian economics will recognize the similarities. Schools have outputs which are difficult to measure. Soviet firms have outputs which are difficult to quantify in quantity and quality terms because of the suspension of the price mechanism. The voucher introduces the possibility of the headteacher being a resource allocator with control over his budget and his labour force. The problem, as in the Soviet Union, is to devise a system of incentives to ensure that the producer supplies those services that are demanded by, in the USSR, the planner, or in the UK, the consumer.

The assertion of voucher advocates is that teachers as budget holders would have incentives to allocate their resources more efficiently. However this conclusion depends on the type of voucher scheme used and the freedom of the headteacher to act as an entrepreneur and manager of his own budget. What is required to test these assertions is experimentation with varying types of incentive and budget scheme. The allocation of the property right in budgets to the teacher has some a priori appeal but the proof of the pudding must come with the eating and this tit-bit has not been sampled yet in most of the UK schooling system.

11.3.4 Vouchers: a conclusion

A discussion of vouchers inevitably opens up a wide debate about the objectives of schooling and the efficiency of alternative means of achieving given education policy ends. Unfortunately the debate about objectives has been poor. Not surprisingly the debate about the alternative means has been limited and poor. Education vouchers are a radical alternative with apparent virtues which beg systematic testing. It is to be hoped that in time the limited US experiments with education vouchers will be replicated and extended in the United Kingdom (Maynard, 1975); Kent County Council, 1978).

11.4 ALTERNATIVE EDUCATION POLICIES II: STUDENT LOANS

Student loans have been advocated as an alternative means of financing higher education in the United Kingdom. This section is concerned with the costs and benefits of such an innovation. After a brief discussion of the student loan proposals, the equity and efficiency characteristics of such a system of higher education finance will be appraised.

11.4.1 Student loans

At present UK students who are offered a place in an approved institution in the higher education sector are eligible generally for a grant from their local authority. This grant is means-tested and usually a student gets his tuition fees paid (around £1500 per year) and is given a maintenance grant to finance his board and lodgings. The means test is a strange mechanism in that students are generally over 18 years of age, and thus independent legally, but their grant has to be supplemented according to family income, by the parents. Thus, on the one hand, the student is freed from the household but in another way she is very much tied to it.

The system of grants is criticized on a variety of grounds. The National Union of Students advocates the abolition of means tests but the public expenditure consequences of such a policy make its adoption unlikely.

The advocates of loans seek to alter the grant system in a more radical fashion. They argue on efficiency and equity grounds that the present system of grants is defective and advocate that students should have to finance their education out of loans which would be repaid over the life-cycle (i.e. the working life of the student).

The obvious initial problem with such a proposal is who would lend students money to finance their education? The human capital they acquire is embodied (i.e. part of their person) and if they leave the country, the lender may not be repaid: the bank or financer has no collateral (security) for his loan to the student. If the state guaranteed the loans part of the collateral problem might be overcome but such an outcome would only be achieved at present at an unknowable cost in terms of public expenditure.

Even if banks were prepared to lend resources to students to finance their education there might still be a problem with a 'brain drain'. If students knew they could avoid repaying their loans by emigrating, some might find the option of living abroad more attractive. This problem is essentially an empirical matter which will be dependent on the size of the loan (will it cover the full cost of education or will the student still be partially subsidized, and if so by how much?), whether the interest rate is subsidized by the state, and the repayment period. The evidence from abroad about this problem is inconclusive (Woodhall, 1970, 1978, and 1980) but does not support the view of some loan advocates who regard it as an irrelevant issue.

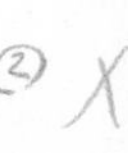

Another criticism made of the loans proposal is that it will act as a disincentive to women and students from poor families. It is not clear whether children from poor families will, if they are unusual enough to get as far as higher education, be deterred by a student loan system. Such an assertion requires careful testing. It is important to recognize that higher education is very much a middle class activity. Although the number of students from the lower social classes increased as the size of the higher education sector increased during the last 20 years, the percentage of children from these groups on the sector has been static. As any appraisal of UCCA statistics show, the social class differences in university applications remain significant (Maynard, 1978) and, as the Nuffield College Study has shown (Halsey, Health and Ridge, 1980), the chances of a working class child entering higher education, let alone the elitist section of secondary education, are significantly less than those of his middle class peers. Given this inequality, the relevant question is whether student loans will increase it or not. If loans do have this effect and this is seen as a policy problem, the policy will have to be amended by offering some form of advantage to students from low income households (e.g. a scholarship scheme).

Student loans may affect female participation in higher education because of their effects on the marriage market. No sensible profit-maximizing male will wish to marry a female with a student debt! Such a negative dowry might have all sorts of effects on mating habits within and without that part of the population receiving higher education! Once again if this effect is substantial and regarded as a policy problem the student loan plan may have to be adapted. Alternatively it could be argued that females should pay back the cost of their education just like men, especially as they retire earlier and produce less over the life-cycle as a consequence. Also because of changing social mores more women are spending more of their life in the labour force and this tendency will facilitate the ability of females to repay their loans.

The arguments over student loans have been long (Prest, 1963; Peacock and Wiseman, 1964), and many of the assertions of the protagonists can only be tested by the adoption of one scheme or another. The relevant criterion by which to judge any student loans scheme is whether it will perform more or less efficiently than the existing policies (Maynard, 1980; Woodhall, 1980).

11.4.2 Student loans and equity

As in our discussion of education vouchers, the question we are addressing here is whether loans will reduce the dispersion in earnings over the life-cycle. The advocate of loans uses an equity argument of the following nature: students are temporarily poor during their education, but, by virtue of their human capital investment in the higher education sector, they may get high lifetime earnings profiles. Why should students, who are temporarily poor but over the life-cycle rich, get a highly subsidized education? Why shouldn't they pay back the whole or a part of the cost of their education out of their high earnings?

This type of argument requires careful analysis. In terms of *Figure 11.1*, a students loan plan will change the cost of higher education, i.e. the shape of the supply curve will alter. The piece of the supply curve particularly affected by the policy change will be the first and second tranches as the loans scheme raises the opportunity cost of investing in human capital. For people such as the poor with no alternative sources of gifts or subsidized loans, the consumption of human capital may decline quite significantly in the absence of compensating policies. The more affluent students may also reduce their consumption for human capital because, for instance, they will no longer get 'minimum' UK government grants covering tuition fees.

Whether these alternatives in human capital consumption will narrow earnings differences over the life-cycle is an empirical question. It seems, at the a priori level, that there are no substantial reasons for optimism.

This lack of optimism may be heightened by a questionning of the assumption that the highly educated will, always and everywhere, receive higher lifetime earnings than their peers in the same age cohorts. Simple neoclassical theory indicated that increased supply and relatively stable demand, particularly in periods of unemployment, might depress the returns to higher education and shift the demand curve in *Figure 11.1* to the left. In the extreme we could argue as Phillip Wicksteed did 100 years ago, that in time the plentitude of highly educated people may depress the remuneration of such people, and the scarce manual workers would be paid more highly than the professionals. Perhaps such a conclusion is unduly pessimistic, implying little real incentive to invest in human capital, and ignores the possibilities of capital substitution in manual trades.

In conclusion the effects of student loans on the distribution of earnings is uncertain and it is possible that unless great care is taken in the design of the particular student loan scheme that is adopted, such an innovation may make the distribution of earnings more unequal.

11.4.3 Student loans and efficiency

The second argument put forward by student loan advocates is that such a reform would improve the efficiency of higher education. Higher education, like schools, is a consumer of large amounts of scarce resources and the activities these resources finance are noticeable by their lack of evaluation. What is the cheapest way of training a student in basic economic skills? What mix of lectures, seminars, tutorials, programme learning and private study gets the student to the required level of proficiency at the cheapest cost?

Such questions are rarely asked in education. Indeed like Adam Smith we might question for whose convenience education at all levels is arranged:

> 'The discipline of colleges and universities is in general contrived, not for the benefit of students, but for the interest, or more properly speaking, the ease of the masters.'
>
> Smith (1776), Book V, Part III; Article II, p. 249.

By its nature education is a task which is executed in isolation, in which output is difficult to measure, and in which professional pressure leads often to the muted operation of the review of practice. Ideally education systems should generate information about teacher performance (as assessed by consumers and producers) and pupil performance. Such information should fuel the process of peer review and mutual criticism of performance by producers.

In fact universities are peculiar places with outmoded methods of operations. Academic staff are supposed to be good administrators, good teachers and good researchers but are generally not well trained for these tasks and could quite profitably benefit all by specializing in one of them. Peer review is limited and regarded as slightly unprofessional in some quarters. Staff have tenure for life and have limited incentives to strive after excellence in teaching, research or administration. The universities generally teach over three 10-week terms and during the other 22 weeks valuable capital equipment may be underutilized.

If students paid for their education would this organization change? It is argued by the proponents of loans that the restoration of the cash nexus would increase the incentive for consumers to appraise producers and seek out the most efficient supplier of skills (e.g. Peacock and Culyer, 1968). Such a process might penalize the inefficient and reward the efficient and thereby encourage the former to mend their ways.

However the level and the nature of the argument is similar to that concerning vouchers. Various predictions can be made from basic theory but their validity can be doubted in the absence of experience and evidence.

11.4.4 Student loans: conclusion

The debate about student loans highlights a lot of very important policy issues. What are the objects of higher education? What is the cost-effective method to achieve these ends? How can incentives be improved so that resource allocators (teachers) are given incentives to use society's scarce resources efficiently?

Student loans may alter incentives and distributional outcomes, and it is possible that a carefully structured loans scheme could be more equitable and efficient than the existing system of grants.

11.5 OVERVIEW

Education policy is based generally on conjecture about the link between inputs and outputs. Little is known about the production function by which human capital is created. The institutions which provide education are little evaluated and the incentives to achieve academic excellence, however defined, are muted and generally depend on the charismatic power of the entrepreneur head-teacher. The power will always be important but it might be more effectively exercised if there were more information about the performance of the system and more significant 'sticks' and 'carrots' to make producers and consumers use resources more efficiently.

Education vouchers and student loans might improve the efficiency of the health care system and their distributional effects could also be more attractive than those of existing institutions. Both of these policies could be used to influence the supply and demand sides of the market for human capital. The supply-side effects would be direct and could give subsidies directly to whatever target group is viewed as 'disadvantaged'. The demand-side effects would be indirect, influencing the production costs of human capital by inducing producers to be more efficient.

The need for vigour and greater research into the production and consumption of education is quite clear. The propensity to think that all is well in the school or the college must be discarded for as Chairman Mao pointed out:

> 'complacency is the enemy of study. We cannot really learn anything until we rid ourselves of complacency. Our attitude towards ourselves should be "to be insatiable in learning", and towards others "to be tireless in teaching".'
>
> Mao Tse-Tung (1966) p. 274

Guide to further reading

A more detailed analysis of the theory of the demand and supply of human capital can be found in the second edition of Becker's *Human Capital* (1976), in particular the Woytinsky lecture. An overview of the merits and problems associated with education vouchers and student loans can be found in Maynard (1975).

Bibliography

BECKER, G. S. (1964, 1976), *Human Capital: a theoretical and empirical analysis with specific reference to education*, Columbia University Press for the National Bureau of Economic Research; New York (first and second editions)

HALSEY, A. H., HEATH, A. F. and RIDGE, J. M. (1980), *Origins and Destination: family, class and education in modern Britain*, Clarendon Press; Oxford

HOUSE OF COMMONS SELECT COMMITTEE ON EDUCATION, SCIENCE AND ARTS (1980), *The Funding and Organisation of Courses in Higher Education*, Minutes of evidence, 21 May 1980, HC papers 363 xii, HMSO; London

JENCKS, C. (1970), *Education vouchers: a report on financing elementary education by grants to parents*, prepared by the Center for the Study of Public Policy for the US Office of Economic Opportunity; Washington, DC.

KENT COUNTY COUNCIL (1978), *Education Vouchers in Kent*, Kent County Council Education Committee, Maidstone

MAYNARD, A. K. (1975), *Experiment with Choice in Education*, Institute of Economic Affairs; London

MAYNARD, A. K. (1978), 'Economic aspects of State intervention', in RODERICK, G. and STEPHENS, M. (eds.), *Higher Education for All?* Falmer Press; Brighton

MAYNARD, A. K. (1980) in HOUSE OF COMMONS SELECT COMMITTEE ON EDUCATION, SCIENCE ·AND ARTS, *The Funding and Organisation of Courses in Higher Education*, Minutes of evidence, 21 May 1980, HC papers 363 xii, HMSO; London, pp. 382–392

PEACOCK, A. T. and WISEMAN, J. (1964), *Education for Democrats*, Institute of Economic Affairs, London

PEACOCK, A. T. and CULYER, A. J. (1968), *The Economics of Student Unrest*, Institute of Economic Affairs; London

PREST, A. R. (1963), *Financing University Education*, Institute of Economic Affairs; London

SELDON, A. (1978), *Charge*! Temple Smith; London

SMITH, A. (1776), *An Inquiry into the Nature and the Causes of the Wealth of Nations*, Everyman edition (1910); London

TSE-TUNG, MAO (1966), *Quotations from Chairman Mao*; Peking

WOODHALL, M. (1970), *Student Loans: a review of experience in Scandinavia and elsewhere*, Harrap; London

WOODHALL, M. (1978), *Review of Student Support Schemes in Selected OECD Countries*, Organisation for Economic Cooperation and Development; Paris

WOODHALL, M. (1980), in HOUSE OF COMMONS SELECT COMMITTEE ON EDUCATION, SCIENCE AND ARTS, *The Funding and Organisation of Courses in Higher Education*, Minutes of evidence, 21 May 1980, HC papers 363 xii, HMSO; London, pp. 389–392

Index